DIVORCE – THE NEW LAW

DIVORCE
THE NEW LAW

District Judge Roger Bird LLB
Stephen Cretney DCL, FBA, QC(Hon)

Family Law
1996

Published by
Family Law
a publishing imprint of
Jordan Publishing Limited
21 St Thomas Street
Bristol BS1 6JS

© Jordan Publishing Limited 1996
Reprinted November 1996

British Library Cataloguing-in-Publication Data

A catalogue record for this book is available
from the British Library.

ISBN 0 85308 376 2

Photoset by Mendip Communications Ltd, Frome, Somerset
Printed in Great Britain by Bookcraft (Bath) Ltd, Midsomer Norton

PREFACE

In this book, we have tried to give a succinct account of the main provisions of the Family Law Act 1996 as it will apply to the divorce process. The reader should be warned that the Act is of formidable complexity, and that even such apparently simple questions as the length of the period for reflection and consideration turn out to be much more complex than might have been imagined. It is evident that family lawyers will need to familiarise themselves with the Act in order to assess its implications for clients well before the date on which the provisions governing the availability of divorce are brought into force; and we have tried to provide the materials to enable this to be done. In particular, the Appendices contain not only the text of the Family Law Act 1996, but also the, heavily amended, text of the Matrimonial Causes Act 1973 as it will be as and when the numerous amendments made by the 1996 Act have been brought into force. Consolidation should be an early priority, but we hope that in the meantime readers will share our feelings of gratitude to the publishers for undertaking the work involved.

In preparing the text, we have (encouraged in this respect by the decision of the House of Lords in *Pepper v Hart*) made numerous references to parliamentary debates, but it should be remembered that many changes of policy – some of considerable significance – were made in response to pressure during the Bill's passage. The fact that the Government should have refrained from seeking to remove a wholly unworkable provision dealing with pension splitting is itself remarkable, but that another provision (equally defective) should have been allowed to be put onto the statute book on the understanding that it would never be brought into force is a remarkable commentary on the realities of the legislative process in present circumstances.

This book was first conceived by Roger Bird. He has contributed the greater part of the text (ie Chapters 2, 3, 4, 6 and 10); while Stephen Cretney has contributed the residue. However, we have each considered the whole work and take equal responsibility for it. On occasions, study of successive prints of the Bill made us almost feel that the tortures inflicted on the martyr whose feast falls today were not the worst that could have been devised; but our task has been lightened by the enormous skills of the publishers whose speedy efficiency could not be surpassed.

ROGER BIRD
STEPHEN CRETNEY
The Feast of St Laurence, Deacon and Martyr, 1996.

CONTENTS

TABLE OF CASES

References in the right-hand column are to paragraph numbers.

TABLE OF STATUTES

References in the right-hand column are to paragraph numbers.

TABLE OF STATUTORY INSTRUMENTS

References in the right-hand column are to paragraph numbers.

CHAPTER ONE

Background to the Family Law Act 1996

Introduction – the Archbishop's group and the Law Commission

1.1 The Divorce Reform Act 1969, which came into force on 1 January 1971, was the outcome of a compromise between a group established by the Archbishop of Canterbury and the Law Commission. The Archbishop's group had concluded that divorce law should no longer be based on the concept of the matrimonial offence; but that the law should allow divorce if a marriage had irretrievably broken down. However, the Archbishop's group believed that such breakdown ought to be established by the court carrying out a detailed inquest into the alleged fact and causes of the death of the marriage: see *Putting Asunder* (1966). The Law Commission agreed that reform of the law was desirable, but it rejected (in part because of the cost involved and in part because it thought that a detailed inquiry would inevitably cause humiliation and distress) the view that the court should carry out a full inquest into the alleged breakdown: see *The Field of Choice* (1966).

After discussion, the Archbishop's group and the Law Commission agreed that irretrievable breakdown should be the sole ground for divorce, but such breakdown was to be inferred either on proof of one or more of certain facts (akin to the matrimonial offences of adultery, cruelty and desertion) or on proof that the parties had been separated for five years (two years if they agreed to divorce): see Appendix to the Law Commission's *Third Annual Report*.

The parliamentary history of the Divorce Reform Act 1969

1.2 A private member's Bill (drafted in the Law Commission) was introduced in 1967 but failed for lack of parliamentary time. The Bill was re-introduced by another private member (Mr Alec Jones) in 1968 and, on this occasion, the Government made parliamentary time available with the Bill eventually receiving Royal Assent on 22 October 1969. The reason why it was not brought into force until 1971 was because the Government had given an undertaking to defer implementation until the Law Commission had reviewed the financial consequences of divorce; and the legislation to give effect to the Law Commission's recommendations on that subject (the Matrimonial Proceedings and Property Act) was not enacted until 1970. The two Acts were eventually consolidated in the Matrimonial Causes Act 1973.

Ground for divorce and financial consequences of divorce: the legislation consolidated

1.3　The Matrimonial Causes Act 1973 (in provisions which will be repealed when the Family Law Act 1996 comes into force) provides that a petition for divorce may be presented to the court by either party to a marriage on the ground that the marriage has broken down irretrievably (s 1(1)); but the Act also provides (s 1(2)) that the court hearing a petition for divorce shall not hold the marriage to have broken down irretrievably unless the petitioner satisfies the court of one or more of five 'facts', *viz*:

(a) that the respondent has committed adultery and the petitioner finds it intolerable to live with the respondent;

(b) that the respondent has behaved in such a way that the petitioner cannot reasonably be expected to live with the respondent;

(c) that the respondent has deserted the petitioner for a continuous period of at least two years immediately preceding the presentation of the petition;

(d) that the parties to the marriage have lived apart for a continuous period of at least two years immediately preceding the presentation of the petition ... and the respondent consents to a decree being granted;

(e) that the parties to the marriage have lived apart for a continuous period of at least five years immediately preceding the presentation of the petition....

The rule preventing divorce in the early years of marriage

1.4　The Divorce Reform Act 1969 retained the rule (which dated from the Matrimonial Causes Act 1937) whereby no petition for divorce could be presented before the expiration of the period of three years from the date of the marriage unless it was shown that the case was one of exceptional hardship suffered by the petitioner or one of exceptional depravity on the part of the respondent. In 1984 the Matrimonial and Family Proceedings Act 1984 (giving effect to recommendations made by the Law Commission in its Report *Time Restrictions on Presentation of Divorce and Nullity Petitions* (1982)) substituted an absolute bar on the presentation of a divorce petition before the expiration of the period of one year from the celebration of the marriage. It was intended thereby to preserve a symbolic assertion of the State's interest in upholding the stability and dignity of marriage, whilst doing away with the need for a petitioner seeking release from marriage to make almost necessarily wounding allegations about the 'exceptional' nature of the matters relied on to obtain the court's leave.

Reform of the law governing the financial consequences of divorce

1.5 As already mentioned, the Matrimonial Proceedings and Property Act 1970 had codified the law governing the financial consequences of divorce. The legislation conferred wide powers on the court to make financial provision and property adjustment orders; and provided that in deciding whether to exercise those powers and, if so, in what manner, the court should have regard to all the circumstances (including certain specified circumstances) and seek to place the parties, so far as it was practicable and, having regard to their conduct, just to do so, in the financial position in which they would have been if the marriage had not broken down and each had properly discharged his or her financial obligations and responsibilities towards the other (MCA 1973, s 25(1)).

However, these guidelines proved to be controversial in their application, and the Matrimonial and Family Proceedings Act 1984 (giving effect to recommendations made by the Law Commission: Law Com No 112, 1981) reformulated the law in three main respects The court was no longer required so to exercise its powers as to place the parties in the financial provision in which they would have been had the marriage not broken down. The necessity of making such financial arrangements as would safeguard the welfare of children of the family was to be a first consideration. The importance of each party doing everything possible to become self-sufficient was emphasised by the introduction of guidelines intended to direct attention to the desirability of the so-called clean break (see *Minton v Minton* [1979] AC 593, HL).

The special procedure

1.6 Perhaps the most important development affecting the divorce process since the coming into force of the Divorce Reform Act 1969 has been the introduction (in 1973, in undefended cases relying on two-years' separation and not involving children; and in 1977 for all undefended cases) of the so-called 'special procedure' which has become in reality the ordinary procedure for dealing with the great majority of cases (*Day v Day* [1980] Fam 29, 32, per Ormrod LJ). The following account of the procedure (given by Waite LJ in *Pounds v Pounds* [1994] 1 FLR 776, CA) explains the process sufficiently for present purposes:

'Following presentation of the petition, the petitioner's solicitor lodges an application for "directions for trial" together with a standard affidavit in the form required to verify the particular ground alleged in the petition. In routine cases . . . the [district judge] gives "directions for trial" by entering the cause in the special procedure list and thereafter considers the evidence filed by the petitioner. If he is satisfied that the petitioner has sufficiently proved the contents of the petition and is entitled to the decree sought and any costs prayed for, he will make and file a certificate to that effect. The court then sends notification to the parties of the date, time and place fixed for the pronouncement of the decree nisi, The parties are also told that their attendance at the pronouncement of decree is not necessary. The actual process of pronouncement of the decree has become reduced to a very brief ceremony of a purely formal character in which decrees are listed together in batches for a collective mention in open court before a judge who speaks (or nods) his assent. The right to a decree absolute 6 weeks thereafter is automatic . . . . [T]he sole truly judicial function in the entire process is that of the [district judge] when granting his certificate. Everything that follows is automatic and administrative, and the open court pronouncement of the decree is pure formality, to which the pronouncing judge . . . has no option but to consent . . .'

It should be noted that the 'pronouncing judge' will now be a district judge: see FPR 1991, r 2.49(2).

Continued criticism of the law governing the divorce process

1.7   The Law Commission in *The Field of Choice* stated that a good divorce law should seek:

 (i) to buttress rather than to undermine, the stability of marriage; and
(ii) when a marriage has irretrievably broken down, to enable the empty legal shell to be destroyed with the maximum fairness, and the minimum bitterness, distress and humiliation.

But it soon began to be questioned whether the 1969 Act had attained those objectives.

First, there was concern that the divorce rate seemed to increase: in 1971 (the first year of the operation of the new law) there had been 110,017 petitions, but by 1993 the number of petitions had increased to 184,171. The divorce rate (13.5 divorces per thousand married couples) was one of the highest in Western Europe. Notwithstanding the emphasis placed by the long title of the 1969 Act on reconciliation as an objective of the law, there was little evidence that the legislation effectively encouraged recourse to reconciliation procedures.

Secondly, it was said that the legislation had not been effective in reducing bitterness, distress and humiliation. On the contrary, the *Report of the Matrimonial Causes Procedure Committee* (Chairman, Mrs Justice Booth DBE, 1985) stated that the bitterness and unhappiness of divorcing couples was frequently exacerbated and prolonged by the fault element in divorce, and this was particularly so where the 'behaviour' fact was relied on. Moreover, divorce procedures did not sufficiently encourage the parties to resolve the consequences of divorce (notably in relation to children and financial matters) in an amicable way; rather, the adversarial approach often taken in the process engendered an atmosphere of hostility and recrimination which was damaging not only for the adults but particularly for the children.

Finally, it was said that those involved in the divorce process often found it confusing or indeed incomprehensible: the law purported to be based on breakdown, but it seemed often to be necessary to make allegations of culpability. As one MP put it in the debates on the Bill for the Family Law Act 1996:

> 'A solicitor will ask a wife seeking divorce "whether, over the life of the marriage, she can think of occasions on which her husband has been difficult". It is a pretty unusual marriage which has not had a fair number of difficult moments over 10 years. The solicitor will then crystallise and distil those examples into 10 or so incidents which, when put together, read in a lurid way, as if the marriage was especially wicked and abnormal, whereas in fact it was probably very normal.
>
> When the petition is passed to the husband, he will immediately hit the roof .... That is hardly a basis for dealing with the sad after-effects of marriage breakdown, particularly from the point of view of the children ...' (*Official Report* (HC) 24 April 1996, col 477, Mr Donald Anderson)

Conciliation (or mediation)

1.8 For some years, attention concentrated on attempts to minimise the bitterness and distress apparently often engendered by the divorce process; and there was much activity intended to promote recourse to conciliation (or mediation). This has been defined as a way of resolving disputes without resort to traditional adjudication through the courts – rather, the parties are to be encouraged, with the assistance of a neutral third party, to reach their own agreements on the matters which have to be resolved. Although the *Matrimonial Causes Procedure Committee* (Chairman, Mrs Justice Booth DBE, 1985) expressed warm support for the use of conciliation (and also made many suggestions for improving court procedures, few of which were in the event implemented) other official enquiries were less supportive (see notably the *Inter-Departmental Committee on Conciliation* (1983)) and the Government was reluctant to make any funding available to the many conciliation schemes established by private initiative in various parts of the country.

The Law Commission's review of divorce law and practice

1.9. In the meantime, the Law Commission had decided to review the ground for divorce, and in 1988 the Commission published a discussion paper (*Facing the Future* (Law Com No 170)) which concluded that, although the law was a considerable improvement on the pre-1969 law, it:

> '... did not, nor could it reasonably be expected to, buttress the stability of marriage by preventing determined parties from obtaining a speedy divorce. Because of the compromise nature of the 1969 Act, the benefits referred to above have been bought at the price of incoherence and increased confusion for litigants. Thus the law is neither understandable nor respected and there is evidence of not inconsiderable consumer dissatisfaction. Attaining the aims of maximum fairness and minimum bitterness has been rendered impossible by the retention of the fault element. The necessity of making allegations in the petition "draws the battle-lines" at the outset. The ensuing hostility makes the divorce more painful, not only for the parties but also for the children, and destroys any chance of reconciliation and may be detrimental to post-divorce relationships. Underlying all these defects is the fact that whether or not the marriage can be dissolved depends principally upon what parties have done in the past. In petitions relying on fault-based facts, the petitioner is encouraged to 'dwell on the past' and to recriminate.
>
> At the same time, the present divorce process may not allow sufficient opportunity for the parties to come to terms with what is happening in their lives. A recent study of the process of "uncoupling" points out that one party has usually gone far down that path before the other one discovers this, by which time it may be too late. Once the divorce process has been started it may have a "juggernaut" effect, providing insufficient opportunity for the parties to re-evaluate their positions. Thus, there is little or no scope for reconciliation, conciliation or renegotiation of the relationship. It is clear that both emotionally and financially it is much less costly if ancillary matters can be agreed between the parties. Where antagonism is created or exacerbated by the petition, or their respective bargaining power distorted, the atmosphere is not conducive to calm and sensible negotiations about the future needs of the parties and their children.
>
> Above all, the present law fails to recognise that divorce is not a final product but part of a massive transition for the parties and their children. It is crucial in the interests of the children (as well as the parties) that the

transition is as smooth as possible, since it is clear that their short and long-term adjustment depends to a large extent on their parents' adjustment and in particular on the quality of their post-divorce relationship with each parent. Although divorce law itself can do little actively to this end, it can and should ensure that the divorce process is not positively adverse to this adjustment. As Lord Hailsham has said, "though the law could not alter the facts of life, it need not unnecessarily exaggerate the hardships inevitably involved." There seems little doubt that the present law is guilty of just this.'

Divorce as a process over time

1.10. The Law Commission's consultation process led it to conclude that there was still 'overwhelming support' for the view that irretrievable break-down should remain the 'fundamental basis' of the ground for divorce. The complaint, it seemed, was not of the breakdown principle itself, but of the legal rules and procedures by which breakdown is established. The Commission produced draft legislation intended to give effect to its proposals for 'divorce after a period for the consideration of future arrangements and for reflection.'

1.11. The Law Commission's proposals formed the basis of a Government Consultation Paper, *Looking to the Future. Mediation and the Ground for Divorce* (Cm 2424, 1993) which, as the title suggests, dealt not only with the legal ground upon which a marriage could be dissolved but also with procedures whereby many of the consequences of marital breakdown would be dealt with by family mediation rather than in the traditional processes of lawyer negotiation and court order. The Consultation Paper concluded that a system such as that recommended by the Commission:

> 'might make the divorce process better than under the present system . . . might reduce the bitterness and feelings of injustice so prevalent in divorce proceedings and . . . consequently minimise the harm suffered by children. Perhaps by encouraging parents to look at how best they can meet their parental responsibilities for the future, rather than dwelling upon the unhappiness and unfairness of the past, the process could be easier for children'.

Having considered the many comments made on the Paper and the results of an attitude survey, the Government accepted that the ground for divorce should (as the Law Commission had recommended) be the irretrievable breakdown of the marriage 'as demonstrated by the sole fact of a period for reflection and consideration': see the White Paper, *Looking to the Future* (1995, Cm 2799, para 4.7).

The Government also accepted many features of the process which the Law Commission had recommended (although it is to be noted that the

Government, contrary to the views of the Law Commission, believed that all arrangements about finance and the upbringing of children should have to be dealt with before the marriage was dissolved: see para **3.1** below).

The Family Law Bill

1.12 The Queen's speech on 15 November 1995 stated that the Government would introduce legislation to reform the law governing divorce, and the Family Law Bill (HL Bill 1) was ordered to be printed on 16 November 1995. The Bill did not have an easy passage through Parliament. One hundred and twelve Conservative MPs, including the Home Secretary and four other Ministers, voted against the Government in a free vote in the House of Commons on whether the fault-based ground for divorce should be retained; whilst five Cabinet Ministers and 15 other Ministers voted in favour of an extended period 'for reflection and consideration'. Influential bodies, including The Law Society, withdrew support from the Bill, and its fate hung in the balance until a very late stage.

However, the Government made substantial concessions on a number of significant matters, and the Bill was eventually given a third reading in the House of Commons by 427 votes to nine. The Family Law Act 1996 received Royal Assent on 4 July 1996; but it is important to note that the Act differs in many respects from the Bill originally introduced and even more from the Bill annexed to the Law Commission's report (which should thus be treated with caution as an explanation of the policies underlying the provisions of the Act). However, the main features of the legislation governing the availability of divorce are readily comprehensible, whilst the Act also incorporates a statement of the general principles underlying those parts of the Act governing divorce[1]. The reader may find it helpful to have at the outset a brief summary of the legal process for divorce under the Family Law Act 1996; and statement of the general principles laid down by the Act.

An outline of the legal process for divorce under the Family Law Act 1996

1.13 The Family Law Act 1996 retains the general principle that the irretrievable breakdown of the marriage is the only ground for divorce (s 3(1)(a)); but such breakdown will be inferred, and can only be inferred (s 5(1)), from:

---

[1] ie Parts II and III of the Act. Part IV of the Act deals with Family Homes and Domestic Violence, and those provisions are analysed in R Bird, *Domestic Violence – The New Law* (Family Law, 1996).

(i) the lodging of a *statement of marital breakdown* with the court (which can only be done after attendance at an *information meeting*);

(ii) the expiration after the making of the statement of a *period for 'reflection and consideration'* (s 7(1), (2)); and

(iii) the making of an *application for a divorce order*. This must evidence compliance with the Act's requirements that the parties' *arrangements for the future* (in respect of *children and financial matters*) should first have been resolved (s 3(1)(c); s 9) and it must be accompanied by a *declaration* that the applicant believes the marriage cannot be saved (s 5(1)(d)). (It should be noted that it is only at this stage that such a statement is to be made: the statement of marital breakdown does not state that the maker believes the marriage to have broken down *irretrievably*, and this conclusion is only to be reached after the expiration of the period for reflection and consideration.)

1.14 In some circumstances, the court may make an *order preventing divorce* (notwithstanding the fact that the marriage has irretrievably broken down and that the other requirements set out above have been satisfied) if it is satisfied that dissolution of the marriage would result in substantial financial or other hardship to a spouse or to a child of the family (s 10).

1.15 The Act also contains provisions governing the availability of *separation orders*.

The general principles underlying the provisions relating to divorce and separation

1.16 Section 1 of the Family Law Act 1996 provides:

'The court and any person, in exercising functions under or in consequence of Parts II and III [of the Act, ie those provisions relating to Divorce and Separation and to Legal Aid for Mediation in Family Matters] shall have regard to the following general principles—

(a) that the institution of marriage is to be supported;

(b) that the parties to a marriage which may have broken down are to be encouraged to take all practicable steps, whether by marriage counselling or otherwise, to save the marriage;

(c) that a marriage which has irretrievably broken down and is being brought to an end should be brought to an end—

(i) with minimum distress to the parties and to the children affected;

(ii) with questions dealt with in a manner designed to promote as good a continuing relationship between the parties and any children affected as is possible in the circumstances; and

(iii) without costs being unreasonably incurred in connection with the procedures to be followed in bringing the marriage to an end; and

(d) that any risk to one of the parties to a marriage, and to any children, of violence from the other party should, so far as reasonably practicable, be removed or diminished.'

1.17 The Lord Chancellor, moving the insertion of a statement of general principles at Report stage in the House of Lords (*Official Report* (HL) 22 February 1996, col 1145), stated that they constitute an assertion of the framework within which the legislation is intended to operate. However, it is to be noted that the insertion of s 1(d) above (domestic violence) was forcefully resisted by the Government on the basis that it was not easy to see how this provision could be relevant to the exercise of functions under Parts II and III of the Act (the provisions conferring powers to deal with domestic violence being found in Part IV): see in particular per Mr Jonathan Evans, Standing Committee E, Fourth Sitting, 7 May 1996. However, at third reading the Government evidently felt unable to carry these objections to a Division; and conceded that the provision could have some (albeit limited) relevance in the course of the divorce and separation process. It appears that the Lord Chancellor may find this provision relevant in making regulations under the Act about such matters as attendance at information meetings; and that it will also inform the actions of those conducting information meetings, mediators and others: per Lord Mackay of Clashfern, *Official Report* (HL) 27 June 1996, col 1065.

Mediation and counselling

1.18 It was always envisaged that mediation in the sense of providing facilities for the parties, with assistance from a neutral third party, to reach their own agreements about the consequences (particularly in terms of arrangements about children's upbringing and financial matters) should have a central part in the new divorce process; and provisions to this end were made in the Act. (The relevant provisions are considered at para **3.21**).

However, the White Paper had indicated that the divorce process was also to be tailored so as to identify savable marriages and to give opportunities to explore any prospect of reconciliation; and in the course of the parliamentary debates on the Bill for the Family Law Act 1996 the Government was criticised for not particularising the means whereby marriage was to be supported. Under pressure, the provisions dealing with marriage support were considerably expanded in an attempt to give effect to the general principles, set out in s 1 of the Act (in particular the provision requiring the institution of marriage to be supported; and the provision stipulating that the parties to a marriage which may have broken down are to be encouraged to take all practicable steps, whether by marriage counselling or otherwise, to save it). It may be helpful to summarise the relevant provisions at this stage.

Provisions relating to counselling and marriage support

1.19 The following provisions of the Family Law Act 1996 ('the Act') are particularly relevant.

Funding for marriage support

First, s 22(1) of the Act provides that the Lord Chancellor, with the approval of the Treasury, may make grants in connection with:

(a) the provision of marriage support services;
(b) research into the causes of marital breakdown; and
(c) research into ways of preventing marital breakdown.

Reflecting the general belief that prospects of reconciliation are sharply reduced with the passage of time, it is provided that the Lord Chancellor is to have regard, in particular, to the desirability of services of that kind being available when first needed: s 22(3).

Provision of marriage counselling

1.20 Secondly, s 23 of the Act makes limited provision for meeting the costs of marriage counselling incurred by those who have started marital proceedings. The Government brought these provisions forward in the final stages of the Bill's progress through the House of Commons; and they empower the Lord Chancellor or a person appointed by him to secure the provision of marriage counselling after the period for reflection and consideration has been started by the making of a statement of marital breakdown. It appears that this provision is intended primarily to allow those eligible for legal aid with a nil contribution to receive counselling without payment: per Lord Mackay of Clashfern, *Official Report* (HL) 27 June 1996, col 1061.

Attendance at information meetings etc.

1.21 Thirdly, information about the availability of counselling and other marriage support services is to be given at information meetings: s 8(9)(a).

Moreover, power has also been taken to require legal representatives to inform the client: (i) about the availability of marriage support services; (ii) to give the client names and addresses of persons qualified to help to effect a reconciliation. A legal representative may also be required to certify that those provisions have been complied with, and whether or not the legal representative has discussed with the client the possibility of reconciliation: s 12(2).

Cooling off period before filing statement

1.22 Fourthly, the Act contains provisions designed to discourage precipitate recourse to legal proceedings. The Bill was amended to prevent a person making a statement of marital breakdown – and thereby starting the period of reflection and consideration running – within three months of his or her attending the meeting: s 8(2). It appears to be intended that if a party does decide to make a statement, he or she is to be required to state the steps taken to explore the possibility of reconciliation: see *Official Report* (HL) 29 February 1996, cols 1689–1692, and note that the Act (s 6(5)) provides that a statement must satisfy any requirements of rules made by the Lord Chancellor.

Reconciliation attempts during period for reflection and consideration

1.23 The Family Law Act 1996 also contains provision intended to allow the parties to 'stop the clock' which starts running on receipt by the court of a statement: it is provided that at any time during the period of reflection and consideration the parties may give joint notice to the court that they 'are attempting reconciliation but require additional time': s 7(7). The effect of such a notice is to suspend the period, but the period can be restarted if either party gives notice that the attempted reconciliation has been unsuccessful: s 7(8)(b).

Ministerial responsibility for marriage support

1.23 Finally, it should be noted (although not mentioned in the Act) that Ministerial responsibility for marriage support services has been transferred from the Home Office to the Lord Chancellor's Department; and an interdepartmental working group (chaired by the Lord Chancellor's Department) has been established in order to identify the needs of couples (for example, in preparing for marriage and for support during marriage, and to establish how those needs might be met). The Committee issued a Consultation Paper in June 1996.

Implementation of the Act

1.24 Statements by Ministers indicated that the provisions of the relevant parts of the Act will not come into force for two years from the date on which the Family Law Act received Royal Assent: see *Official Report* (HL) 30 January 1996, cols 1409–1410; (HC) 25 March 1996, col 740. Time was needed not only to settle the subordinate legislation but also to give an opportunity to assess pilot schemes in respect of information meetings and other aspects of the legislation. The reader may think, in the light of the massive infrastructure apparently necessary, that the Ministerial forecasts could well turn out to have underestimated rather than overestimated the length of time required to ensure that this should be in place.

Arrangement of the text

The text is arranged as follows:

Chapter One   – The Background to the Family Law Act 1996
Chapter Two   – Commencing Marital Proceedings
Chapter Three – The Period for Reflection and Consideration
Chapter Four – Divorce Orders
Chapter Five – Preventing or Delaying Divorce
Chapter Six   – Financial Relief in Divorce and Separation Cases
Chapter Seven – Children in the Divorce Process
Chapter Eight – Separation Orders under the Family Law Act 1996
Chapter Nine – Nullity and Other Forms of Matrimonial Relief
Chapter Ten   – Transitional Provisions

Chapter Two

Commencing Marital Proceedings

Introduction

2.1 At the heart of the new system of divorce law and procedure is the period for reflection and consideration. This cannot begin until a statement of marital breakdown has been received by the court. However, this statement cannot be filed at court until the applicant has fulfilled the requirements of the information session.

These are the three essential characteristics of the new system. The period for reflection and consideration will be discussed in Chapter 3; in this chapter, the two preliminary matters will be considered in turn.

2.2 In this chapter, the statement of marital breakdown will be referred to as 'the statement'. Section 20(1) and (2) provide that the filing of the statement is to be treated as the commencement of proceedings, which are to be known as 'marital proceedings'. Subsection (3) goes on to provide that marital proceedings 'are also' separation and divorce proceedings. It might seem to follow from this that marital proceedings, which exist between the filing of the statement and the application for a divorce order pursuant to s 3, are, in some way, distinct from the eventual divorce proceedings. This cannot be the case; the divorce proceedings are part of the same marital proceedings as those initiated by the statement.

2.3 The only time-limit which it is necessary to bear in mind at this stage is that imposed by s 7(6), which provides that a statement made before the first anniversary of the marriage is ineffective for the purposes of any application for a divorce order; this does not preclude a statement for the purpose of a separation order. For the purposes of divorce, therefore, a statement made on or after the first anniversary of the marriage is effective. Given that attendance at the information meeting must have preceded the making of the statement, and the absence of any provision in the Act as to when such attendance may take place, it seems to follow that an aspiring applicant for divorce may attend an information meeting at any time during the first year of the marriage. It also seems to follow that a statement may be made perhaps many years after the applicant has attended an information meeting.

The information meeting

2.4   The thinking behind the information meeting was explained by the Lord Chancellor in the second reading debate in the House of Lords in the following way:

> 'The provisions in the Bill are that the breakdown would be established by the passage of an absolute period of time without that period being abridged in any circumstances. The provision would require a person wishing to initiate proceedings to attend a compulsory information session before the period of time starts to run which might lead to divorce. This will not only mark the seriousness of the step being taken but also ensure that essential information is conveyed to people contemplating divorce in the most effective way possible. Information provided will include information about the various services available to help people, including marriage guidance, mediation and legal services. I believe that this will be done most objectively and effectively if done by those who provide the services. It will also deal with alternative options to divorce and the consequences of divorce for the parties and their children'. (*Official Report* (HL) 30 November 1995, col 702)

In a later debate[1], the Lord Chancellor explained why the word 'meeting' was to be substituted for the original choice of 'session'; it was thought that the expression 'information session' had connotations of large, communal events which might prove intimidating to some people. There were also concerns as to privacy.

2.5   Section 8(2) provides that a party making a statement must (except in prescribed circumstances) have attended an information meeting not less than three months before making the statement. The exceptions to the rule, permitted by the prescribed circumstances, will be considered at para **2.9** below. The Act will be unworkable if rules of court do not provide for some method of proving attendance at an information meeting, so it may be confidently predicted that some form will be devised for this purpose.

Section 8(3) provides that different information meetings must be arranged with respect to different marriages; this is intended to require the meeting to be an individual (rather than a group) encounter.

There are, in fact, three different sets of circumstances under which parties may attend an information meeting. The first is where a person wishing to file a statement attends alone. The second is where both parties to the marriage wish to file the statement; both must attend an information meeting, but s 8(4) provides that they may attend either separate meetings or the same meeting.

The third set of circumstances relates not to the filing of a statement but to an application to be made by the party who did not file the statement; here, the

---

[1] 22 February 1996 – see *Official Report* (HL), col 1180.

position will be that one party has filed a statement and either that party or the other party wishes to make an application to the court with respect to a child of the family, or make an application of a prescribed description relating to property or financial matters or to contact. In these circumstances, both the party wishing to make such an application and a party wishing to resist the application must, if they have not done so already, attend an information meeting (s 8(5)).

2.6 To summarise, therefore, attendance at an information meeting is compulsory for anyone wishing:

(a) to file a statement, whether solely or jointly;
(b) in the case of a party other than the party who has filed the statement:
    (i) to apply for an order with respect to a child of the family; or
    (ii) to apply for an order relating to property or financial matters; or
    (iii) to oppose an application for such an order,

unless they fall within one of the prescribed exceptions.

2.7 The question of who will be qualified to conduct an information meeting remains to be decided. One possibility has always been that the person conducting the meeting would be a court official. However, it now seems to be the case that organisations or individuals will be, as it were, franchised for this purpose.

Section 8(7) provides that an information meeting must be conducted by a person who is qualified and appointed in accordance with prescribed provisions and who will have no financial or other interest in any marital proceedings between the parties. The Lord Chancellor intends to assess a number of pilot projects before making a final decision as to the format.

Exactly what is required to happen at the information meeting remains to be determined by regulation, but the explanation given by the Lord Chancellor and quoted above gives a useful indication of what form the meeting is likely to take. Further guidance is offered by s 8(8) and (9) which prescribe the matters with which the regulations may in particular deal.

Subsection (6) defines an information meeting as:

    '... a meeting organised ... for the purpose—
    (a) of providing, in accordance with prescribed provisions, relevant information to the parties attending about matters which may arise in connection with the provisions of, or made under, this Part [ie the provisions as to divorce] or Part III [ie the provisions as to legal aid and mediation]; and
    (b) of giving the party or parties attending the information meeting the opportunity of having a meeting with a marriage counsellor and of encouraging that party or those parties to attend that meeting.'

Subsection (8) provides that the regulations may, in particular, make provision about the places and times of such meetings, for written information to be given to persons attending, and for the giving of information to parties (otherwise than at information meetings) in cases where the requirement to attend meetings does not apply. This is all fairly general, and does not reveal very much, except that some of the information which the parties attending will receive will be written. It seems also to be envisaged that some of the material to which the parties will be exposed will be in the form of a video[2].

2.8   It is to subsection (9) that one must look for more detail about what the regulations will contain about the nature of the information to be imparted. This provides that the regulations must, in particular, make provision for the giving of information about the following:

(a)   marriage counselling and other marriage support services;
(b)   the importance to be attached to the welfare, wishes and feelings of children;
(c)   how the parties may acquire a better understanding of the ways in which children can be helped to cope with the breakdown of a marriage;
(d)   the nature of the financial questions that may arise on divorce or separation, and services which are available to help the parties;
(e)   protection available against violence and how to obtain support and assistance;
(f)   mediation;
(g)   the availability to each of the parties of independent legal advice;
(h)   the principles of legal aid and where the parties can get advice about obtaining legal aid;
(i)   the divorce and separation process.

The detail will be contained in the regulations, but this gives a good idea of what the information meeting will be like. The purpose of (a) is to bring home to parties the possibility of saving the marriage, while (b) and (c) are designed to emphasise the importance of children in the divorce process. Compliance with (d) should cover the financial consequences of divorce, and the range of options open to the court, while compliance with (f) will explain the availability of mediation; mediation is considered in more detail in Chapter 3 at para **3.21**. The purpose of (g) and (h) is that it should be explained that people are entitled to be separately legally advised and represented, and the availability or otherwise of legal aid. Finally, (i) will deal with the legal process itself, so that parties will know what they face. No doubt one matter which will be emphasised in the meeting will be the requirement that arrangements for the future must be made before a divorce order can be granted.

2.9   In the second reading debate in the House of Lords, the Lord Chancellor said that the objects of the information session were:

'to give information so as to be sure that anyone contemplating the divorce process has all the information that we can furnish in an objective

---

[2] The Lord Chancellor – *Official Report* (HL) 22 February 1996 Hansard, col 118.

way about conciliation, counselling, lawyers, mediation and anything else that may be helpful.' (*Official Report* (HL) 30 November 1995, col 786)

He made it clear that the form and structure of the meeting was yet to be decided, and that it would be necessary to experiment with pilot studies before a final decision was taken (ibid, cols 786 and 787).

2.10 The Act envisages certain exemptions from the requirement to attend the information meeting. These will be prescribed by regulation, but it is possible to speculate as to the classes of persons who may be exempt. First, it is necessary to bear in mind that attendance at the information meeting is designed for several purposes. The first of these is to qualify to be able to file a statement of marital breakdown. It is difficult to see who could justifiably claim exemption from this, except someone who was physically disabled and unable to attend, persons in custody or, perhaps, a person who, although domiciled in England and Wales, was resident abroad and unable to visit this country for this purpose.

Another class of persons who may be exempt comprises those who wish to take, or defend, ancillary proceedings relating to children or financial matters. Here, the question of urgency may arise. It is not envisaged that attendance at a meeting will be necessary before application is made for an occupation order or non-molestation order, for obvious reasons, but domestic violence and urgency can be factors leading to applications in divorce proceedings relating to children or for financial support, and there is likely to be some exemption here.

The statement of marital breakdown

2.11 Opening the second reading debate in the House of Lords, the Lord Chancellor in referring to the period for reflection and consideration, said that this period:

'... would be commenced by the lodging of a neutral statement. By that I mean a statement which does not make allegations and does not, at that early stage, state that the marriage has already broken down and that the maker of the statement wants a divorce. The spouse or spouses making the statement would be required to declare that he, she or they believe the marriage to have broken down and declare that they understand that the purpose of the period which will follow before an application to the court can be made for either a separation or a divorce order will be for reflection on whether the marriage can be saved and consideration of the arrangements for the future should divorce be proceeded with.' (*Official Report* (HL) 30 November 1995, col 702)

Section 5(1)(a) refers to the statement as:

'a statement [. . .] made by one (or both) of the parties that the maker of the statement (or each of them) believes that the marriage has broken down;'

By s 5(1)(b), the statement must comply with the requirements of s 6.

2.12   The main element of s 5(1) is, therefore, that the statement must state that the maker of the statement believes that the marriage has broken down. It does not state that the marriage has broken down irretrievably; this can only be established at the end of the period for reflection and consideration.

The additional requirements of s 6 may be summarised as follows:

(a)   the maker, or makers of the statement must state that he, she or they is or are aware of the purpose of the period for reflection and consideration as described in s 7;

(b)   he, she or they must also state that they wish to make arrangements for the future.

By s 6(4) and (5), the statement must be given to the court in accordance with rules of court to be made under s 12, and may have to contain such other matters as may be prescribed. Section 12 prescribes certain matters for which the rules may provide and which can therefore be confidently predicted as being likely to be contained in the rules.

2.13   The matters for which s 12 provides, and the effect of this on the contents of the statement may be summarised as follows:

(a)   the form will be required to be a prescribed form, and rules will provide for information to accompany the form;

(b)   the person making the statement will be required to state whether or not, since attending the information meeting, he has made any attempt at reconciliation;

(c)   rules may govern the way in which the statement is to be given to the court; there is little to say about this, since it is implicit that statements have to be filed at court;

(d)   the statement will be served by the court on the other party;

(e)   rules may specify circumstances under which service on the other party may be dispensed with, or effected otherwise than by delivery to that party; clearly, there will have to be provision for dispensing with service where one party cannot be found, and for ordering substituted service where one party is elusive;

(f)   a party who has made a statement may be required to provide the court with information about the arrangements that need to be made in consequence of the breakdown; and

(g)   rules may provide for the time, manner and (where attendance in person is required) place at which such information is to be given.

The last two provisions have to be read together. It seems to be envisaged that the court may require a person who has made a statement to supply further information either to the court or to the other party. Section 12(1)(f) refers to a person 'who has made' a statement, so it must follow that the information would not be contained in the statement itself. Presumably, the court would not do this of its own motion, so there will have to be a procedure for the other party to apply to the court for an order for further information.

The matters set out below in (h) to (j) are variations on the same theme:

(h) where a statement has been made, either or both parties may be required:
    (i) to prepare and produce such other documents; and
    (ii) to attend in person at such places and for such purposes, as may be specified.

Again, it seeems to be envisaged that one or other party may be able to ask the court to order delivery of further documents or information, and also to order a party to attend for some specified purpose (this will be best considered in Chapter 3 where the period for reflection and consideration is discussed):

(i) rules may provide for the information and assistance which is to be given to the parties and the way in which it is to be given; and
(j) finally, rules may require that parties be given, in such manner as may be specified, copies of specified documents and information.

2.14 The provisions as to rules set out above make no mention of the jurisdiction of the court. However, s 19 deals with the question of the court's jurisdiction 'to entertain marital proceedings' and provides, in subsection (2), that this jurisdiction is exercisable only if either at least one of the parties is domiciled in England and Wales, or has been habitually resident in England and Wales for at least one year ending with the statement date, or nullity proceedings are pending in relation to the marriage when the marital proceedings commence (see para **9.2**). The effect of the latter provision seems to be to allow proceedings for divorce to be instituted by a respondent to nullity proceedings.

Divorce and separation proceedings[3] are begun by the filing of the statement, so the court will need to be satisfied that either the person making the statement or the other party to the marriage falls within one of the requirements set out in s 19(2). Presumably, therefore, the statement will contain a declaration to that effect.

2.15 The matters set out above enable one to predict what the requirements are likely to be in connection with the form of the statement, its filing and service, and certain consequential matters. Section 12(2) then goes on to provide for the making of rules which will impose requirements on the legal representatives 'of a party to a marriage with respect to which a statement has been made or is proposed to be made'. These requirements will therefore have

---

[3] Nullity proceedings are not within the definition of 'marital proceedings'; see s 20 and Chapter Nine below.

to be observed by legal representatives for either the party making the statement or the party receiving it.

The rules may provide for the following requirements to be imposed on the legal representatives:

'(a) to inform that party, [ie the party for whom the legal representative acts], at such time or times as may be specified—

    (i) about the availability to the parties of marriage support services;

    (ii) about the availability to them of mediation;

    (iii) where there are children of the family, that in relation to the arrangements to be made for any child the parties should consider the child's welfare, wishes and feelings;

(b) to give that party, at such time or times as may be specified, names and addresses of persons qualified to help—

    (i) to effect a reconciliation; or

    (ii) in connection with mediation; and

(c) to certify, at such time or times as may be specified—

    (i) whether he has complied with the provision made in the rules by virtue of paragraphs (a) and (b);

    (ii) whether he has discussed with that party any of the matters mentioned in paragraph (a) or the possibility of reconciliation; and

    (iii) which, if any, of those matters they have discussed.'

2.16 Some of the matters set out above will be familiar to solicitors specialising in family law. The requirement to certify whether or not a reconciliation has been discussed has existed (in cases where the petitioner is not on the 'Green Form' scheme) since 1970, and the extent to which it has become a mere formality has depended on the individual practitioner. The other matters, now contemplated, such as the requirement to inform the client about marriage support and mediation, have been the stock-in-trade of the good family lawyer without compulsion for some time, and the rules will therefore only require them to do what they are doing already.

2.17 In conclusion, therefore, it may be said that the statement will be in a prescribed form, and will have to be filed in a prescribed way, after which it will be served by the court. Where a legal representative is involved, it will have to be accompanied by certain certificates from him.

The filing of the statement initiates the marital proceedings. Thereafter, the court may require further information from either party. Discussion of the next stages is contained in Chapter Three.

When a statement may not be effective

2.18 Section 6(7) sets out the circumstances in which a statement is ineffective for the purposes of Part II of the Act, ie for the purpose of obtaining a divorce or separation order. They are:

'(a) that a statement has previously been made with respect to the marriage and it is, or will become, possible—
  (i) for an application for a divorce order, or
  (ii) for an application for a separation order,
  to be made by reference to the previous statement;
(b) that such an application has been made in relation to the marriage and has not been withdrawn;
(c) that a separation order is in force.'

These three possibilities are distinct. No doubt, (a) is intended to establish the principle that there can only be one statement in relation to one marriage at the same time. This is consistent with the fact that, by s 5(2), the application for a divorce order or separation order does not have to be made by the person who made the statement. However, complications may arise because of s 7(6) which provides that a statement which is made before the first anniversary of the marriage is ineffective for the purposes of any application for a divorce order; the corollary of this is that such statement would be effective for the purpose of a separation order, and, indeed, it must follow that someone seeking a separation order may make a statement at any time after the celebration of the marriage, provided he or she had attended an information meeting three months earlier.

If one party makes a statement after, say, 11 months of marriage, this would be a statement by reference to which a separation order could be made. If the other party sought a divorce, he would normally have to make a statement on or after the first anniversary of the marriage. However, any statement which he made in such circumstances would be ineffective, because of the first statement. The party who did not want a divorce would, therefore, be able to delay the grant of the divorce order by these means. The other party would have to wait for one year to elapse from the end of the period for reflection and consideration triggered off by the first statement (see s 5(3)(b); on the face of it, this could cause a delay of up to 21 months, in straightforward cases, before the party seeking a divorce could file his statement.

It seems that the only way in which this delay could be circumvented would be by the respondent applying for a separation order himself, based on the applicant's statement, at the appropriate time, and then applying for this to be converted to a divorce order on the second anniversary of the marriage (see Chapter Eight, para **8.14**).

This is a curious result which, one suspects, was not intended by the Government.

Termination of marital proceedings

2.19 It may be convenient to record here how marital proceedings come to an end. Section 20(6) provides that this happens:

'(a) on the making of a separation order;

(b) on the making of a divorce order;

(c) on the withdrawal of the statement by a notice in accordance with section 5(3)(a);

(d) at the end of the specified period mentioned in section 5(3)(b), if no application under section 3 by reference to the statement is outstanding;

(e) on the withdrawal of all such applications which are outstanding at the end of that period;

(f) on the withdrawal of an application under section 4(3).'

2.20 The only point to be considered is withdrawal of a statement. Section 5(3)(b) refers only to a joint withdrawal of a statement, and there is no provision for a unilateral withdrawal. If follows that, once a statement has been filed, it can only be withdrawn by consent. As will be seen in Chapter Four, either party can present an application for a divorce order after the period for reflection and consideration has passed, based on a statement filed by either party, and subject to the other matters which must be proved.

CHAPTER THREE

The Period for Reflection and Consideration

Introduction

3.1 At the heart of the system established by the Act is the period for reflection and consideration. As was seen in Chapter Two, this begins 14 days after the filing of the statement, and it is only possible to apply for a divorce or separation order after the ending of that period. During that period, it is intended that the parties should reflect on the consequences of their intended actions, consider saving the marriage, and complete all necessary arrangements for the future, either on a consensual basis or by contested litigation.

In the words of the Lord Chancellor:

> 'The period should be sufficiently long to give parties a realistic timescale within which to reflect on whether the marriage could be saved but also a realistic time within which the practical questions about children, home and finances could be resolved.' (*Official Report* (HL) 30 November 1995, col 702).

Later in the same debate, the Lord Chancellor outlined the thinking behind one of the most important features of the new procedure:

> 'A very important requirement in the Bill is the requirement that parties decide all arrangements relating to their children, finance and home before a separation or divorce order can be made. This is an important and significant change from the Law Commission's recommendations. In making this change the government have been influenced by those who responded to their consultation paper who were of the view that parties who marry should discharge their obligations undertaken when they contracted their earlier marriage, and also their responsibilities which they undertook when they became parents, before they became free to remarry. The Bill provides for certain narrow exceptions to the requirement that all arrangements should be decided before divorce, in order to protect vulnerable parties, such as those who are sick, disabled or being prevented from making arrangements by vindictive and obstructive spouses, and also to protect the children of such parties.' (ibid, col 703)

3.2 These intentions are reflected in statutory form in s 7(1), which provides for, when a statement has been made, a period for the parties:

> '(a) to reflect on whether the marriage can be saved and to have an opportunity to effect a reconciliation, and
> (b) to consider what arrangements should be made for the future.'

In the Bill as originally presented to Parliament, the period for reflection and consideration (which will hereafter be referred to as 'the period') was to be one year. In the House of Commons on 23 April 1996, on a free vote, an amendment was carried which extends the period by six months in certain circumstances; the Government decided to accept this change. Another amendment was later carried, the result of which is that a statement of marital breakdown may not be presented until three months after the information meeting; this resulted in yet another amendment to change the period for reflection and consideration to nine months. The result is that the overall period from the date of the information meeting must be not less than one year (it may be more, depending on how promptly the statement is filed) and this may be extended by six months.

In this chapter, therefore, the following questions must be addressed:

(a) the length of the period;
(b) extensions to the period;
(c) expiry of the period;
(d) the conduct of proceedings during the period.

These will be considered in turn.

The length of the period

3.3 Marital proceedings are commenced by the filing of a statement. By s 7(3), the period for reflection and consideration is nine months beginning with the fourteenth day after the day on which the statement is received by the court; as has been seen, this date must be not less than three months after the information meeting. The intention behind the provision for 14 days is that it allows time for the court to serve the statement on the other party. The effect is therefore, that the minimum period from the information meeting is 54 weeks.

However, this period can be extended in certain circumstances, and must be extended in others. The possible extensions are complicated, and can be summarised as follows:

(a) extension by order under s 7(4) – (delay as to service);
(b) extension by joint notice under s 7(8) – (with a view to reconciliation);
(c) extension by six months by operation of s 7(10) and (13) – (one party seeks further time);

(d) extension by six months by operation of s 7(11) and (13) – (child under 16);

(e) provisions for disapplying (c) and (d).

These will be considered in turn.

Extension under section 7(4): delay in service

3.4 The period for reflection and consideration is fixed to give the other party to the marriage nine months (or, in some cases, 15 months) from service of the statement to reflect and consider, on the assumption that service of the statement will be completed within 14 days. It is always possible that service will not be effected within this period, and s 7(4) therefore provides for extension of the period in those circumstances.

The effect of s 7(4)(a) is that this provision only applies where the statement has been made by one party; it would obviously not be appropriate in the case of a joint statement.

By s 7(4)(b), the provision applies where: 'rules made under s 12 require the court to serve a copy of the statement on the other party'.

Presumably this is what the rules to be made will, in fact, require. If this proves not to be the case, s 7(4) will either have to be amended or will be of no effect.

3.5 However, on the assumption that both these requirements are satisfied, it is only necessary to consider the third condition, contained in s 7(4)(c), namely, 'failure to comply with the rules causes inordinate delay in service'.

If all these requirements are fulfilled, 'the court may, on the application of that other party, extend the period for reflection and consideration'.

Extension is not granted by the court of its own motion; the other party has to make an application to the court, presumably on notice to the party who made the statement. It will be for the party applying to satisfy the court that the delay in service has been 'inordinate'. From this, it would seem that normal delay will not be enough, so that delay of a few days or, arguably, a few weeks, would not per se lead to an extension. Quite what 'inordinate' means in this context must remain to be seen.

It is also to be noted that the power of the court to extend the period is discretionary. The basis on which the court should exercise its discretion is not specified. It would have been simpler if the Act had provided for an automatic extension of whatever time beyond 14 days it actually takes to serve the statement; however, this is not the case, so this provision may well be the subject of litigation.

3.6 In the event of the court deciding to exercise its discretion to extend the period, s 7(5) provides that the extension may be:

'... for any period not exceeding the time between—
(a) the beginning of the period for reflection and consideration; and
(b) the time when service is effected.'

It cannot, therefore, exceed the period of delay, or go beyond the date of actual service, but may be any shorter amount of time. Again, it must be said that there is nothing in the Act to guide the court as to what the period should be except, of course, the general principles in Part I.

Extension under section 7(8): joint reconciliation attempts

3.7   s 7(8) is designed to govern the position where the parties to the marriage think that the period for reflection and consideration is insufficient for that purpose. By s 7(7), subsection (8) applies:

'... if, at any time during the period for reflection and consideration, the parties jointly give notice to the court that they are attempting a reconciliation but require additional time.'

Where this is the case, the effect of subsection (8) is that:

'The period for reflection and consideration—
(a) stops running on the day on which the notice is received by the court; but
(b) resumes running on the day on which either of the parties gives notice to the court that the attempted reconciliation has been unsuccessful.'

Subject to the cut-off period referred to below, therefore, the giving of a joint notice to the court results in time ceasing to run for the purpose of the period for reflection and consideration. Time begins to run again when notice is given by one party that the attempt at a reconciliation has been unsuccessful.

3.8   This interruption of the period is subject to s 7(9), which must be borne in mind by anyone giving a notice under s 7(8). This provides that, where the period is interrupted by a notice under s 7(8), and the interruption is for a continuous period of more than 18 months:

'... any application by either of the parties for a divorce order or for a separation order must be by reference to a new statement received by the court at any time after the end of the 18 months.'

The result of this, in practical terms, is that once 18 months have elapsed from the date of receipt by the court of the s 7(8) notice, the statement which initiated the marital proceedings and the period for reflection and consideration ceases to have any effect, as does the period which has elapsed until then.

It is then necessary to start all over again, with a new statement and a new period for reflection. This is the case whether the length of the period which had elapsed before the s 7(8) notice was one week or nine months.

Extension under section 7(10) and (13): one party seeks further time

3.9 Subsections (10) and (13) are the result of the first occasion during the passage of the Bill when the House of Commons (on a free vote) disregarded the advice of the Government and voted for an amendment proposed by a backbencher.[1] The effect of the amendment is that, to put it one way, the period for reflection and consideration can be extended by a further six months, making a total period of 15 months from the date of the statement, in certain circumstances. It might, however, be more accurate to describe the additional time of six months as a period during which there is a bar to proceeding further with the marital proceedings.

This may happen whenever subsection (13) applies, which may be in either of two sets of circumstances; the first of these arises when subsection (10) applies, and is considered in this paragraph. The second arises under subsection (11) and is considered at para **3.12**. Both these provisions come into effect by operation of law, once the appropriate procedure is employed, but there are two sets of circumstances in which they respectively will, or may, not apply; these are considered in paras **3.13–3.14**.

When s 7(13) applies, the period for reflection and consideration is extended by six months without invalidating the application for a divorce order. The significance of the extension is clear enough; where s 7(13) applies, the time between the filing of the statement and the application for a divorce order must be at least 15 months. The need to insert the words 'without invalidating the application for a divorce order' means that, if an application for a divorce order has been made and is delayed by the giving of a notice under subsection (10), the application itself is not rendered of no effect but remains, as it were, on ice. It might also mean that, where time would otherwise 'run out', by virtue of s 5(3)(b), this would not be the case where the delay had been caused by a six-month extension under subsection (13).

3.10 Section 7(10) sets out the first set of circumstances in which subsection (13) may apply. These are that one party has applied to the court for a divorce order, when:

'(a) the other party [ie not the party who filed the request for the divorce order] applies to the court, within the prescribed period, for time for further reflection; and

---

[1] Mr Edward Leigh, MP on 24 April 1996.

(b) the requirements of section 9 (except any imposed under section 9(3)) are satisfied.'

3.11. The first requirement is, therefore, that the non-initiating party must, at some time after the other party has applied for a divorce order, apply to the court for time for further reflection; since, subject to subsection (12), this will result in an extension of time without any order of the court, the application will presumably be made on a prescribed form. The application must be made 'within the prescribed period'; this clearly means a period to be prescribed by the rules for the making of such an application. Given that the application can only be made after one party has applied for a divorce order, there will have to be provision for notice to be given of one party's intention to apply for a divorce order.

The second requirement relates to the requirements of s 9. Section 9(3) need not be considered here since it relates to cases to which s 26(1) of the Marriage Act 1949 applies (for more detail, see para **4.25**). The remainder of s 9 relates to the making of arrangements for the future which must be completed before a divorce order can be granted; this is considered in more detail in Chapter Four, but the position may be summarised by saying that a party seeking a divorce order has to produce either a court order or negotiated agreement relating to financial matters, or has to show that one of certain exemptions from this requirement applies, and the court must have made a declaration as to the children under s 11.

The result of this seems to be that while a notice under s 7(10) can be given at any time during the prescribed period from the application for a divorce order, the six-month extension only comes into effect after the applicant for a divorce order is in a position to satisfy the court as to arrangements for the future, and, in the absence of any notice, that a divorce order should be granted. Whenever it comes into effect, it will run on from the end of the nine-month period. The total period for reflection and consideration cannot, therefore, exceed 15 months, but a non-initiating party will be in a position to bring about a delay at a late stage, if so advised, subject to subsection (12).

Extension under section 7(11) and (13): children cases

3.12 As was seen above, a six-month delay can be caused by the non-initiating party giving notice under s 7(10). This may, or may not, happen. In effect, the provisions enable a party resisting divorce to delay it for six months, notwithstanding the fact that the marriage may have broken down; indeed, given the fact that notice under s 7(10) can only be given if the applicant has applied for an order under s 3, which itself means that the applicant must have been in a position to satisfy the court as to arrangements for the future, such arrangements for the future should have been made.

Section 7(11) is somewhat different, since it provides circumstances in which subsection (13) will come into effect and bring about a six-month extension in all cases to which subsection (11) applies; these are:

> 'Where any application for a divorce order is made [and] ... there is any child of the family under the age of sixteen when the application is made.'

This is likely to be the case in a considerable proportion of cases. Subject to subsection (12), therefore, (see para **3.13** below) the period for reflection is 15 months wherever there is a child of the family who is under the age of sixteen.

The provision applies by reference to the age of the child at the date of applying for the divorce. In cases where a child is nearly sixteen, it is not necessary to wait until after the child's sixteenth birthday before applying, because subsection (14) provides that a period which has been extended under subsection (13) and has otherwise come to an end, comes to an end on there ceasing to be any children of the family to which subsection (11) applied.

The fact that the application under s 3 must be made in order to initiate the period of six months is difficult to reconcile with the underlying policy of the period for reflection and consideration, and may give rise to difficulties of interpretation.

Exceptions to section 7(13)

3.13   As was seen above, the extension of the period by six months in the two sets of circumstances prescribed by s 7(10) and (11) are not immutable, and the extension can be nullified in two cases; the first of these is by operation of law and the second can only occur as a result of an order of the court.

By s 7(12)(a), subsection (13) does not apply, and the period is not, therefore, extended if:

> 'at the time when the application for a divorce order is made, there is an occupation order or a non-molestation order in force in favour of the applicant, or of a child of the family, made against the other party;'

Domestic violence is not the subject of this book[2], but it will be recalled that Part IV of the Act contains new and complicated provisions as to non-molestation and occupation orders or injunctions. Where this is the case, and the order is still in force at the date of the application for a divorce order (which can only be at the end of nine months from the date of the filing of the statement), the six-month extension does not apply. It should be noted that occupation and non-molestation orders are almost invariably limited in time, so it may well be that courts granting such orders will be asked to bear these provisions in mind, to avoid unnecessary delay.

---

[2] For a full treatment of the topic, see R. Bird, *Domestic Violence – The New Law* (Family Law, 1996).

This provision applies only when the applicant for the divorce order is a party to the marriage in whose favour the order was made; if, therefore, one party makes and files the statement, and the other subsequently obtains the order, the disapplication of the six-month extension only occurs if the other party applies for the divorce order.

Subsection (12)(a) applies as a matter of course if the appropriate order can be produced; it, therefore, seems not to be necessary to apply to the court for an order disapplying subsection (13).

3.14   The second set of circumstances in which subsection (13) may be disapplied is contained in subsection (12)(b), which provides that this is the case if:

> 'the court is satisfied that delaying the making of a divorce order would be significantly detrimental to the welfare of any child of the family.'

Subsection (12)(b) applies only, therefore, if one or other of the parties applies to the court for an order to that effect. It is necessary to prove to the court, on the balance of probabilities, that delay would be detrimental to the welfare of a child; and in this context the court will no doubt wish to take into account the general principles embodied in s 1 of the Act: see para **1.16** above.

It is only possible to speculate as to what the approach of the court may be. Any application based on financial grounds, for example that an order for property adjustment or lump sum should be able to take effect as soon as possible, might be met by the reply that, by ss 22B and 23B of the Matrimonial Causes Act 1973, the court may, when making such an order, provide that it take effect before divorce where hardship can be shown, and that, since that power exists, it cannot have been the purpose of subsection (12)(b) to provide for that eventuality. The court has to concentrate on the welfare of a child of the family, and nothing else. It is difficult to see obvious examples of cases where this requirement may be satisfied. One such example might be where the parent with care wished to remarry.

Expiry of the period

3.15   The period for reflection and consideration does not last indefinitely and, if no application is made for a divorce or separation order within a certain time, the statement (the filing of which initiated the marital proceedings) and the period itself, will cease to have any effect and can no longer be the basis for the grant of a divorce or separation order. Some of these provisions as to expiry of the period have been referred to above, but it may be helpful to summarise them here.

The basic rule is contained in s 5(3)(b), which provides that an application may not be made under s 3 (for a divorce or separation order) by reference to a particular statement if:

'a period of more than one year ("the specified period") has passed since the end of the period for reflection and consideration.'

Where the period is nine months, this means that the time-limit is one year, nine months and two weeks from the date on which the court receives the statement.

3.16 Section 5(4) provides that any period during which an order preventing divorce is in force is not to count towards the one-year period referred to in subsection (3)(b). This is a reference to orders which may be made on grounds of hardship, and this subject is discussed in more detail in Chapter Five, paras **5.5** et seq.

It is to be noted that an order preventing divorce does not stop the time running for the calculation of the period which has elapsed since the filing of the statement, but only in respect of the time since the end of the period for reflection and consideration; in other words, if an order preventing divorce is made and then discharged, the time during which it was in force will count for the purposes of s 5(1)(c) (to establish that the period for reflection and consideration has ended), but will not count for the calculation of the period following the end of the reflection and consideration period, which may be described as the 'lapse period'.

3.17 As was seen above (para **3.7**), by s 7(8), the period for reflection and consideration stops running when the parties jointly give notice that they are seeking a reconciliation but need more time; accordingly, that time is ignored in calculating whether the period has elapsed. However, s 7(9), which imposes an absolute deadline when the period is interrupted for a continuous period of 18 months, must be borne in mind.

Provision for reconciliation during the period

3.18 As was seen in paras **3.1–3.2** one of the purposes of the period for reflection and consideration is intended to be an opportunity for the parties to consider reconciliation, and that intention is enshrined in s 7(1)(a). This is reinforced by s 1, which sets out the general principles underlying the Act, in particular:

'that the parties to a marriage which may have broken down are to be encouraged to take all practicable steps, whether by marriage counselling or otherwise, to save the marriage' (s 1(b)).

It was also seen, in Chapter Two, that information about marriage counselling services and provision for reconciliation is given when the parties attend the information meeting.

It is, therefore, beyond doubt that one of the purposes of the Act is the encouragement of reconciliation where that is possible, and this is given statutory form in s 23.

Section 23(2) provides that marriage counselling may only be provided under this section at a time when a period for reflection and consideration is running in relation to the marriage, or has been interrupted under s 7(8) (but not for a continuous period of more than 18 months). In other words, it may be provided after the filing of the statement, before the grant of a divorce or separation order, and as long as the statement would still be effective.

The class of persons able to take advantage of this provision of counselling is severely limited. Subsection (3) provides that marriage counselling may only be provided under this section for persons who would not be required to make any contribution towards the cost of mediation provided for them under Part IIIA of the Legal Aid Act 1988, as to which see para **3.29** below.

No doubt as a corollary to this, subsection (4) provides that persons for whom marriage counselling is provided under this section are not to be required to make any contribution towards the cost of the counselling.

Finally, by subsection (5), marriage counselling is only to be provided under the section if it appears to the marriage counsellor to be suitable in all the circumstances.

Arrangements for the future

3.19   If reconciliation is not achieved, the principal purpose of the period for reflection and consideration is the consideration of arrangements for the future and, if possible, agreement between the parties relating to these. When the requirements for the grant of a divorce order are considered in Chapter Four, it will be seen that, subject to certain exceptions, satisfactory arrangements for the future have to be made, in one way or another, before such an order can be made. By s 9, such arrangements may be in the form of either:

(a)   a court order dealing with the financial arrangements;
(b)   a negotiated agreement relating thereto;
(c)   a declaration that they have made their financial arrangements; or
(d)   a declaration that there are no significant assets and no financial arrangements to be made.

There are certain exceptions to these requirements, which will be considered in Chapter Four, but the matters set out above are those which have to be addressed.

In addition, the court must make a declaration in respect of the children, pursuant to s 11. This, too, will be considered in Chapter Four, but the arrangements for the children are, clearly, one of the important issues to be addressed during the period.

3.20   The parties to the marriage have, therefore, at least nine months, in some cases 15 months, and, in any event, unless they apply to extend the lapse period (see s 5)6), not more than 21 months from the date of the statement in which to resolve these matters. This may be done in one of two ways, namely, by negotiation and agreement or by contested litigation. When the matter is dealt with by contested litigation, the procedure, and the principles set out in Chapter Six (financial issues), and Chapter Seven (children) will have to be applied. When agreement is reached, this may take the form of either a consent order or a negotiated agreement.

In any of these cases, mediation is clearly intended to play an important part, and the next section of this chapter will, therefore, deal with this subject.

Mediation

3.21 When the parties embark on the legal process, they will already have received information about the availability of mediation at the information meeting. One of the overriding objects of the Act, contained in s 1(c)(ii) and (iii), is that issues between the parties should be dealt with in a manner designed to promote as good a continuing relationship between the parties as possible, and without incurring unnecessary costs. These matters, together with the statements of Government Ministers and others, show that great importance is placed on mediation in the context of the Act, and that, in the eyes of many, it is the key to the thinking behind the Act.

3.22 Although it is unnecessary to consider legal aid in detail, it should be noted that Part III of the Act deals entirely with legal aid for mediation in family matters. The Lord Chancellor is authorised to empower the Legal Aid Board to fund mediation services, and make payments for mediation. The intention is that the Board will make contracts with mediation services, thereby funding them to carry out the mediation for which the Act provides. Provision is made for legally aided parties to be able to participate in mediation at either no cost to them, or such cost as is consistent with their means and assessed by reference to the legal aid regulations.

3.23 It is curious that, in an Act which already places so much importance on mediation, the term is only defined by s 26, and then exclusively in the context of legal aid and in a somewhat circular form. However, for the purposes of this book, mediation may be defined as the process by which parties to an actual or potential dispute are assisted to come to a negotiated agreement; the emphasis is on the result being their agreement and not a solution which someone else has made for them. Mediation has most commonly been encountered in disputes relating to children, such as contact or residence, but it has been increasingly used in financial disputes.

Guidance as to the proper approach of mediators in the context of the Act can be gained from s 27, which inserts a new s 13B into the Legal Aid Act 1988 (references to sections, subsections etc in this paragraph relate to the amended 1988 Act). Subsection (3) provides that a person is not to be granted mediation in relation to any dispute unless mediation appears to the mediator suitable to the dispute and the parties and all the circumstances.

Subsection (6) provides that any contract entered into by the Legal Aid Board for the provision of mediation, must require the mediator to comply with a code of practice; by subsection (7), the code must require, inter alia:

(a) that parties participate in mediation only if willing and not influenced by fear of violence or other harm;
(b) that cases where either party may be influenced by fear of violence or other harm are identified as soon as possible;
(c) that the possibility of reconciliation is kept under review throughout mediation; and
(d) that each party is informed about the availability of independent legal advice.

By subsection (8), where there are one or more children of the family, the code must also require the mediator to have arrangements designed to ensure that the parties are encouraged to consider:

(a) the welfare, wishes and feelings of each child; and
(b) whether and to what extent each child should be given the opportunity to express his or her wishes and feelings in the mediation.

3.24 A new section 15(3F) inserted in the 1988 Act deals with mediation and legal aid, and attempts to overcome the possible (in the eyes of some critics) problem of the relationship between mediation and conventional methods of resolving disputes. Subsection (3F) provides that:

'a person shall not be granted representation for the purpose of proceedings relating to family matters, unless he has attended a meeting with a mediator—
(a) to determine—
(i) whether mediation appears to be suitable to the dispute and the parties and all the circumstances, and
(ii) in particular, whether mediation could take place without either party being influenced by fear of violence or other harm; and
(b) if mediation does appear suitable, to help the person applying for representation to decide whether instead to apply for mediation.'

Subsection (3G) provides that subsection (3F) does not apply in relation to Part IV of the Family Law Act (domestic violence cases), s 37 of the Matrimonial Causes Act 1973, nor to cases under Parts IV and V of the Children Act 1989.

The reference to 'representation' in subsection (3F) means the grant of legal aid for such representation, and has no application to non-legal aid cases.

Subsection (3H) contains provision to direct the exercise of the Legal Aid Board's discretion in this respect. When deciding whether, in relation to proceedings, it is reasonable that a person should be granted legal aid, the Board:

> '(a) must have regard to whether and to what extent recourse to mediation would be a suitable alternative to taking the proceedings; and
>
> (b) must for that purpose have regard to the outcome of the meetings held under subsection (3F) and to any assessment made for the purposes of section 13B(3).'

3.25 The court's powers with regard to mediation are contained in s 13 of the Family Law Act. The effect of s 13 may be summarised as follows:

(a) the power to give a direction under s 13 arises at any time after the court has received a statement (s 13(1));

(b) a direction may then be given at any time, including in the course of 'proceedings connected with the breakdown of the marriage' (s 13(2)); these are defined by s 25, and include applications with respect to a child of the family under Parts I to V of the Children Act 1989 and applications under Part IV of the Act (domestic violence etc). The power to give a direction continues once the statement has been filed (provided it is not withdrawn), and after a divorce or separation order has been made;

(c) a direction may be given on the application of either party or on the initiative of the court (s 13(3));

(d) the direction which the court may give is to require each party to attend a meeting arranged in accordance with the direction (s 13(1)); the Act does not specify where the meeting will take place, nor who will conduct it. However, from statements made during the parliamentary passage of the Bill[3], it is clear that the meeting will be conducted by a mediator whose role will be to explain the purpose of mediation under the Act; it will not, therefore, be conducted by a judicial officer or court official. This is also implicit in subsection (5), as to which see (g) below;

(e) the meeting is for the purpose of:
   (i) enabling an explanation to be given of the facilities available to the parties for mediation in relation to the disputes between them; and
   (ii) providing an opportunity for each party to agree to take advantage of those facilities (s 13(1)(a) and (b)).

The purpose of the meeting is, therefore, explanation. It appears that no mediation as such will be carried out at this meeting, but it is intended that parties will come to see the benefits of mediation as a result of the meeting, and will agree to go through the process;

(f) the parties are to be required to attend the same meeting, unless:
   (i) one or both of them ask for a separate meeting; or
   (ii) the court considers separate meetings to be more appropriate (s 13(4)).

---

[3] See eg the Lord Chancellor, *Official Report* (HL), 14 March 1996, col 40.

This would be the case where, for example, there had been violence, or an injunction was in force;

(g) the direction itself must specify a person chosen by the court to arrange and conduct the meeting; that must be with the consent of such person (s 13(5)). The direction must also require this specified person to produce to the court, at such time as the court may direct, a report stating:

    (i) whether the parties have complied with the direction; and

    (ii) if they have, whether they have agreed to take part in any mediation (ibid).

3.26   Although the direction made by the court under s 13 will 'require' the parties to attend a meeting, it is not clear what the sanction for disobeying such a direction would be. Certain consequences as to adjournments may follow (as to which see para **3.27**), but beyond that it would seem that the court's powers are of an exhortatory, rather than a coercive, nature. It has been said that there may be certain effects on entitlement to legal aid, but at present it is not known whether this is so.

3.27   Section 14 makes certain provisions as to adjournments, which clearly must be read in conjunction with the provisions as to directions which may be given under s 13. Subsection (1) provides that the court's power to adjourn any proceedings connected with the breakdown of a marriage (as to the meaning of 'connected' see para **3.25** at (b)), includes power to adjourn:

'(a) for the purpose of allowing the parties to comply with a direction under s 13; or

(b) for the purpose of enabling disputes to be resolved amicably.'

Subsection (2) provides that, in determining whether to adjourn for either purpose, the court shall have regard in particular to the need to protect the interests of any child of the family. By subsection (3), if the court adjourns for either purpose, the period of the adjournment must not exceed the maximum period prescribed by rules of court; at present, such rules are not available.

3.28   Subsection (4) prescribes the purpose for which an adjournment may be ordered under s 14. Unless the only purpose of the adjournment is to allow the parties to comply with a direction under s 12, the court must order one or both of the parties to produce to the court a report as to:

'(a) whether they have taken part in any mediation during the adjournment;

(b) whether, as a result, any agreement has been reached between them;

(c) the extent to which any dispute between them has been resolved as a result of any such agreement;

(d) the need for further mediation; and

(e) how likely it is that further mediation will be successful.'

It follows from this that the court will not order an adjournment under s 13 if there is no useful purpose to be served. Where this provision is invoked, the court must order a report; the matters set out from (a) to (e) must be addressed.

Legal aid

3.29 Although legal aid merits a separate section in this chapter, due to its practical importance for the practitioner, it will be seen that much of the relevant material is contained in the immediately preceding section on mediation. Indeed, Part III of the Act, which contains all the provisions relating to legal aid, is headed 'Legal Aid for Mediation in Family Matters', and the question of whether there will be any restrictions on the availability of legal aid must be answered by reference to this Part.

3.30 The reader's attention is, therefore, drawn to the new s 15(3F) of the 1988 Act, which is discussed at para **3.24**. The other principal provision to be noted in this context is the new s 15(3H), which provides that the Legal Aid Board, in determining whether, in relation to family proceedings, it is reasonable that a person should be granted representation,

'(a) must have regard to whether and to what extent recourse to mediation would be a suitable alternative to taking the proceedings; and

(b) must for that purpose have regard to the outcome of the meeting held under subsection (3F) and to any assessment made for the purposes of section 13B(3).'

Section 13B(3) relates to an assisted person's liability to pay to the Board a contribution towards the cost of mediation.

PROGRESS CHART FOR PERIOD FOR REFLECTION AND CONSIDERATION

3.31 EVENT	**TIME**
1. SMB filed at court (s 12(1)(c))	Day 1
2. SMB served by court (s 12(1)(d))	Add 14 days (s 7(3))
3. [Only where inordinate delay in service, and respondent applies for more time] Court extends time to not later than actual date of service (s 7(4))	Add as ordered (s 7(5))
4. (i) Both parties apply for more time (s 7(7)) (ii) 18 months elapse from Event 4(i) (s 7(9)) (iii) notice that reconciliation unsuccessful (s 7(8))	Time stops (s 7(8) SMB ceases to be effective (s 7(9)) Time restarts (s 7(8))
5. Nine months elapse from Event 2 (s 7(3))	Add 9 months to Event 2 (s 7(3))
6. Applicant applies for DO under s 3	
7. EITHER Child under 16 (s 7(11)) OR Before specified period elapses, respondent applies for time (s 7(10)) Unless either (i) OO or NMO in effect (s 7(12)(a)) or (ii) applicant satisfies court that delay significantly detrimental to child of family (s 7(12)(b))	Add 6 months (s 7(13)) (see para **3.9**)
8. Child attains 16, and no other reason for extension (s 7(14))	Extra time stops (s 7(14))
9. One year elapses from Event 5 or 7 (as applicable) (s 5(3)(b))	SMB ceases to be effective (s 5(3)(b))

Key: SMB – Statement of Marital Breakdown
     OO   – Occupation Order
     NMO – Non-Molestation Order
     DO   – Divorce order

Note: It must be said that what appears above is a simplified account of what may happen when the Act is in force, and that there are potential areas of considerable complication which cannot be reflected in such a chart.

CHAPTER FOUR

Divorce Orders

Introduction

4.1 The essential elements of the new procedure for obtaining a divorce order have been summarised in earlier chapters. It has been seen that at the heart of the procedure is the period for reflection and consideration; in effect a nine months, or sometimes 15 months, enforced wait after filing the statement of marital breakdown. The applicant cannot make the statement until he has attended an information meeting, and, at the end of the period, cannot be granted a divorce until he has satisfied the court as to certain arrangements for the future. The information meeting is considered in more detail in Chapter Two para **2.4** et seq, and the statement in Chapter Two para **2.10** et seq.

It is necessary to bear in mind that, when the time comes to apply for a divorce order, the process is entirely retrospective; the court is concerned to look back at what has happened over the period of reflection and consideration, and to satisfy itself that the formalities have been complied with.

Who can apply?

4.2 Either party to the marriage may apply for a divorce order. As will be seen, an application for a divorce is made under s 3, and the purpose of the formalities is in part to show that a statement of marital breakdown has been made pursuant to s 5; s 5(2) provides that the s 5 statement and the application under s 3 need not be made by the same person. It follows that, once the statement of marital breakdown is filed the process can become irreversible, since although the person making the statement may change his mind he can only withdraw the statement with the consent of the other party; there is no provision in the Act for the unilateral withdrawal of a statement of marital breakdown. The result is that the respondent to the statement may apply for a divorce or separation order based on the other party's statement.

Time-limits

4.3 Apart from the period for reflection, there are no time-limits as such. However, this is subject to two qualifications. First, in the case of divorce, it would not have been possible to file the notice of marital breakdown, and so start the time running, before the first anniversary of the marriage (s 7(6)). Secondly, time can run out if an application for a divorce order is not received within certain time-limits. The effect of s 5(3) is that a statement of marital breakdown (one of the essential elements of the divorce process) cannot be relied upon if more than one year has passed since the end of the period for reflection and consideration; this period is itself normally nine months, but, as was seen in Chapter Three, it may be extended by up to six months.

Documents and evidence to be produced

4.4   The applicant for a divorce order, who may be either party to the marriage (and not necessarily the one who initiated the proceedings), has to satisfy the requirements of s 3. He must, therefore, prove that:

(a) the marriage has broken down irretrievably;
(b) the s 8 requirements about information meetings are satisfied;
(c) the s 9 requirements as to arrangements for the future are satisfied;
(d) the application has not been withdrawn;
(e) time has not 'run out' by virtue of s 5(3).

In addition, the court will need to satisfy itself that no order under s 10 preventing divorce has been made.

4.5   The first matter to be addressed is, therefore, proof that the marriage has broken down. This can be done only if the requirements of s 5 are satisfied. These requirements are

(a) compliance with the rules as to the statement of marital breakdown;
(b) the passage of the period for reflection and consideration since the date of the statement of marital breakdown;
(c) the making of a declaration under s 5(1)(d), to the effect that the marriage cannot be saved.

The first essential element for this purpose is the statement of marital breakdown, the requirements for which are contained in s 6. The required contents of the statement of marital breakdown, stipulations as to filing and service of this document, and other relevant topics are set out in more detail in Chapter Two. For present purposes, therefore, it need only be said that the court will need to be satisfied that the statement has been properly made, after attendance at an information meeting, and duly filed and served.

Similarly, the period for reflection and consideration is dealt with in detail in Chapter Three, and it need only be said here that the court will have to satisfy itself that the necessary period has passed.

4.6   The final element in proof of irretrievable breakdown is the declaration under s 5(1)(d). This is a declaration by the party making the application that, having reflected on the breakdown, and having considered the requirements of Part II of the Act as to the parties' arrangements for the future, the applicant believes that the marriage cannot be saved. No doubt a printed form will be available for this purpose.

By s 5(2), the declaration need not be by the same person who made the statement as to marital breakdown.

4.7   In addition to providing that the marriage has broken down irretrievably, the applicant must also satisfy the court as to the requirements of s 8 relating to the information meeting. In a sense, this is a circular process, since it is not possible to file a statement of marital breakdown without proof of having attended an information meeting; the stipulation as to information meetings in s 3(1)(b) is, therefore, superfluous. Information meetings, in the context of the preliminaries to the statement of marital breakdown, are considered in more detail in Chapter Two.

4.8   The applicant must also satisfy the court as to the requirement of s 9 relating to arrangements for the future. Section 9(2) sets out a list of possible ways of doing this. There are also certain stipulated exceptions. The detail as to arrangements for the future is set out at para **4.10** et seq.

The position as to orders preventing divorce on the ground of hardship is considered in more detail in Chapter Five. It should merely be noted here that the court must satisfy itself that no such order is in effect before granting a divorce order.

Summary of procedural requirements

4.9   The following checklist may assist in summarising the position. The questions which the court, and practitioners, must ask are (a negative answer to any question will mean that a divorce order cannot be granted):

(1) has a statement of marital breakdown been filed at the court?[1]
(2) have nine months elapsed since filing?
(3) has the period for reflection etc been extended by operation of s 7(13) and, if so, has the appropriate period elapsed since filing the statement?
(4) has a declaration under s 5(1)(d) been filed?
(5) have the requirements of s 9(2) been complied with?

In addition, the following questions must be answered in the negative; a positive answer to any will mean that a divorce order cannot be granted.

(6) Have the parties jointly given notice withdrawing the statement of marital breakdown?

---

[1] It will not be possible for the statement to have been validly filed unless one year has passed since the celebration of the marriage, and the applicant has attended the required information meeting.

(7) Has more than one year elapsed since the end of the period of reflection and consideration?
(8) Has the application for a divorce order been withdrawn?
(9) Is an order preventing divorce in effect under s 10?

Arrangements for the future

4.10 As was seen in Chapter Three, one of the purposes of the period for reflection and consideration is that the parties should consider their position, and conclude arrangements as to children and financial matters. This may be achieved by negotiation and agreement, and there are many incentives for parties to participate in mediation. If agreement cannot be reached, the issues in dispute will have to be litigated and, subject to certain exceptions, the proceedings concluded before an application for a divorce order is made. The intention of the legislation is that, when the time comes to apply for a divorce order, the applicant should be able to show that all necessary arrangements for the future have been made. These arrangements fall into two categories, namely, those relating to finance and those relating to children. These will be dealt with in turn.

4.11 'Financial arrangements' are defined by para 6 of Sch 1 as having the same meaning as in s 34(2) of the Matrimonial Causes Act 1973. This definition is:

> '... provisions governing the rights and liabilities towards one another when living separately of the parties to a marriage (including a marriage which has been dissolved or annulled) in respect of the making or securing of payments or the disposition or use of any property, including such rights and liabilities with respect to the maintenance or education of any child, whether or not a child of the family.'

4.12 Section 9(2) provides that one of the following must be produced to the court:

> '(a) a court order (made by consent or otherwise) dealing with their financial arrangements;
> (b) a negotiated agreement as to their financial arrangements;
> (c) a declaration by both parties that they have made their financial arrangements;
> (d) a declaration by one of the parties (to which no objection has been notified to the court by the other party) that—
>> (i) he has no significant assets and does not intend to make an application for financial provision;
>> (ii) he believes that the other party has no significant assets and does not intend to make an application for financial provision; and

(iii) there are therefore no financial arrangements to be made.'

Subject to the exceptions contained in Sch 1, which are dealt with at para **4.17**, the applicant for a divorce order has to produce one of the documents set out above. These will now be considered briefly, in turn.

4.13 A 'court order' may be either by consent or be the result of a disputed application. It will have to be a final order, which disposes of the issues between the parties. It will have, therefore, to contain either a periodical payments order or an order dismissing the claim for periodical payments. It will have also to deal with lump sum and property adjustment orders, either by making such orders or dismissing the claims.

Where the court has jurisdiction to make an order in respect of children of the family, for example in the case of stepchildren, they will also have to be dealt with in the order.

Where the order is by consent, the court will have to perform the role, at present performed under the MCA 1973, s 33A and FPR 1991, r 2.62, of approving the order. When the order was made before the application for a divorce order, this will already have been dealt with, but if the proposed order is presented to the court with the application for the divorce order it will be, in effect, the result of a negotiated agreement and it would be undesirable if it had to be considered on different criteria. This point will be further considered below.

By para 4(1) of Sch 1, s 9 is not to be read as requiring any order or agreement to have been 'carried into effect' (for example by transferring the property in respect of which a transfer order has been made) at the time when the court is considering whether arrangements for the future have been made by the parties. The fact that an appeal is pending against an order is to be disregarded.

4.14 A 'negotiated agreement' is defined by para 7 of Sch 1. It means:

'. . . a written agreement between the parties as to future arrangements—
  (a) which has been reached as the result of mediation or any other form of negotiation involving a third party; and
  (b) which satisfies such other requirements as may be imposed by rules of court.'

The requirements of rules of court are not yet known, so it is only possible to comment on (a). It is unclear who would qualify as a 'third party'. This might mean an independent person who was in a position to offer disinterested and independent advice to both sides. Alternatively, it might mean a solicitor acting for one or other party, but this is less certain since, for this purpose, the solicitor might well not be regarded as independent from his client. It may be, therefore, that an independent outside person must be involved, and if this is right, an agreement negotiated by solicitors would not qualify as a 'negotiated agreement'.

As was seen above, it is unclear whether the court will have to exercise any inquisitorial role in respect of the terms of the agreement.

Presumably, the negotiated agreement should deal with the same areas as should be covered by a court order, and the comments at para **4.13** are repeated.

4.15   The third way in which the applicant for a divorce order may satisfy the requirements of s 9(2) is by a 'declaration' by both parties that they have made their financial arrangements. Paragraph 8 of Sch 1 deals with declarations generally, by providing that they:

'(a) must be in a prescribed form;
(b) must, in prescribed cases, be accompanied by such documents as may be prescribed; and
(c) must, in prescribed cases, satisfy such other requirements as may be prescribed.'

At the present stage, this does not greatly assist in discerning what is intended by this provision. Parties seeking a divorce order will have to ask themselves what is the difference between a declaration on the one hand and a negotiated agreement on the other.

One answer is that, as was seen above, a mediator or third party has to be involved in a negotiated agreement; this is not the case with a declaration. It appears that the parties will not have to divulge to the court what arrangements they have made; it will be sufficient to say that they have made their arrangements. It follows that the court will not be required to approve such arrangements.

It is not clear what steps the court will have to take to ensure that both parties voluntarily agree whatever undivulged terms they have agreed, nor what their capacity for arriving at a fully informed decision may be. Nor is it clear what the status of any arrangements the parties may have made will be. In the case of a negotiated agreement, presumably the court would accord to such an agreement the same sort of status as a court order, should either party seek to resile from or vary it. This could not be the case in respect of the arrangements contemplated here, and it is not necessary to be pessimistic to foresee considerable litigation arising out of this provision.

4.16   The final way in which to satisfy the court regarding the financial arrangements is a 'declaration' by one of the parties that he and the other party have 'no significant assets', that neither party intends to apply for financial provision and that, accordingly, there are no arrangements to be made. This declaration will be subject to para 7 of Sch 1, in the same way as the previous type of declaration, and it is not yet known what the prescribed requirements will be. It can be said that it is the Government's intention that the declarations should be statutory declarations pursuant to the Statutory Declarations Act 1834, with the result that a false declaration would incur penalties; however, such a false declaration would not invalidate the divorce (see *Official Report* (HL) 27 June 1996, col 1112, per the Lord Chancellor).

The intention is clear: many divorcing couples have no assets at all, and it would be a waste of time and resources to make them go through the same procedures as those who really do have something to divide.

It is to be noted that either party may make the declaration, although presumably it will normally be the party applying for the divorce order who does so. Rules will provide for the service of the declaration on the other party, and for a certain time to elapse before the court may take it that there is no objection. Clearly, there is a degree of overlap between this provision and the declaration by both parties that they have made their arrangements; parties falling into the 'no assets' category could just as easily make a joint declaration that they had made their arrangements.

It remains to be seen what would be the position if one of the parties subsequently made an application for financial relief. It would be arguable that the person who had made the declaration, at least, would be estopped from making such an application, save in the case of a drastic change of circumstances. It also remains to be seen what the role of the court is to be in looking behind any such declaration; for example, it may be asked whether the court should accept such a declaration at its face value when there are young children of the family.

4.17   As was mentioned above, there are exceptions to the provisions of s 9(2). Section 9(7) provides that if the court is satisfied, on an application made by one of the parties after the end of the period for reflection and consideration, that the circumstances of the case are those set out in either para 1, 2 or 3 of Sch 1, it may make a divorce order or a separation order even though the requirements of subsection (2) have not been satisfied. The provisions of these paragraphs must, therefore, be examined.

4.18   Paragraph 1 of Sch 1 contains 'The first exemption'. The circumstances here must be that:

'(a) the requirements of section 11 have been satisfied;
(b) the applicant has, during the period for reflection and consideration, taken such steps as are reasonably practicable to try to reach agreement about the parties' financial arrangements; and
(c) the applicant has made an application to the court for financial relief and has complied with all requirements of the court in relation to proceedings for financial relief but—
   (i)   the other party has delayed in complying with requirements of the court or has otherwise been obstructive; or
   (ii) for reasons which are beyond the control of the applicant, or of the other party, the court has been prevented from obtaining the information which is required to determine the financial position of the parties.'

Subparagraph (a) is clear enough; the applicant will always have to satisfy the court in respect of s 11 matters (welfare of children), and this is considered further at para **4.23**. The applicant has then, in all applications based on this exemption, to satisfy the court of his own lack of delay in two respects. First, it is necessary to show that he has taken such steps as are reasonably practicable to try to reach agreement as to financial matters. Secondly, as a separate requirement, he must have made an application to the court for financial relief and have complied with all the procedural requirements of the court.

4.19 Attention then moves to matters beyond the control of the applicant, who has to prove one of two things. First, he may establish that the other party has delayed in complying with the procedural requirements or has been obstructive. There may be room for debate here, for example as to whose fault it is that the application has been delayed.

Secondly, the applicant may seek to show that for reasons beyond the control of either party, the court does not have the information it needs to dispose of the financial relief application. In the parliamentary debate on this point, the Lord Chancellor explained the thinking behind this provision as follows:

> 'That part of Schedule 1 was intended to provide for specific circumstances whereby a party was unable to put before the court sufficient information to enable a decision to be made about financial matters. For example, that may occur where there is outstanding separate litigation relating to the ownership of land, or, indeed, to personal injury damages. The total amount of the asset in question might be difficult to assess. Such matters would affect the assessment of the total value of the parties' assets, so a final decision for a division of assets may take some years.' (*Official Report* (HL) 30 January 1996, col 1414)

The examples given by the Lord Chancellor are not, of course, exhaustive, but they indicate why this provision is there.

4.20 Paragraph 2 contains 'the second exemption'. The first two requirements are as in the first exemption.

The remaining requirements for the circumstances in which this exemption might apply are then set out as follows:

> '(c) because of—
>> (i) the ill health or disability of the applicant, the other party or a child of the family (whether physical or mental), or
>> (ii) an injury suffered by the applicant, the other party or a child of the family,
>> the applicant has not been able to reach agreement with the other party about those arrangements and is unlikely to do so in the foreseeable future; and
> (d) a delay in making the order applied for under section 3—
>> (i) would be significantly detrimental to the welfare of any child of the family; or

(ii) would be seriously prejudicial to the applicant.'

In this case, therefore, it is not necessary to have made an application to the court. Indeed, it is implicit in the requirement that it would not have been possible for such an application to have proceeded very far, because of the ill health of, or injury to, one of the parties or a child. It is also part of the requirement that no end is in sight and that no resolution will be reached in the foreseeable future.

However, it is necessary to go further than that. It is necessary to show that delay in granting a divorce order would be 'significantly detrimental' to the welfare of a child, or 'seriously prejudicial' to the applicant. The difference in the wording of the two possible scenarios is, presumably, dictated by the need to link the reference to the child to the child's welfare. What circumstances may be found to come within the definition of 'seriously prejudicial' can only be a matter for conjecture at the present time.

4.21 The 'third exemption' is found in para 3 of Sch 1. Once again, it is necessary to have satisfied the court under s 11 (welfare of children). The remaining requirements are as follows:

'(b) the applicant has found it impossible to contact the other party; and
(c) as a result, it has been impossible for the applicant to reach agreement with the other party about their financial arrangements.'

This is quite clear. Presumably, in most cases in which these circumstances apply, there will have been an order dispensing with service of the statement and other divorce papers on the other party.

4.22 In all the exemptions set out in Sch 1, it will, of course, be necessary to make an application to the court for leave for the exemption to apply. No doubt such application will be to the district judge, and, apart from the third exemption, will be on notice to the other party.

4.23 In addition to the financial arrangements, the applicant for a divorce order has to comply with the requirements of s 11 relating to 'children of the family'. Section 9(5) provides that, 'the requirements of section 11 must have been satisfied'.

Section 11 replaces s 41 of the MCA 1973, which was the provision governing the way in which the court dealt with children on divorce, usually under the 'special procedure'. The new section repeats much of the old s 41, but in a greatly expanded form. The basic function of the court remains the same; the district judge has to perform two functions, the first of which is to make a declaration as to whether or not there are any children to whom s 11 applies. The second relates to the arrangements. Before the enactment of the Children Act 1989 the court had to declare whether or not it was 'satisfied' with the arrangements for the children. This was changed by the 1989 Act, and the court now has to consider whether or not it should exercise any of its powers under that Act with respect to any of them.

4.24   The full extent of the new provisions is dealt with in Chapter Seven at para **7.12** et seq. For present purposes, it need only be said that the extent of the courts' enquiry has, on the face of it, been very considerably enlarged. To put this in perspective, it must be remembered that this exercise is performed by the district judge by his reading a standard form completed by the petitioner. This is part of the 'special procedure' under the pre-1996 law, and will be part of what will no doubt be the special procedure under another name when the 1996 Act takes effect. It seems inevitable that new forms of 'statements of arrangements' will have to be devised to try to cater for the new requirements, but, in any event, the ability of the district judge to fulfil his obligations under the new provisions will be severely limited. It remains to be seen, therefore, whether s 11 will be more than a cosmetic addition to this statute.

Jewish and Quaker marriages
4.25   The final 'arrangement for the future' in respect of which the court must be satisfied is likely to be of fairly limited application. Section 9(3) provides that, if the parties were married in accordance with usages of a kind mentioned in s 26(1) of the Marriage Act 1949, and are required to co-operate if the marriage is to be dissolved in accordance with those usages, the court may, on the application of either party, direct that there must also be produced to the court a declaration by both parties that they have taken such steps as are required to dissolve the marriage in accordance with those usages. Such a direction may be given only if the court is satisfied that in all the circumstances of the case it is just and reasonable to give it, and the direction may be revoked by the court at any time.

Although s 26(1) of the 1949 Act covers Jewish marriages and Quaker marriages, the marriages with which this subsection is designed to deal are Jewish marriages, since, evidently, there are no comparable Quaker usages. This provision is intended to enable the court to exercise pressure on Jewish husbands to deliver the *get* (or bill of divorcement) to their wives without which the wife will be unable to remarry in accordance with rabbinical law.

CHAPTER FIVE

Preventing or Delaying Divorce

Introduction

5.1   In most respects, the 1996 Act is going to spell the end of the defended divorce suit. The sole ground on which the making of a divorce order can be opposed is substantial hardship, pursuant to s 10. This subject is considered in more detail at para **5.5** et seq.

However, there are other ways in which the progress of a divorce may be inhibited and, in extreme circumstances, blocked. These have all been considered at the appropriate places in this book, but it may be helpful to summarise them all in one chapter.

These provisions may be summarised as follows:

(a) application under s 7(4);
(b) notice under s 7(10);
(c) non-compliance with s 9.

For the sake of completeness, mention must be made of stay of proceedings under Sch 1 to the Domicile and Matrimonial Proceedings Act 1973. Schedule 3 to the 1996 Act amends Sch 1 to the 1973 Act but there are no changes in substance; the amendments relate entirely to the changes of nomenclature needed to bring the 1973 Act into line with the 1996 Act. This subject will, therefore, not be pursued further.

The three matters set out above will now be considered in turn and detailed consideration will then be given to the hardship bar embodied in s 10.

Application under section 7(4)

5.2   Section 7(4) provides that where rules of court provide for the court to serve a copy of the statement of marital breakdown on the other party, and failure to comply results in inordinate delay in service, the other party may apply to the court for an extension of the period for reflection and consideration. What constitutes 'inordinate delay' remains to be clarified, but a party who has not been properly served and wishes for further time should be aware of the right to make this application.

Application under section 7(10)

5.3   The period for reflection and consideration is nine months from the filing of the statement where there is no child under 16 years old at the date of application for a divorce order, and 15 months where there is such a child. In the former case, either party may apply to the court for time for further reflection, and, in that event, the period will be extended by six months; no reason need be given, and no enquiry can be made into the bona fides of the applicant. The use of this provision would fail automatically if s 7(12)(a) is applied (occupation order or non-molestation order in force); otherwise, the only way in which the extension could be prevented would be where the applicant for a divorce could satisfy the court that subsection (12)(b) applied (delay detrimental to welfare of child).

Non-compliance with section 9

5.4   As was seen in Chapter Four, it is not possible to obtain a divorce order unless either the requirements of s 9 relating to arrangements for the future are satisfied (ie production of court order, negotiated agreement etc), or the court is satisfied that the case falls within one of the exceptions set out in Sch 1. While deliberate delay is not a policy which could be advocated as a tactical device, the fact remains that it may be used as such, and the applicant for a divorce order must be alert to this.

Orders preventing divorce: section 10

5.5   The Divorce Reform Act 1969 included a provision (subsequently embodied in the Matrimonial Causes Act 1973, s 5) which gave the court a discretion to dismiss a divorce petition founded solely on the basis of five years' living apart if the court was satisfied that the dissolution of the marriage would result in grave financial hardship to the respondent and that it would in all the circumstances be wrong to dissolve the marriage. The Law Commission recommended that this bar should apply to applications for divorce under the new law. The Government initially accepted this recommendation which would, however, be potentially applicable in all cases rather than only in five-year separation cases.

The Government's Divorce White Paper stated, at para 4.47, that the 'jurisprudence on the use of this bar is now well established'; and that, although the bar was likely to be invoked only 'very rarely', retention would nevertheless prevent hardship arising 'in a few cases' and that the bar might well be useful in other cases as a 'bargaining chip' to the weaker partner.

Although the Divorce White Paper stated that the Government did not intend to change the present statutory wording 'or the way in which the law in this area is now applied', it also believed that the 'extent and usefulness of the bar may not necessarily be clear from previously decided cases'.

5.6   In the debates on the Family Law Bill, doubts were expressed about the validity of the White Paper's view that the bar 'in its present form provided significant protection' from the hardship which could arise as a result of divorce, even where that hardship is not financial (para 4.46); and the Government introduced amendments which seem significantly to extend the scope of the bar (see *Official Report* (HL) 4 March 1996, col 27).

5.7   Section 10 of the Act provides that, if an application for a divorce order has been made (which, as pointed out in Chapter Four above can only be done after the expiration of the period for reflection and consideration, and after the applicant has stated the basis on which he proposes to satisfy the court about the arrangements for the parties' future) the court may, on the application of the other party, order that the marriage is not to be dissolved.

What has to be established

5.8   The court may only make an order preventing divorce if it is satisfied (the burden of proof thus being on the applicant: see *Reiterbund v Reiterbund* [1975] Fam 99):

(a)   that dissolution of the marriage would result in substantial financial or other hardship to the other party or to a child of the family; and

(b)   that it would be wrong, in all the circumstances (including the conduct of the parties and the interests of any child of the family), for the marriage to be dissolved (s 10(2)).

5.9   The language and structure of this provision is based on that of s 5 of the Matrimonial Causes Act 1973, and it is anticipated that authorities on the construction of that provision will often be relevant. However, the 1996 Act has made two significant alterations in the statutory language: first, the level of hardship need only be 'substantial' (as distinct from 'grave'); secondly, the 1996 Act allows the court to make an order on the basis that such hardship will be caused to a child of the family (although it is to be noted that applications under the section can only be made by a spouse). It should also be noted that the 1996 Act contains provisions envisaging that the courts will have effective powers to make pension adjustment orders; and it may be that statutory provisions to this end will reduce the number of cases in which divorce can be shown to cause serious financial hardship (see para **5.13**). In the light of these considerations, it is not easy to predict the effect of the 'hardship' bar now contained in s 10 of the Act; but in view of its potential significance its provisions must be considered in some detail.

Hardship must result from the dissolution of the marriage

5.10   The law cannot create or restore a family unit nor can it compel a couple to live together. The most that it can do is to prevent the legal relationship of husband and wife from being terminated; and the power to make an order preventing divorce is therefore concerned exclusively with the consequences of divorce, not those of separation (see *Talbot v Talbot* (1971) 115 SJ 870). What has to be compared is the applicant's position as a divorced (as distinct from a separated) spouse, and the child's position as the child of divorced parents (as distinct from his position as the child of separated parents). It is, however, to be noted that 'hardship' is defined so as to include the loss of a chance to obtain a future benefit (as well as the loss of an existing benefit (s 10(6)).

Hardship must be 'substantial'
5.11   The bar created by the comparable provision of the Divorce Reform Act 1969 required proof of 'grave' hardship (see eg *Reiterbund v Reiterbund* [1975] Fam 99; *Le Marchant v Le Marchant* [1977] 1 WLR 559). The substitution of the word 'substantial' for 'grave' is manifestly intended to substitute a different and less demanding criterion; and the Lord Chancellor stated that the effect of the change would be to reduce the statutory criterion to 'as low a standard as it can go' consistently with the principle that the law does not in any case take account of insubstantial considerations (see *Official Report* (HL) 4 March 1996, cols 25–33). It was pointed out that the Act uses ordinary language and it may therefore be relevant to note that the word 'substantial' is defined by the Oxford English Dictionary to mean 'having substance; not imaginary, unreal, or apparent only; true, solid, real'. It appears from the parliamentary debates that the word 'substantial' was intended to indicate to a lay person that he 'would have to be able to identify something on which the court could find as occasioning hardship'; and it may be that the question will be put in terms of a direction to a jury: 'would a right thinking person come to the conclusion that the hardship suffered was substantial?' (Cf *Livingstone-Stallard v Livingstone-Stallard* [1974] Fam 47, 54, per Dunn LJ.)

Hardship to child suffices
5.12   Under the bar created by the Divorce Reform Act 1969, the court had to be satisfied that divorce would result in grave hardship *to the respondent*, although it was held that in assessing the extent of such hardship the court could properly consider the overall family picture (see *Lee v Lee* (1973) 117 SJ 616 and para **5.19**). But in the light of further consideration during the debates on the Family Law Bill, the Government decided to extend the provision to encompass hardship caused by the divorce to children as well as parties to the marriage. It was apparently intended that the hardship which has to be established should be objective hardship of some kind, such as the need to sell a house specially adapted to meet the needs of a disabled child (see *Lee v Lee* (1973) 117 SJ 616), rather than merely the child's feelings of hurt and distress (see *Official Report* (HL) 4 March 1996, cols 30–31). But it is to be anticipated that in some cases reliance may be placed on research studies which are said to demonstrate that the dissolution of marriage by divorce (as distinct from the well-known sequelae of parental conflict – such as poor self-esteem, impaired school performance, increased likelihood of early and short personal relation-

ships with sexual partners – often incidental to separation) is capable of causing damage to children (see M. Cockett and M.J. Tripp, *The Exeter Family Study. Family Breakdown and its Impact on Children* (Exeter, 1994, reprinted 1996).

Financial hardship

5.13 In the light of the court's extensive powers to make financial provision and property adjustment orders on divorce, it was often difficult to establish that the granting of a decree would itself cause a spouse any financial hardship. However, the termination of the status of marriage would negative a spouse's entitlement to a widow's pension under the National Insurance scheme and would also often affect one spouse's expectations of benefiting as a widow or dependant under the other's occupational pension scheme; and the limitations on the court's powers to make financial orders in respect of pension expectations meant that divorce could have seriously adverse consequences. Most of the cases in which the grave hardship bar available under the 1969 legislation was successfully invoked were in fact based on loss of pension expectations; and it was even said (albeit at a time of high inflation and before Index Linked Government Securities were available for investment) that loss of an index-linked pension was prima facie grave financial hardship to a wife (see *Le Marchant v Le Marchant* [1977] 1 WLR 559, 561). For example, in *Parker v Parker* [1972] Fam 116, it was held that a 47-year-old wife's loss of a police pension payable in the event of her surviving her husband was a grave hardship; and decrees were refused on this ground in *Julian v Julian* (1972) 116 SJ 763, and in *Johnson v Johnson* (1981) Fam Law 116. Reference should also be made to *Dorrell v Dorrell* [1972] 1 WLR 1087; *Brickell v Brickell* [1974] Fam 31; *Purse v Purse* [1981] Fam 143. It should also be noted that the loss of even a small sum of money was held to be capable of constituting grave hardship in the case of those of small means (*Dorrell v Dorrell* [1972] 1 WLR 1087, 1093). However, it might not be possible to establish grave hardship if the loss would be made good by increased payments of means tested benefits (*Reiterbund v Reiterbund* [1974] 1 WLR 788; *Jackson v Jackson* [1993] 2 FLR 848); but such cases should perhaps be treated with some caution in view of changing Government attitudes to the availability and scale of income-related welfare benefits.

5.14 Section 10(6) of the Act defines 'hardship' so as to include the loss of a chance to obtain a future benefit (as well as the loss of an existing benefit); and this provision would seem particularly apt in relation to pension expectations. But, in considering the scope of the court's power to make an order preventing divorce, account needs to be taken of the coming into force of provisions of the Pensions Act 1995 giving the court power to 'earmark' pension payments for one spouse's benefit (see the Pensions Act 1995 (Commencement No 5) Order 1996, SI 1996/1675; Divorce etc Pensions Regulations 1996, SI 1996/1676), and the provisions of s 16 of the 1996 Act which are evidently intended to give the court extended powers to order the division of pension rights but cannot confidently be said to be effective in achieving that objective (see the statement of the Government's intention to introduce any legislation necessary to make the provisions effective: *Official Report* (HL) 27 June 1996, per Lord Mackay of Ardbrecknish at col 1090). It is clear that it will remain essential for an applicant to lead evidence demonstrating precisely what hardship would be caused by the dissolution of the marriage (*Reiterbund v Reiterbund* [1974] 1 WLR 788). Subject to that point, it can be assumed that all of the fact situations in which 'grave' hardship was established under the old law would now meet the 'substantial' hardship criterion; but it is not easy to make rational predictions as to whether the court would hold that substantial hardship had been established on facts such as those which arose in *Mathias v Mathias* [1972] Fam 287 (wife unsuccessfully argued that she would be caused grave hardship by the loss of her right to have a maintenance award deducted from her husband's army pay and by the loss of the financial security which a serving soldier enjoyed).

Hardship other than financial hardship
5.15   As was the case under the 'grave hardship' bar provided by the Divorce Reform Act 1969, the court's power to make an order preventing divorce is not confined to cases of financial hardship; and it is open to a spouse to allege that he will suffer substantial hardship other than financial hardship. However, it seems that in practice such hardship was rarely alleged under the old law (see *Rukat v Rukat* [1975] Fam 63, 75, per Ormrod J) and there was no reported case in which a plea based on such hardship prevented the dissolution of a marriage.

Religious convictions
5.16   Many of the cases decided under the 1969 Act were based on the applicant's religious susceptibilities; and the outcome of the case-law seemed to be that, on the one hand, it was not sufficient to show that divorce was contrary to the applicant's religion and would cause unhappiness and a sense of shame; but, on the other hand, if the applicant could show that she lived in a community in which social and religious attitudes and conventions were such that divorce would make her an outcast, the burden of showing that divorce would cause her hardship might be made out (see *Banik v Banik* [1973] 1 WLR 860, where the wife's pleadings were held to establish a prima facie case of grave hardship; but on examination of the evidence, it was held that this was not the case: *Banik v Banik (No 2)* (1973) 117 SJ 874; and see *Parghi v Parghi* (1973) 117 SJ 582; *Grenfell v Grenfell* [1978] Fam 128; *Balraj v Balraj* (1980) Fam Law 110; *Rukat v Rukat* [1975] Fam 63).

Failure to deliver a *get*
5.17   It should be noted that hardship was sometimes caused to Jewish wives by the granting of a divorce to a husband who then became free to remarry, but who might deny his wife the right to remarry in accordance with the requirements of rabbinical law by refusing to deliver to her the *get* (or bill of divorcement) requisite under that law. It would appear that pressure might be

exercised on such a husband by the threat to seek an order preventing divorce, coupled with a condition that no application be made to cancel the order unless and until the *get* was delivered (see para **5.23**).

5.18 In general, however, it seems pointless to speculate how the court will approach pleas of hardship founded on religious conviction; but it may be relevant to note that the House of Commons defeated on a division an amendment stating that hardship included hardship attributable to the fact that the person concerned has a deeply held religious belief that marriage is indissoluble (*Official Report* (HC) 17 June 1996, col 630; and see the debate at cols 561–581).

Other hardship flowing from loss of status

5.19 There may well be other cases in which, on the facts, a plea of substantial hardship can be founded (eg where a woman is entitled to housing in right of her husband's employment); whilst under the old law it was held, in *Lee v Lee* (1973) 117 SJ 616[1], that the fact that divorce would mean that a house adapted for the needs of a disabled child would, on the facts, have to be sold on divorce thereby depriving the wife of the possibility of caring for the child (whereas the house might be retained if the spouses merely separated) sufficed on the unusual facts of the case to justify withholding a decree. It appears to be envisaged that under the 1996 Act an order preventing divorce might be made in such circumstances, remaining in force at least until new arrangements had been made (see *Official Report* (HL) 4 March 1996, col 31, per Lord Mackay of Clashfern).

Exercise of the court's discretion to make order preventing divorce

5.20 If, but only if, the court is satisfied that the dissolution of the marriage would result in substantial financial or other hardship to the other party or to a child of the family, it will proceed to the next stage and consider whether it would be 'wrong in all the circumstances' for the marriage to be dissolved (Family Law Act 1996, s 10(2)(b)). The Act specifically refers to the conduct of the parties and the interests of any child of the family as matters to be taken into account, but it seems unlikely that the omission of a specific reference, such as appeared in the Divorce Reform Act 1969 'grave hardship' bar (see Matrimonial Causes Act 1973, s 5(2)) to the interests of the parties to the marriage or other persons concerned was intended to have any particular significance.

Relevance of general principles

5.21 In contrast, the requirement to exercise a discretion to keep in existence a marriage which, by definition, has irretrievably broken down would seem to make it important for the court to refer to the general principles underlying this Part of the Act which are set out in s 1 and discussed at para **1.16**.

---

[1] The Court of Appeal agreed with this reasoning (see (1974) Fam Law 48), although it allowed the husband's appeal because the son had died after the first instance decision.

It seems probable that guidance from the appeal courts will be required as to the approach which the court should adopt to striking a balance between what may well appear to some to be the conflicting principles of supporting the institution of marriage on the one hand, and bringing a marriage which has irretrievably broken down to an end with minimum distress to the parties and to the children affected (cf s 1(a) and s 1(c)(i)) on the other. These would not appear to be easily justiciable issues; but it is to be noted that in the course of the Parliamentary debates on the Bill for the Family Law Act, the Chancellor of the Duchy of Lancaster gave an assurance on behalf of the Lord Chancellor that the new provision preventing divorce would be:

> 'transmitted to judges in such a way that they will realise that when people involved in divorces say that they do not wish to be divorced against their will, their feelings will be taken into account.' (*Official Report* (HC) 25 March 1996, col 749).

The debates made it clear that there is a body of opinion which would wish the hardship bar to be applied much more often than was the case under the 1969 legislation.

Effect of an order preventing divorce

5.22 The most important effect of the making of an order preventing divorce is that the court may not make a divorce order so long as the prohibition is in force (Family Law Act 1996, s 3(2)). Equally, so long as an order preventing divorce is in force, no order can be made converting a separation order into a divorce under the procedure laid down by s 4 of the Act (s 4(2)(a); see para **8.14**). An order preventing divorce also stops the running of the lapse period of one year which follows the period for reflection and consideration (s 5(4); see para **3.16**). In contrast, an order preventing divorce can have no effect on the running of the period for reflection and consideration, since applications for such an order can only be made if an application for divorce has been made, and that can only be done after the end of the period (see para **4.5**).

Cancellation of order preventing divorce

5.23 The 1995 Divorce White Paper stated, at para 4.47, that the Government proposed the hardship bar should be revocable on a change of circumstances, since if 'divorce would no longer cause hardship, it is unjust that the bar should remain'. Effect is given to this policy by s 10(3) of the Act which provides that the court must cancel an order preventing divorce on the application of either or both parties, unless the court is still satisfied that dissolution of the marriage would result in substantial financial or other hardship to the other party or to a child of the family; and that it would be wrong in all the circumstances for the marriage to be dissolved. However, it is provided (s 10(4)) that if an order preventing divorce is cancelled, the court may make a divorce order in respect of the marriage only if an application is made under s 3 (or s 4(3) in cases in which a separation order falls to be converted into a divorce order); and it will presumably therefore be necessary for the requirements about declarations and about the parties' arrangements for the future to be satisfied afresh.

Imposition of conditions on application for cancellation

5.24   Section 10(5) of the Act provides that an order preventing divorce may include conditions which must be satisfied before an appplication for cancellation of the order may be made. No doubt, on occasions the court will simply order that no such application be made for a period of time; but it may well be that conditions will be imposed relating to financial matters (eg that the husband should give information about financial matters or undertakings to effect transactions which the court lacks the power to order: cf *Dorrell v Dorrell* [1972] 1 WLR 1087). It also seems that the power could be used to require a Jewish husband, as the price of obtaining the freedom to remarry, to deliver a *get* to his wife thereby enabling her to remarry in accordance with her religious law (see further, para **5.17**).

CHAPTER SIX

Financial Relief in Divorce and Separation Cases

Introduction

6.1   The broad areas in which the 1996 Act affects ancillary relief are set out in s 15(2). This provides that:

> 'The main object of Schedule 2 [which amends that part of the MCA 1973 dealing with financial relief] is—
>
> (a) to provide that, in the case of divorce and separation, an order about financial provision may be made under that Act before a divorce or separation order is made; but
>
> (b) to retain (with minor changes) the position under that Act where marriages are annulled.'

Section 15(3) goes on to say that Sch 2 also makes minor and consequential amendments to the 1973 Act connected with the changes mentioned in subsection (1).

In fact, the changes effected by the Act are more extensive than might appear from the objects mentioned in s 15(2), and these must be examined in detail. The changes relating to pensions are discussed at para **6.28**.

To assist the reader to understand the full extent of these amendments, the Matrimonial Causes Act 1973 is set out in its amended form in Appendix 2.

6.2   The first of the changes is in respect of the arrangements for the future. One of the underlying principles of the Act is that the parties should have dealt with their financial and other arrangements during the period for reflection and consideration, and, as was seen in Chapter Four, that an applicant for a divorce order must produce to the court either a court order or negotiated agreement relating to financial issues, or must satisfy the court, in effect, that this is not practicable. It is intended, therefore, that financial disputes are to be resolved before the making of a divorce order. This is a reversal of the pre-1996 position; it has already been considered in detail in Chapter 4.

Section 15(2) does not, therefore, give the whole picture when it says that an order about financial provision '*may* be made ... before a divorce order or separation order is granted'; the truth is that any such order *must* be made unless the applicant falls within some exception to the rule.

6.3   The 'minor and consequential amendments' referred to in subsection (3) deal principally with the orders which the court can make, and when they should take effect. Under the pre-1996 law, it was necessary to have a decree nisi before an order of a capital nature could be made, and a decree absolute before it could take effect. This has all had to be reconsidered.

There are provisions in the Act which deal with pensions, and these will have to be considered. Finally, the potentially important changes as to the conduct of the parties must be discussed.

6.4   The matters to be dealt with in this chapter are, therefore, as follows:

(a) orders which the court may make;
(b) the time when orders may be made, and when they may take effect;
(c) new provisions as to variation;
(d) new provisions as to pensions;
(e) new provisions as to conduct;
(f) procedure.

It must be emphasised that this is not a comprehensive text on financial relief; the matters covered in this chapter relate only to the changes brought about by the 1996 Act, and matters closely associated with such changes. The references to the 1973 Act are, of course, references to the Act as amended by the 1996 Act.

Orders which the court may make

6.5   Section 21 of the Matrimonial Causes Act 1973 now provides for two classes of orders for financial relief, namely, financial provision orders and property adjustment orders.

'Financial provision orders' comprise the following:

(a) periodical payments orders;
(b) secured periodical payments orders;
(c) orders for payment of a lump sum (lump sum order).

'Property adjustment orders' comprise:

(a) an order for transfer of property to the other party or to a child;
(b) an order for settlement of property;
(c) an order for variation of settlement;
(d) an order extinguishing or reducing an interest in a settlement.

This does not change the substance of the previous law. However, there are changes in detail.

When can orders be made?

6.6 Any of these orders may be made at 'the appropriate time' (MCA 1973, s 22A(1) and s 23A(1)). The appropriate time is defined by s 22A(2) as any time:

'(a) after a statement of marital breakdown has been received by the court and before any application for a divorce order or for a separation order is made to the court by reference to that statement;

(b) when an application for a divorce order or separation order has been made under section 3 of the 1996 Act and has not been withdrawn;

(c) when an application for a divorce order has been made under section 4 of the 1996 Act and has not been withdrawn;

(d) when an application for a divorce order has been made following the cancellation of an order preventing divorce under section 10 of that Act and has not been withdrawn;

(e) after a divorce order has been made;

(f) when a separation order is in force.'

The effect of this is that an order may be made at any time after a statement has been filed, provided it has not been withdrawn (which can only be done by consent), whether or not a divorce order or a separation order has been granted. However, certain restrictions as to time are imposed by s 22B. The effect of these is as follows:

(1) Except for an interim periodical payments order, the court may not make a financial provision order during any period which has to be disregarded in determining the period for reflection and consideration fixed by s 7(8) of the 1996 Act (s 22B(2)); this refers to the provision whereby, if both parties notify the court that they are attempting a reconciliation and require more time, the period for reflection and consideration stops running until the court is notified that the attempted reconciliation has been unsuccessful.

(2) No financial provision order of any description may be made where, by virtue of s 5(3) or s 7(9) of the 1996 Act, it has ceased to be possible for an application for a divorce order or a separation order to be made by reference to the statement filed, or for such an order to be made (s 22B(3)); this refers to the fact that a divorce order may not be made if more than one year has passed since the end of the period for reflection and consideration, or if the period for reflection and consideration is extended beyond 18 months. In those circumstances, time has run out, the statement ceases to have any effect, and the marital proceedings are, in effect, dead.

(3) Section 22B(4) deals, in effect, with the time when an application for financial provision must be made. The effect of the provision is that an

application must be made before a divorce order or separation order is made, and, if not, can only be made with leave of the court.

Subject to the restrictions in s 22B, therefore, the court may make orders for financial provision or property adjustment at any time after a statement has been filed. The question of when such orders may take effect is a separate one, and is dealt with at para **6.10**.

How many orders?

6.7   Section 22A(3) deals with the number of financial provision orders which the court may make. The court may make:

'(a) a combined order against the parties on one occasion;
(b) separate orders on different occasions;
(c) different orders in favour of different children;
(d) different orders from time to time in favour of the same child.'

However, the amended MCA 1973 follows the previous law in restricting the number of orders which may be made. Accordingly, subsection (3) concludes by providing that the court:

'may not make in favour of the same party more than one periodical payments order, or more than one order for payment of a lump sum . . . .'

The effect of this is that, once an order for periodical payments (other than an interim order) has been made, it can only be altered by a variation order. As will be seen when variation is considered at para **6.17**, a lump sum order cannot be varied, save where it is payable by instalments, and accordingly continues to be a 'final order'.

The position as to the number of property adjustment orders which may be made is expressed differently, but is similar in effect. Section 23A(1) provides that the court may, at the appropriate time (as defined above), 'make one or more property adjustment orders'. However, this is qualified by s 23A(2), which provides that, when the court makes more than one property adjustment order, 'each order must fall within a different paragraph of section 21(2) . . .'

In other words, the court may make an order that one party transfer a property to the other party, and, on the same or a later occasion, order settlement of property, or variation of a settlement; having exercised its power to make one class of property adjustment order, it cannot do so again.

6.8   Section 23A(3) directs the court as to the exercise of its jurisdiction, by providing that:

'the court shall exercise its powers under this section, so far as is practicable, by making on one occasion all such provision as can be made by way of one or more property adjustment orders in relation to the marriage as it thinks fit.'

This must be regarded as an overriding directive, and, taken with the other provisions set out above, the intention of the legislation is clearly that orders of a capital nature should be treated as final orders. Whether that intention will be realised in practice remains to be seen, and the provision for 'interim lump sums' considered at para **6.15** gives rise to some doubts in this respect.

Restrictions on periodical payments

6.9 Before the coming into force of the amendments effected by the 1996 Act, s 25A(3) of the MCA 1973 provided that, if the court considered that no continuing obligation should be imposed on either party to make or secure periodical payments in favour of the other party, the court might dismiss the application with a direction that the applicant should not be entitled to make any further application.[1] This subsection has been replaced by a new s 25A(3), which provides that:

'if the court—
(a) would have power under section 22A or 23 above to make a financial provision order in favour of a party to a marriage ("the first party"), but
(b) considers that no continuing obligation should be imposed on the other party to the marriage ("the second party") to make or secure periodical payments in favour of the first party,
it may direct that the first party may not at any time after the direction takes effect apply to the court for the making against the second party of any periodical payments order or secured periodical payments order and, if the first party has already applied to the court for the making of such an order, it may dismiss the application.'

The express power to dismiss has, therefore, in effect been retained in this form.

For the sake of completeness in this context, mention must be made of ss 22B(4) and 23B(4), which apply respectively to financial provision orders and property adjustment orders; their effect is that once a divorce order has been made or a separation order is in force, no financial provision order nor property adjustment order may be made except in relation to an application made before the divorce or separation orders or on a subsequent application with leave of the court. Clearly, finality is one of the aims of these provisions; it would only be in exceptional circumstances that an application for financial relief would be allowed to survive the grant of a divorce or separation order,

---

[1] The effect of an order for dismissal which omitted the restriction on further applications was considered in *Richardson v Richardson* [1994] 1 FLR 286.

and one suspects that leave to make such an application after divorce or separation would be granted only sparingly.

When may orders take effect?

6.10   Under the pre-1996 law, no financial orders, except orders of a temporary or interim nature, could be made until decree nisi, and they could not take effect until decree absolute (for an exception see *Barry v Barry*, discussed at para **6.13**). The fact that any order may now be made at any time after the filing of the statement of marital breakdown, coupled with the fact that there is now to be one divorce order, with no delay between orders nisi and absolute, has meant that the Act has to provide for the problem of when the order should take effect.

This raised issues of principle for the draftsman of the legislation. On the one hand, it could be, and was, argued that since the purpose of the period for reflection and consideration was to allow parties to investigate the possibility of reconciliation, this purpose might be frustrated if the parties were permitted to rush into litigation and if the court made orders which could be implemented and which might have an irreversible effect. On the other hand, practitioners in this field submitted that long delays between the making of an order and its taking effect could have unfortunate consequences, and would impose an artificial stalemate.

6.11   In respect of property adjustment orders, the solution is contained in s 23B. This provides that no property adjustment order may be made so as to take effect before the making of a divorce order or a separation order unless the court is satisfied:

'(a) that the circumstances of the case are exceptional; and
 (b) that it would be just and reasonable for the order to be so made.'

Clearly, (b) presents few difficulties; the court would have to decide whether, in effect, it was fair to grant the leave sought, bearing in mind the interests of both parties.

However, (a) is more difficult. The starting point for the court would have to be the general prohibition on allowing orders to take effect before a divorce or separation order. It would then have to decide whether the circumstances of the instant case were exceptional; given that every case turns on its own facts, the court would have to decide how exceptional, or far from the norm, a particular case was before it would qualify for this description.

In relation to consent orders parties will, of course, bear in mind that there will be nothing to prevent them from implementing whatever arrangements they have agreed. Presumably, orders made in such cases would contain a lengthy preamble, consisting of undertakings, or recitals of what had already been done, and the order would be confined to dismissals of all claims.

6.12   The position as to lump sum orders is exactly the same, s 22B(4) being in identical terms, mutatis mutandis, with s 23B(4).

Interim orders

6.13   Under the pre-1996 law, the court had power to make various interim orders. In respect of periodical income orders, it could make orders for maintenance pending suit before decree absolute, and interim periodical payments thereafter. The position as to orders of a capital nature was more limited. Section 23(3) of the Act permitted the court to order payment of a lump sum for the purpose of enabling the recipient to meet liabilities or expenses reasonably incurred. This was expressed to be without prejudice to the court's general power to make a lump sum order. There was no statutory power to make an interim order for sale nor a property adjustment order. However, it was decided in *Barry v Barry* [1992] 2 FLR 233 that the court had an administrative power of appropriation which it could exercise before decree, by, for example, ordering the sale of a property and the payment of all or part of the proceeds to one party, provided the funds were sufficient to be taken into account at the final hearing.

6.14   The position is now somewhat different. First, the term 'maintenance pending suit' has had to disappear because of the new terminology. As was seen above, any financial provision order can be made at any time after the filing of the statement of marital breakdown. Section 22A(4) now provides that:

> 'If it would not otherwise be in a position to make a financial provision order in favour of a party or child of the family, the court may make an interim periodical payments order, an interim order for the payment of a lump sum, or a series of such orders, in favour of that party or child.'

The court therefore has power to make interim periodical payments orders in cases where it is not yet possible to deal with the matter on a final basis. (However, it may not do so before the statement has been made and filed because only then do proceedings start.)

6.15   As has been seen, s 22A(4) also deals with interim lump sum orders, and here the intention seems to be, in effect, to repeat the old s 23(3). The provision for interim lump sum orders is an innovation. As mentioned above, there was provision, under the old s 22(3), for interim lump sum orders to meet urgent expenses; these were expressly to be taken into account as and when the court made a final lump order.

Here, there is no guidance to the court as to the circumstances in which it should make an interim lump sum order, nor is there any provision that such an order is without prejudice to the final order or that it must be taken into account on the making of the final order.

6.16   There is no express provision for interim property adjustment orders. The position is explained at paras **6.6** and **6.10**.

Variation orders

6.17   As before, it is only intended in this section to draw attention to those parts of ss 31 to 33 which have been changed by the 1996 Act. However, these changes are considerable. In addition to the changes which are necessary to give effect to the 1996 Act, it seems that the opportunity to make certain other changes has been taken. The changes may be summarised as follows:

(a)   changes to give effect to new nomenclature;
(b)   provisions as to when variation orders may take effect;
(c)   new powers for the court when discharging periodical payments orders;
(d)   provisions to govern the position where the parties are reconciled.

6.18   The first matter to be considered is that of which types of orders may now be varied. The list is contained in s 31(2), and, although the terminology is in some cases now different (eg maintenance pending suit has been deleted), the types of orders which may be varied have not been substantially changed. It should be noted that subsection (2)(dd) refers to deferred orders made under s 21(1)(c); this is a reference to deferred lump sum orders relating to pensions, and this provision was inserted by the Pensions Act 1995. Pensions, generally, are discussed at para **6.28**.

6.19   Subsection (4B) deals with the question of when a variation order may take effect. It provides that:

'no variation—
(a)   of a financial provision order made under section 22A above, other than an interim order, or
(b)   of a property adjustment order made under section 23A above,
shall be made so as to take effect before the making of a divorce order or separation order in relation to the marriage, unless the court is satisfied that the circumstances of the case are exceptional, and that it would be just and reasonable for the variation to be so made.'

The wording repeats ss 22B(1) and 23B(1).

6.20   By subsection (7A), subsection (7B) applies:

'where, after the dissolution of a marriage, the court—
(a)   discharges a periodical payments order or secured periodical payments order made in favour of a party to the marriage, or
(b)   varies such an order so that payments under the order are required to be made or secured only for such further period as is determined by the court.'

The situation envisaged is, therefore, that there has been a periodical payments order which the court considers it appropriate to discharge or to limit to a finite period; in other words, the court imposes a clean break. Before this enactment, the position was that which was found in *S v S* [1987] 1 FLR 71, where the court thought it right to discharge a periodical payments order which had been made in favour of the former wife of a successful popular entertainer upon his undertaking to pay her a lump sum, but held that, in the absence of such an undertaking, it would not be able to order the lump sum; there is, in fact, no reported case in which such an undertaking has been accepted as being adequate (see eg *Boylan v Boylan* [1991] 1 FLR 282).

These subsections are designed to remedy that lacuna, and follow a recommendation of the Law Commission (Law Com 192 paras 6.8–6.10). It may be noted that the Act provides no guidelines to assist the court in making a decision in such a case. It is possible that such an application would be made, say, 20 years after the periodical payments order had been made, at which stage the court, presumably, would have to rehearse the issues between the parties de novo, and, in more substantial cases, consider updated *Duxbury* calculations.

6.21   Subsection (7B) provides that the court has power, in addition to any other power it may have, to make supplemental provision consisting of:

'(a) an order for payment of a lump sum in favour of a party to the marriage;

(b) one or more property adjustment orders in favour of a party to the marriage;

(c) a direction that the party in whose favour the original order discharged or varied was made is not entitled to make any further application for—

  (i) a periodical payments or secured periodical payments order, or

  (ii) an extension of the period to which the original order is limited by any variation made by the court.'

The court now has, therefore, power to order either a lump sum or a property adjustment order, or both, as 'compensation' for the loss of periodical payments.

The effect of subsections (7C) to (7F) is that the same restrictions as apply to financial provision orders and property adjustment orders, for example requiring the court to make only one property adjustment order of each class in s 21(2), apply to orders made on variation. By subsection (7C), any lump sum order made on variation may be ordered to be paid by instalments.

6.22   The provisions of s 31A are required because of the power of the court to make financial provision orders and property adjustment orders before a divorce order has been made; some provision had to be made to deal with the position where, for some reason, the divorce did not proceed.

It might have been thought that some provision would be made for the situation where, a property adjustment order or financial provision order having been made, and having taken effect, no divorce order is then granted. However, this is not the case, and, in the circumstances just described, the only remedy of an aggrieved spouse would be to apply to set aside the order or to seek leave to appeal out of time.

Section 31A is confined to the situation where parties are agreed that an order should be discharged and, in some cases, it is a condition that they have been reconciled before a divorce order is granted. As such, it will be of very limited practical effect, since, it may be thought, if the parties are sufficiently ad idem to make a joint application to set aside an order, very little turns on the outcome of the application. (The provision seems to be designed for those who do not really need it.)

6.23   Section 31A(1) provides that where, at any time before the making of a divorce order:

> '(a) an order ("a paragraph (a) order") for the payment of a lump sum has been made under section 22A above in favour of a party;
> (b) such an order has been made in favour of a child of the family but the payment has not yet been made; or
> (c) a property adjustment order ("a paragraph (c) order") has been made under section 23A above,
> the court may, on an application made jointly by the parties to the marriage, vary or discharge the order.'

The court therefore has discretion to make the order as sought, or any other order, but the provision is limited to joint consensual applications.

6.24   When an order is made under s 31A(1), it is not essential that the parties have been reconciled, although, no doubt, this will frequently be the case. However, subsections (2), (3) and (4) confer additional powers on the court, and it is provided by subsection (6) that the court may not make such orders unless it appears to it that there has been a reconciliation between the parties to the marriage.

Subsection (2) provides that where the court varies or discharges a paragraph (a) order (ie a lump sum order) it may order the repayment of an amount equal to the whole or any part of the lump sum. The only comment to make on this is that, given that the parties are reconciled and are making a joint application, one wonders why this provision is thought to be necessary and whom it is designed to help.

6.25   Subsection (3) deals with the position where the court varies or discharges a paragraph (c) order (ie a property adjustment order), and the order has taken effect. Here, the court may:

> '(a) order any person to whom property was transferred in pursuance of the paragraph (c) order to transfer—

    (i) the whole or any part of that property, or

    (ii) the whole or any part of any property appearing to the court to represent that property,

in favour of a party to the marriage or a child of the family; or

(b) vary any settlement to which the order relates in favour of any person or extinguish or reduce any person's interest under that settlement.'

Subsection (4) is a linked provision, since it provides that, where the court acts under subsection (3), it may:

'make such supplemental provision (including a further property adjustment order or an order for the payment of a lump sum) as it thinks appropriate in consequence of any transfer, variation, extinguishment, or reduction to be made under paragraph (a) or (b) of that subsection.'

6.26 Once again, it is difficult to conceive of circumstances in which these provisions will be invoked. The subsection can only come into effect when the court is satisfied that the parties have been reconciled, and on a joint application. Even conceding that there may be cases where such reunited couples think it prudent to undo the legal requirements which have previously been imposed on them, one might think that there would be a degree of overkill in making new property adjustment orders to reflect the process of adjustment which they had agreed.

6.27 Finally, subsection (7) provides that the court shall not make an order under subsection (3) or (4) above unless it appears to it that the order will not prejudice the interests of any child of the family or any person who has acquired any right or interest in consequence of the property adjustment order and is not a party to the marriage or a child of the family.

Pensions

6.28 Provisions of the Pensions Act 1995 intended to give the court power to 'earmark' pension payments for the benefit of a divorced spouse were brought into force in respect of petitions filed on or after 1 July 1996: see para **5.14** above; but, in the course of the Parliamentary debates on the Family Law Bill, the Government came under renewed pressure to introduce effective measures whereby the parties' expectations under pension schemes could be re-allocated on divorce. The Government was defeated on a division (see *Official Report* (HL) 29 February 1996) and an amendment was made to the Bill.

However, as the Minister of State in the Department of Social Security put it, this amendment 'expressed the principle but did not will the means to put it into practice'; and in the House of Commons further provision (now to be found in s 16 of the Act) was made in an attempt to will the means, albeit in the absence of a full policy on many important matters, by giving the Lord

Chancellor extensive powers to make regulations, extending even to the power to amend primary legislation. The Minister of State made it clear that this was an unsatisfactory procedure, and that further primary legislation would be required (see *Official Report* (HL) 27 June 1996, col 1090).

The position is, therefore, that the Government has stated that it is 'fully committed to the principle of pension splitting'; in July 1996, the Government published a Consultation Paper *The Treatment of Pension Rights on Divorce* (Cm 3345) seeking views on a wide range of issues. It is intended in due course to publish a White Paper containing a full package of policy proposals, 'followed by legislation as soon as it is practicable' (ibid). The principle of pension splitting has been preserved on the face of the Bill; but it seems certain that the provisions which will ultimately govern this complex matter will be different from those of s 16. In the circumstances, it is not proposed to comment on the details of the section (which appears quite inadequate to achieve the objectives of its promoters).

Conduct

6.29   Before the coming into force of the Act, the approach of the courts to the relevance of the conduct of the parties in relation to financial relief was well settled, and conduct was only an issue in the comparatively rare cases in which it would be inequitable to disregard it. It is possible that this attitude may have to change, because of an amendment to s 25 of the MCA 1973 effected by the Act.

In the course of the debates on the 1996 Act, it became clear that there was a perception among some MPs that conduct was not accorded the prominence by the courts which they considered it should have. The Parliamentary Secretary to the Lord Chancellor's Department stated that 'anecdotal evidence' suggested that 'if conduct was taken into account' only conduct of a financial nature was normally considered (*Official Report* (HC) 16 May 1996, col 371). Ministers had earlier successfully resisted attempts to highlight conduct, but in the House of Commons on Second Reading the Minister was eventually driven to concede that the court's practice did not satisfy everyone, and that conduct was 'extremely important' (*Official Report* (HC) 25 March 1996, col 738).

Accordingly, the Government brought forward an amendment to s 25(g), adding, after 'parties', the words:

> 'whatever the nature of the conduct and whether it occurred during the marriage or after the separation of the parties or (as the case may be) dissolution or annulment of the marriage.'

In moving this amendment, the Parliamentary Secretary said that the purpose of the amendment was:

'to emphasise that conduct of the parties of whatever nature, should it be inequitable to disregard it, has to be taken into account and that it is not only conduct in the course of ancillary relief proceedings that has to be considered.' (Mr Jonathan Evans, Standing Committee E, *Official Report* (HC) 16 May 1996, col 371).

It is difficult to predict the likely impact of this amendment on the approach of the courts. On the one hand, it may be said that the amendment was designed to clarify, rather than change, the law. On the other hand, it may be presumed that Parliament must have intended to change the law in some respects. It seems certain that litigants will be encouraged by these amendments to persist in making allegations of conduct in circumstances in which they would formerly have been advised that to do so would be pointless.

Procedure

6.30 There is nothing in the 1996 Act to govern procedure as such, and this will be the subject of amendments to the FPR 1991. Nevertheless, it is possible to speculate as to what the changes are likely to be.

There is no prohibition on the issuing of an application for financial relief at any stage; indeed, the fact that all proceedings have to have been completed within the period for reflection and consideration, which may be as little as nine months, will be an encouragement to parties to proceed with their litigation promptly. There are provisions which only allow the making of an application after the making of a divorce order with leave of the court, but they are designed to ensure that there is some finality, and that parties do not present a spurious agreement to secure their divorce and then seek to litigate later. The emphasis is, therefore, on getting proceedings under way and completing them within the period.

6.31 Proceedings for financial relief may only be instituted when the marital proceedings exist, which is after the statement has been filed. The statement cannot be filed until three months after the information meeting, which leaves a potential gap for those applicants who are in need of urgent financial relief. Such an applicant will have to apply to a magistrates' court, or to the county court under s 27 of the MCA 1973. As to the latter remedy, s 27 has been amended by Sch 8 to the 1996 Act, to provide that, on an application under that section, the court may make 'one or more financial provision orders against the respondent in favour of the applicant or a child of the family'. (The reference to 'child of the family' must, of course, be read subject to s 8 of the Child Support Act 1991.)

6.32 Subject to what has been said, there is little to add about procedure; on the face of it, this will be the same as under the 1973 Act. However, it may well be that procedure in financial relief cases will be changed as a result of a pilot project initiated by the Lord Chancellor on the advice of his Advisory Group on Ancillary Relief, and governed by a Practice Direction dated 25 July 1996. It may be that recommendations arising out of these pilots will have been made by the time the Act comes into force.

CHAPTER SEVEN

Children in the Divorce Process

Introduction

7.1 The Family Law Act 1996 is not primarily concerned with the law relating to children; but anxieties about the impact of marital breakdown on children were voiced both by the Law Commission and in the Government's 1995 White Paper. In the course of the debates on the Bill for the Family Law Act amendments were made which are intended to minimise the damage done to children by the divorce process. Although the main provisions relating to children involved in marital breakdown are still to be found in the Child Support Act 1991 and in the Children Act 1989, it may be helpful to bring together in this chapter the provisions of the 1996 Act which have particular relevance to children.

The interrelationship of the Children Act 1989 and the Family Law Act 1996: procedures available for resolving questions about the welfare of children

7.2 Paragraph 60 of Sch 8 to the 1996 Act amends the Children Act 1989, s 8(4), so that proceedings under the 1996 Act constitute 'family proceedings' for the purposes of that Act[1]; and the Children Act 1989 is also amended so that for the purposes of any reference in that Act to 'family proceedings' powers which under the Children Act 1989 are exercisable in family proceedings are also exercisable in relation to a child, without any such proceedings having been commenced or any application having been made to the court under the Children Act if: (a) a statement of marital breakdown under s 5 of the 1996 Act (as to which see para **2.11**) with respect to the marriage in relation to which that child is a child of the family has been received by the court; and (b) it may, in due course, become possible for an

---

[1] The relevant part of Sch 8 to the Family Law Act 1996 is headed 'Amendments connected with Part IV' (which is that part of the Act dealing with Family Homes and Domestic Violence) but, presumably, the amendment to the Children Act definition of 'family proceedings' is not confined to applications under Part IV of the 1996 Act. It is not, at first impression, easy to understand why the draftsman should have thought it necessary to add the more specific provision contained in the new s 8(5) and discussed below; but the view taken in the text is that the apparent duplication must have been intended to minimise any doubt about the circumstances in which the court could make an order of its own motion under the Children Act 1989, s 8 (and exercise its other powers under that Act) in divorce-related matters (see para **7.5** below).

application for a divorce order or for a separation order to be made by reference to that statement (Children Act 1989, s 8(5) as inserted by the Family Law Act 1996, Sch 8, para 41(4)). (In this, and other provisions of the Act, 'child of the family' has the same meaning as in the Matrimonial Causes Act 1973, s 52 (see Hershman and Macfarlane, *Children Law and Practice*, (Family Law) para **D[637]**).)

Effect of attendance at an information meeting

7.3 As noted above (para **2.2**), although attendance at an information meeting is the first step in the divorce process established by the 1996 Act, it does not count as the start of proceedings (Family Law Act 1996, s 20(1)). Accordingly, if it is desired to seek the intervention of the court in respect of the questions relating to the welfare of a child, proceedings under the Children Act 1989 will have to be started by a person (such as the child's parent) who is entitled, under that Act, to apply for an order or by another person who obtains the leave of the court to make the application (Children Act 1989, s 10(1), see also, in respect of applications by local authorities, s 31).

7.4 Since attendance at an information meeting does not constitute the start of marital proceedings (and it is evidently hoped that in some cases matters may be resolved by the parties deciding to take no further legal action) the fact that a person has attended such a meeting does not bring 'family proceedings' into being. Accordingly, such attendance will not bring into operation the court's power under the Children Act 1989 to make orders of its own motion.

Effect of a statement of marital breakdown in respect of proceedings under the Children Act 1989

7.5 The Family Law Act 1996, s 20(1), provides that the receipt of a statement by the court is to be treated as the commencement of proceedings; and it would seem to follow from the fact that such proceedings are now defined as 'family proceedings' that the court could thereafter exercise its powers under the Children Act 1989 in respect of the children of the family. However, possibly for the avoidance of any doubt, para 41(4) of Sch 8 to the 1996 Act specifically amends s 8 of the Children Act to empower the court to exercise its powers under that Act if a statement has been received by the court without any application having been made or any proceedings started, so long as it may, in due course, be possible for an application for a separation or divorce order to be made by reference to that statement (see para **7.2**). Once a statement has been received, therefore, it is clear beyond doubt that the court has power to make an order of its own motion under the Children Act 1989 (see Children Act 1989, s 10(1)(b))[2].

---

[2] An alternative explanation is that the amendment effected by Sch 8, para 60, is (contrary to the view expressed above) confined to applications under Part IV of the Family Law Act 1996.

Effect of making of divorce or separation order

7.6 The Family Law Act 1996, s 20(6) provides that marital proceedings come to an end, inter alia, on the making of a separation or divorce order; and it seems to follow that thereafter there are no longer any 'family proceedings' in existence for the purpose of the Children Act 1989. However, applications for orders under that Act may continue to be made by those entitled to do so in terms of the Children Act or with leave of the court. Moreover, the court may on application by such a person, or on the application of the person on whose application a s 8 order had been made, or on the application of a person named in a contact order (Children Act 1989, s 10(6)) vary an existing s 8 order.

Jurisdiction to make Children Act orders

7.7 The question whether the court has jurisdiction to make orders relating to children has to be resolved by reference to the provisions of the Family Law Act 1986, as amended. An underlying principle of that Act was that a court in England and Wales should have jurisdiction to make residence and other orders under s 8 of the Children Act 1989 if the court was exercising its matrimonial jurisdiction in respect of the parents' marriage (see Family Law Act 1986, s 2A(1)). For this purpose, the relevant question in respect of divorce proceedings was whether those proceedings were 'continuing' (see s 2A(1)(a)(ii)); and an extensive meaning was attached to that concept (see s 42(2)), with proceedings to be treated as continuing until the child attained the age of 18 (whether or not a decree had been granted). However, it did not follow that the court would necessarily exercise this jurisdiction if it would be more appropriate for matters relating to the child to be dealt with elsewhere (see *Re S (Jurisdiction to Stay Application)* [1995] 1 FLR 1093, where the child had been cared for in Scotland for many years after the parental divorce).

7.8 The Family Law Act 1996 significantly restricts this jurisdiction. In effect, a case is only to be treated as a 'matrimonial' case for the purpose of conferring jurisdiction if a statement of marital breakdown has been filed and it is or may become possible for a divorce order to be made by reference to it; or if an application for a divorce order in relation to the marriage has been made and not withdrawn (Family Law Act 1986, s 2A(1) as substituted by the Family Law Act 1996, Sch 8, para 37(3)). The court may, of course, still have jurisdiction to make residence and other s 8 orders if another basis of jurisdiction (usually the child's habitual residence) exists. The complex details of this subject are outside the scope of the present work.

Proceedings under the Children Act 1989 as proceedings connected with breakdown of a marriage

7.9 The powers of the court, after receiving a statement of marital breakdown, to give a direction under s 13 of the Family Law Act 1996 requiring each party to attend a meeting at which mediation facilities can be explored have been analysed at para **3.25**. In the present context, it is particularly to be noted that such a direction may also be given in the course of 'proceedings connected with the breakdown of a marriage'; and this expression is defined by s 25 of the Act to include inter alia, proceedings under Parts I to V of the Children Act 1989 with respect to a child of the family if, at the time of those proceedings, either:

(a) a statement has been received by the court by reference to which it is or may be possible for an application for a divorce or separation order to be made; or

(b) an application for such an order has been made and not withdrawn; or

(c) a divorce order has been made, or a separation order is in force in relation to the marriage.

It will be apparent that there is considerable potential for broadening the scope of the mediation direction in cases (eg of difficulty over contact) and, presumably, minimising adversarial litigation over such issues.

General principles in relation to exercise of functions in connection with the divorce process

7.10   As already noted, s 1 of the 1996 Act provides that the court and 'any person, in exercising functions under or in consequence of Parts II and III' of the Act (ie those provisions relating to divorce and separation and to legal aid for mediation in family matters) is to 'have regard to' certain 'general principles'. These include two matters of particular relevance to children affected by marital breakdown.

First, the principle that a marriage which has irretrievably broken down and is being brought to an end should be brought to an end with minimum distress to the parties and to the children affected (s 1(c)(i)), and with questions dealt with in a manner designed to promote as good a continuing relationship between the parties and any children affected as is possible in the circumstances (s 1(c)(ii)).

Secondly, the principle that 'any risk to one of the parties to a marriage, and to any children, of violence from the other party should, so far as reasonably practicable, be removed or diminished' (s 1(d)). These matters must be taken into consideration, not only by the courts in adjudicating on matters which call for the exercise of a discretion, but by those exercising functions in respect of the grant of legal aid, and by others involved including, for example, those providing information at information meetings (the rules governing which are to provide for the giving of information about, inter alia the importance to be attached to the welfare, wishes and feelings of children; and how the parties may acquire a better understanding of the ways in which children can be helped to cope with the breakdown of a marriage (s 8(9)(b) (c)), and also, it would seem, to those who are responsible for listing and other administrative arrangements in connection with procedures under the Act. These general principles are intended to have a pervasive influence; but it may be that other more specific provisions of the 1996 Act will have more immediate impact.

Children and the length of the divorce process

7.11   As already noted, the fact that there is a child of the family under the age of sixteen at the date of the application for a divorce order has the consequence that the period for reflection and consideration is extended by six months (although that extension does not apply if an occupation or non-molestation order is in force, and may not apply if the court considers that delaying the making of the divorce order would be significantly detrimental to the welfare of any child of the family) (Family Law Act 1996, s 7(11), (13); see also para **3.14**). There are also comparable provisions in relation to applications to convert a separation order into a divorce order (s 4(4)(a); see also para **8.14**).

Arrangements for the future in relation to children

7.12   As already noted, it is provided that the court may only make a divorce order or a separation order if the requirements imposed by the Act about the parties' arrangements for the future are satisfied (s 3(1)(c)); and, in respect of children, the relevant requirement is that the provisions of s 11 of the Act relating to the welfare of the children are satisfied (s 9(5)). The court's power under s 4 of the Family Law Act 1996 to convert a separation order into a divorce order is subject to a similar requirement (s 4(3)); and, accordingly, the court will need to take account of children born subsequent to the making of the separation order in such cases (see per Mr Gary Streeter MP, *Official Report* (HC) 17 June 1996, col 594).

7.13   The provisions of s 11 of the Act are similar in structure to those formerly contained in s 41 of the Matrimonial Causes Act 1973 (as amended by the Children Act 1989); and, as originally introduced, the Bill for the Act made only such changes in that section as were required by the novel terminology to be employed in the legislation. However, the Government came under considerable pressure during the Bill's passage through Parliament to give greater prominence to the interests of children involved in the divorce process and, eventually, it was decided that it would be helpful to have the full text of the relevant provision on the face of the Act and also (as the Lord Chancellor put it) to 'enhance its provision' (*Official Report* (HL) 27 June 1996, col 1074). The Act therefore repeals s 41, and substitutes a new provision concerned with the welfare of children.

7.14   As was the case with the Matrimonial Causes Act 1973, s 41, the new provisions apply to any child of the family who has not reached the age of sixteen at the date when the court considers the requirements of the section;

and also to any child of the family who has reached that age at that date and in relation to whom the court directs that the section should apply.

7.15   The first two subsections of the new provisions reproduce the effect of the provisions of s 41, *viz*:

'(1) In any proceedings for a divorce order or a separation order, the court shall consider—

(a) whether there are any children of the family to whom this section applies; and

(b) where there are any such children, whether (in the light of the arrangements which have been, or are proposed to be, made for their upbringing and welfare) it should exercise any of its powers under the Children Act 1989 with respect to any of them.

(2) Where, in any case to which this section applies, it appears to the court that—

(a) the circumstances of the case require it, or are likely to require it, to exercise any of its powers under the Children Act 1989 with respect to any such child,

(b) it is not in a position to exercise the power, or (as the case may be) those powers, without giving further consideration to the case, and

(c) there are exceptional circumstances which make it desirable in the interests of the child that the court should give a direction under this section,

it may direct that the divorce order or separation order is not to be made until the court orders otherwise.'

However, the remaining provisions are new, *viz*:

'(3) In deciding whether the circumstances are as mentioned in subsection (2)(a), the court shall treat the welfare of the child as paramount.

(4) In making that decision, the court shall also have particular regard, on the evidence before it, to—

(a) the wishes and feelings of the child considered in the light of his age and understanding and the circumstances in which those wishes were expressed;

(b) the conduct of the parties in relation to the upbringing of the child;

(c) the general principle that, in the absence of evidence to the contrary, the welfare of the child will be best served by—

  (i) his having regular contact with those who have parental responsibility for him and with other members of his family; and

  (ii) the maintenance of as good a continuing relationship with his parents as is possible; and

(d) any risk to the child attributable to—
    (i) where the person with whom the child will reside is living or proposes to live;
    (ii) any person with whom that person is living or with whom he proposes to live; or
    (iii) any other arrangements for his care and upbringing.'

7.16 It appears that the intention of those responsible for moving these new provisions was to direct the court more clearly to the possibility that it should exercise its powers under the Children Act 1989 (which, once a statement of marital breakdown has been filed, can, as pointed out above, be exercised on the court's own motion) and, in making that decision, to the desirability of giving greater weight to the child's own views (see per Mr Elfyn Llwyd MP, *Official Report* (HC) 17 June 1996, cols 587–590). However, as the Lord Chancellor pointed out, the purpose of the guidelines is to guide the court in deciding whether or not to exercise its Children Act powers; and it is not intended to change any of the provisions of the Children Act itself (see *Official Report* (HL) 27 June 1996, col 1074). The duty imposed on the court by this section remains (as it was under s 41 of the Matrimonial Causes Act 1973) comparatively restricted in scope: it is first to consider whether the court should exercise its powers under the Children Act 1989 and, secondly, if the court is not in a position to do so without further consideration, to decide whether there are exceptional circumstances such as would make it desirable to hold up the dissolution of the marriage (or the making of a separation order). It is, accordingly, only in relation to the decision whether the circumstances of the case are such as to require it, or are likely to require it, to exercise its powers under the Children Act 1989 that the 'paramountcy' principle and the matters specifically referred to in s 11(4) are relevant.

7.17 Moreover, contrary to the assumption apparently made by Mr Elfyn Llwyd in moving the amendment in question, there is no provision in the Act requiring the court to obtain an expression of the child's views (cf *Official Report* (HC) 17 June 1996, col 588). However, the provisions dealing with separate representation noted below may be relevant in this context; and it appears that the Government has under consideration a provision to be made by rule requiring parents to state in their application for an order whether they have consulted the children and taken account of their views; whilst if the matter is dealt with by mediation provided under the Legal Aid Act 1988, the mediator's code of practice will require the making of arrangements designed to ensure that the parties are encouraged to consider the welfare, wishes and feelings of each child, and whether and to what extent each child should be given the opportunity to express his or her wishes and feelings in the mediation (Legal Aid Act 1988, s 13B(8)(b) as inserted by the Family Law Act 1996, s 27).

7.18 Under the Family Proceedings Rules 1991, r 2.39, the question of arrangements for the children was considered in accordance with s 41 by the district judge on the basis of written statements made by the parents (although the district judge had power to give directions requiring, for example, the filing of further evidence, the preparation of a welfare report, or the attendance of the parties); and it is difficult to understand, in the absence of fuller explanations of the procedural framework which the Government have in mind, quite how s 11 is to achieve the objectives sought by its promoters. Notwithstanding the valiant efforts made by Mr Jonathan Evans, the Parliamentary Secretary in the Lord Chancellor's Department, to explain the comparatively limited scope of the jurisdiction, it appears that this may not have been fully appreciated. First, the provisions of s 41 were concerned primarily to ensure that unsuitable arrangements for children should not be allowed to go by default by reason of the lack of parental opposition to them; and, secondly, that (as Mr Evans put it) it was an underlying principle of the Children Act 1989 that parents should take responsibility for their children and that orders should not be made unless they were necessary in the children's interests (Standing Committee E, *Official Report*, 16 May 1996, col 350). There must be some doubt as to whether the provisions of s 11 will prove to have clarified 'the court's position and that of children in the divorce process' (per Mr Gary Streeter, the successor to Mr Evans as Parliamentary Secretary in the Lord Chancellor's Department, in welcoming the new provisions (*Official Report* (HC) 17 June 1996, col 593). It is important to keep in mind the explanation given by the Lord Chancellor:

> 'Essentially, ... the function of the court under this procedure remains the same as under the current law; namely, consideration of whether there are children of the family to whom the section should apply and, where there are any such children, whether it should exercise any of its powers under the Children Act 1989. The court has no jurisdiction ... to make a residence or contact order under this provision. Such orders, if they are to be made, must continue to be made under the Children Act itself. In exercising jurisdiction under that Act, the court will apply the welfare criteria set out in section 1(3) of that Act.
>
> In order to clarify the status of the various factors set out [in the statute] ... I should point out that their purpose is to guide the court when it is deciding whether or not it should exercise its Children Act powers. These factors are not intended to change any of the provisions of the Children Act itself. In particular I would point out that the reference to conduct in [s. 11(4)(b)] is intended to mean conduct towards the child by its parents and not conduct between the parents towards each other. I believe there has been some misunderstanding about that.' (*Official Report* (HL) 27 June 1996, col 1074)

Representation of children

7.19 As will have become apparent, concern was expressed in the course of the Parliamentary debates about the extent to which the voice of the child (as distinct from the voice of those purporting to speak for him or her) was heard in divorce proceedings. The Government, in response, accepted a provision empowering the Lord Chancellor by regulations to provide for the separate representation of children in proceedings which relate to any matter in respect of which a question has arisen, or may arise under, inter alia, Part II of the 1996 Act (Divorce and Separation), the Matrimonial Causes Act 1973, and the Domestic Proceedings and Magistrates' Courts Act 1978: see the Family Law Act, s 64.

The Lord Chancellor pointed out that it will be important to ensure that any 'arrangements complement existing arrangements, do not duplicate them and so far as practicable, do not place children at risk or exacerbate conflict between spouses by unnecessarily dragging children into disputes between their parents'. He pointed out that this would be a 'difficult and sensitive task' and that, accordingly he intended 'to consult widely both with children's organisations and with those who currently represent the interests of children in court proceedings before attempting to devise an effective system and to make any regulations under this provision' (*Official Report* (HL) 27 June 1996, col 1075). It appears that the intention is, in due course, to mount a number of pilot projects.

CHAPTER EIGHT

Separation Orders under the Family Law Act 1996

Introduction

8.1 Under the Matrimonial Causes Act 1973, a petition for judicial separation could be presented to the court by either party to the marriage on the ground that one of the 'facts' from which the court could infer irretrievable breakdown – adultery, behaviour, desertion, or living apart for the requisite period – had been established (MCA 1973, s 17(1)). The court was obliged to inquire so far as it reasonably could into the facts alleged by the petitioner and into any facts alleged by the respondent; but it was provided that the court was not to be concerned with the question whether the marriage had broken down irretrievably (MCA 1973, s 17(2)). Provided that the requirements of the MCA 1973, s 41, about the arrangements for children were complied with, the court was bound to grant a decree on proof of one of the relevant facts.

8.2 The effect of the grant of a decree of judicial separation was that thereupon it ceased to be 'obligatory for the petitioner to cohabit with the respondent' (MCA 1973, s 18(1)); and it was provided that if while a decree of judicial separation was in force and the separation was continuing, either of the parties died intestate, the intestate's property should devolve as if the other party to the marriage was dead (MCA 1973, s 18(2)). Moreover, the court had power on or after the making of a decree of judicial separation to make financial provision and property adjustment orders.

8.3 It appears that applications for judicial separation were made by those who accepted that their marriage was over but, for religious or other reasons, did not seek a divorce; and by those who sought redress within the first year of the marriage (and were thus, by reason of the prohibition contained in MCA 1973, s 3, unable to start divorce proceedings). The Government's White Paper *Looking to the Future* (1995, Cm 2799, para 4.49), reported that there was strong support in the responses to consultation for the retention of judicial separation as an alternative remedy for those who needed to make proper arrangements for living apart, but had objections to divorce, or no wish to remarry; and the White Paper stated that judicial separation enabled those with religious/ideological objections to divorce to achieve a comprehensive rearrangement of their affairs, without ending their marriage.

Separation orders: the provisions of the Family Law Act 1996

8.4 The provisions of the Act relating to separation orders mirror those already explained applying to divorce orders. The court must, on an application by one or both of the parties to a marriage which has not been withdrawn, make a separation order if (but only if):

(a) the requirements imposed by s 8 of the Act about information meetings (see para **2.4**) and by s 9 of the Act about the parties' arrangements for the future (see para **4.10**) have been satisfied;
(b) the marriage has broken down irretrievably. For this, as for divorce, a marriage is to be taken to have broken down irretrievably if (but only if) a statement complying with the requirements of s 6 of the Act has been made (see para **2.1**[1]), the relevant period for reflection and consideration (see para **3.3**) has ended, and the application for the order is accompanied by the stipulated declaration that after reflection and consideration the applicant believes the marriage cannot be saved (s 5(1)(d); para **4.6**).

Applications in the first year of marriage

8.5 A statement of marital breakdown made in the first year of marriage is to be effective for the purposes of obtaining a separation order (whereas it will be ineffective for the purposes of any application for a divorce order[2]). However, it will not, in practice, be possible for the court to make a separation order within the first year of the marriage because of the requirements about the period of time which must elapse between attendance at the information meeting (three months) and the start of the period for reflection and consideration (see below).

The length of the period for reflection and consideration

8.6 The Family Law Act 1996 provides that the period for reflection is nine months beginning with the fourteenth day after the day on which the statement of marital breakdown is received by the court (s 7(3); see further, para **3.3**). The court may, where the statement is made by one party and failure to comply with the rules causes inordinate delay in service, extend that period for a period not exceeding the time between the beginning of the period and the time when service is effected (s 7(4); see further, para **3.4**). It should, however, be noted that the statutory provisions whereby the period for reflection and consideration may be extended if application for further reflection is made by one party or in cases in which there is a child of the family under the age of 16 (s 7(10)–(13); see further para **3.9**), do not apply where application is made for a separation order.

---

[1] Note the possibility that a person wishing to delay the making of a divorce order in respect of a short marriage may be able to do so by making a statement (para **2.18**).
[2] See para **2.18** for the complications to which this may give rise.

Jurisdiction to make orders

8.7   The court's jurisdiction to entertain proceedings for separation is part of its jurisdiction to entertain marital proceedings; and is exercisable (as explained at para **2.14**) on the basis of the domicile of one or both parties, their habitual residence, or the fact that nullity proceedings were pending (s 17(2)). However, as explained at para **8.11** below, once a separation order has been made, the court continues to have jurisdiction even if this would not otherwise be the case.

The period within which application must be made for a separation order

8.8   An application for a separation order may not be made by reference to a particular statement if a period of more than one year (the 'specified period' prescribed by the Family Law Act 1996, s 5(3)(b)) has passed since the end of the period for reflection and consideration (s 5(3)).

Although the period for reflection and consideration may be extended by six months in certain cases, it appears that this only occurs retrospectively on the making of an application for a divorce order (s 7(10), (11)) and that any such extension only applies in relation to the application for a divorce order which is being sought (s 7(13)). Accordingly, it appears that the 'period for reflection and consideration' for the purpose of computing the period within which a separation order may be sought will always be nine months.

Competing applications for divorce and separation

8.9   It will, in many cases, be possible for one party to apply for a separation order and the other to apply for a divorce order; but the Act (s 3(3)) provides that if the court is considering an application for a divorce order and an application for a separation order in respect of the same marriage, it must proceed as if it were considering only the application for a divorce order.

Effect of order preventing divorce on applications for separation order

8.10   The fact that an order preventing divorce (made under the Family Law Act 1996, s 10; see para **5.5**) is in force does not prevent the court from making a separation order on an appropriate application (cf s 3(2)). However, in one respect it appears that the fact that such an order has been made may affect separation proceedings. Section 5(4) provides that any period during which an order preventing divorce is in force is not to count towards the so-called lapse period (ie the specified period of one year from the end of the period for reflection and consideration (s 5(3)(b); para **3.15**) at the end of which no application for a separation or divorce order can be made). It would thus seem, in theory, to be possible – contrary to the policy that proceedings should not be allowed to be hanging over the heads of the parties indefinitely – for application to be made for a separation order perhaps many years after the making of the statement. However, in practice it seems likely that separation orders will usually be sought contemporaneously with the application for an order preventing divorce.

Effects of a separation order

8.11 The Family Law Act 1996, in contrast to the Matrimonial Causes Act 1973, does not contain a general provision stating the effect of a separation order; and the provision of the MCA 1973 stating that after the making of such an order it is no longer obligatory for the parties to cohabit, has been repealed without replacement (Family Law Act 1996, Sch 10). Section 21 of the 1996 Act does, however, perpetuate the rule that where a couple remain separated under a separation order which is in force between them, neither shall be entitled to take under the intestacy of the other. In practice, however, the main significance of the separation order procedure is likely to be that it constitutes a means whereby the court's extensive powers to make financial provision and property adjustment orders can be exercised. As shown in Chapter Six, the court has power to make such orders 'at the appropriate time', and this term is defined (see MCA 1973, ss 22A(2), 23A(1), as inserted by the Family Law Act 1996, Sch 2, paras 3 and 5) to extend:

(a) to any time after a statement of marital breakdown has been received by the court and before any application for a divorce or separation order has been made by reference thereto;

(b) when an application for a separation order has been made and has not been withdrawn; and

(c) when a separation order is in force.

8.12 In appropriate cases the court may make substantial orders (see *W v W (Judicial Separation: Ancillary Relief)* [1995] 2 FLR 259 – although it is understood the judicial separation petition in that case was replaced by a divorce petition, but no reference to that fact is made in the judgment).

8.13 The making of a separation order brings to an end the marital proceedings started by the receipt of a statement of marital breakdown by the court (Family Law Act 1996, s 20(6)(a)). However, notwithstanding this fact, the court will continue to have jurisdiction to entertain an application made by reference to the separation order (eg an application to convert it into a divorce order, see below) and may exercise any other jurisdiction conferred on it in consequence of such an application (s 20(3), (4)). Hence, the court will still have jurisdiction even if the parties are no longer either domiciled or resident here.

Conversion of separation into divorce order

8.14 Although it was in the great majority of cases possible for one party effectively to convert a judicial separation into a divorce once the parties had lived apart for five years, this could only be done by filing a divorce petition in the usual way (see *Butler v Butler, The Queen's Proctor Intervening* [1990] 1 FLR 114). The Law Commission recommended that it should be possible for one or both spouses to apply to have a separation order converted into a divorce order; and s 4 of the 1996 Act provides a procedure whereby the court must, on the application of either or both parties, convert a separation order into a divorce order without further formality. However, the court cannot exercise this power:

(a) until after the second anniversary of the marriage (thereby seeking to achieve consistency with the policy under which a statement made within the first year of the marriage is ineffective for the purposes of divorce, and a period for reflection and consideration must elapse between the making of the statement and the application for divorce) (s 4(1));

(b) if and so long as an order preventing divorce under s 10 of the 1996 Act is in force (s 4(2));

(c) if there is a child of the family under the age of 16 at the time of the application for conversion of the separation order, or if the application for conversion is made by one party and the other party applies to the court for time for further reflection (s 4(4)). However, these provisions do not apply if, at the time when the application for conversion is made, there is an occupation order or non-molestation order made under Part IV of the Act (Family Homes and Domestic Violence) in favour of the applicant or a child of the family against the other party, or if the court is satisfied that delaying the making of a divorce order would be significantly detrimental to the welfare of any child of the family (s 4(5)(a) and (b)). Moreover, the provisions mentioned cease to apply:

   (i) at the end of the period of six months beginning with the end of the period for reflection and consideration by reference to which the separation order was made; or

   (ii) if earlier, on there ceasing to be any child of the family under the age of 16 (s 4(5)(c)).

Duration of separation orders

8.15 A separation order comes into force on being made (Family Law Act 1996, s 2(2)) and remains in force while the marriage continues or until cancelled by the court on the joint application of the parties s 2(3)).

General

8.16 As noted above, the Family Law Act 1996 usually applies to separation orders as it does to divorce and, in general, references in the text of this book to divorce orders also apply to separation orders. The reader should, of course, check whether this is so by reference to the text of the legislation printed at Appendix One.

CHAPTER NINE

Nullity and Other Forms of Matrimonial Relief

Introduction

The Government's *White Paper* stated, at para. 4.52 that 'consultees did not view the law of nullity as relevant to a revision of the divorce law' and that the 'possibility that the ground for nullity of wilful refusal to consummate the marriage should be removed because the need to prove fault was not supported'. However, for two sometimes related reasons the practitioner should not ignore the consequences of the legislation in relation to nullity.

First, it is possible that in the past some of those who would have had grounds for seeking to annul a voidable marriage (particularly in cases of sexual incompatibility) have preferred to obtain relief by the simple and everyday procedure of divorce; whereas, under the new law, some clients (particularly the elderly wishing to remarry) may find that the delay now inevitably involved in divorce tips the balance in favour of nullity.

Secondly, the task of preserving the law of nullity unchanged has resulted in much complex drafting. Perhaps the most striking example is that the provisions of s 41 of the Matrimonial Causes Act 1973 – restrictions on decrees affecting children – have been preserved intact so far as they relate to nullity proceedings (see the Family Law Act 1996, Sch 10), notwithstanding the fact that they have, as shown at para **7.12**, been replaced by the provisions of s 11 of the Family Law Act 1996 in the case of divorce and separation. In the circumstances, it seems appropriate to list the more important drafting changes made by the legislation in their application to nullity petitions, and to give the briefest summary of the effect of those provisions.

9.2   First, however, two provisions relating to nullity in which, exceptionally, minor changes have been made to the law relating to nullity should be mentioned.

Interim lump sum orders available in nullity
It is now provided that before granting a decree in any proceedings for nullity of marriage, the court may make against either or each of the parties to the marriage an interim order for the payment of a lump sum or a series of such orders in favour of the other party (Matrimonial Causes Act 1973, s 23(2)(a) as amended by the Family Law Act 1996, Sch 2, para 4).

Jurisdiction to make orders in marital proceedings if nullity proceedings pending

Under the Domicile and Matrimonial Proceedings Act 1973, s 5, the court had jurisdiction to make divorce, judicial separation or nullity decrees on the basis of the parties' domicile or habitual residence in England and Wales; and the court also had jurisdiction to grant nullity decrees in cases in which one of the parties had died domiciled here or had been resident here at the date of death. Section 5(3) of the 1973 Act in effect gave the court power to entertain supplemental petitions or cross-petitions for divorce, judicial separation or nullity (whether or not those jurisdictional provisions were satisfied at the time the supplemental or cross-petition was filed) provided that it had had jurisdiction when the original proceedings were filed, and those proceedings were still pending. The removal of the concept of cross-petitioning enabled the draftsman to simplify these rules; and it is now provided that the court has jurisdiction to entertain marital proceedings (as defined in the Family Law Act 1996, s 20(2) – in effect, separation and divorce proceedings) if nullity proceedings are pending in relation to the marriage when the marital proceedings are begun by the court receiving a statement of marital breakdown. The fact that nullity proceedings are pending cannot (contrary to fears expressed in the House of Lords debates: *Official Report* 23 January 1996, col 1151), in any circumstances affect the right of the respondent to make a statement and seek a divorce or separation order.

Nullity under the amended Matrimonial Causes Act 1973

9.3   The provisions setting out the *grounds* upon which a marriage is void or voidable are unchanged (MCA 1973, ss 12–14). The provision stipulating that every decree of nullity is in the first instance to be a *decree nisi*, not to be made absolute until the relevant period has expired has been redrafted (see now MCA 1973, s 15 as substituted by the Family Law Act 1996, Sch 8, para 6); and the same is true of the provisions governing interventions by the Queen's Proctor (see now MCA 1973, s 15A as substituted by the Family Law Act 1996, Sch 8, para 6). The provisions of the MCA 1973, ss 23 and 24, governing the court's powers to make *financial provision and property adjustment orders*, have been extensively redrafted (see MCA 1973, ss 23 and 24 as substituted by the Family Law Act 1996, Sch 2, paras 4 and 6), in part to give effect to the general policy that such powers should in nullity proceedings continue only to be exercisable on or after the making of a decree and only effective when the decree has been made absolute, and in part to be congruent with the style of drafting adopted in relation to the extensive changes of substance made in relation to the powers available in divorce and separation.

It should also be noted that the power to make orders for *maintenance pending suit* (MCA 1973, s 22) has been replaced by a power exercisable before granting a nullity decree to make interim orders (Family Law Act 1996, Sch 10; MCA 1973, s 23(2) as substituted by the Family Law Act 1996, Sch 2, para 4).

Other forms of matrimonial relief

9.4   The court's *power to make a decree of presumption of death and dissolution of marriage* (MCA 1973, s 19) remains substantially unchanged (see the amendments made by the Family Law Act 1996, Sch 8, para 7). However, it is possible that the draftsman has deprived the court of its power to make financial provision and property adjustment orders ancillary to the grant of such a decree (a power occasionally exercised in cases in which it transpired, after the grant of the decree, that the respondent was still alive: see *Deacock v Deacock* [1958] P 230).

9.5   The power of the High Court and county court to make *orders for financial provision in the case of neglect to maintain* a spouse or child of the family is extended to give the court power, in certain circumstances, to make a lump sum order by way of maintenance (MCA 1973, s 27(5) as amended by the Family Law Act 1996, Sch 8, para 13). It is possible that such proceedings will become more common since some applicants will wish to obtain a court order for financial support during the three months which must elapse between attendance at an information meeting and the making of a statement of marital breakdown (which will be effective to start marital proceedings).

9.6   Finally, the grounds upon which *magistrates' courts have power to make financial orders* under the Domestic Proceedings and Magistrates' Courts Act 1978, s 2 have been amended in order to 'reflect the change in the divorce law' (1995 White Paper, para 4.51). This has been done by removing the provisions under which the court could make orders on the ground that a spouse had behaved in such a way that the applicant could not reasonably be expected to live with him or that the applicant had been deserted by her spouse (Family Law Act 1996, Sch 10, repealing the Domestic Proceedings and Magistrates' Courts Act 1978, s 1(c) and (d)). The result is that the only ground upon which a financial order can be made in such proceedings is the respondent's failure to provide reasonable maintenance for the applicant or a child of the family (Domestic Proceedings and Magistrates' Courts Act 1978, s 1(a), (b)). Again, it is possible that such proceedings will now be used in the three-month period following attendance at an information meeting.

CHAPTER TEN

Transitional Provisions

10.1 Part II of the Act is to come into force on a day to be appointed, which may be in January 1999 (see Chapter One, para **1.24**). Until then, the provisions of the Matrimonial Causes Act 1973 will continue to have effect. When the 1996 Act comes into force, the Parts of the 1973 Act relating to divorce and judicial separation will be repealed.

10.2 The first matter with which transitional provisions have to deal is, therefore, petitions which have been filed before the appointed day. By para 5(1) of Sch 9, except for para 6 of the Schedule (considered at para **10.4**):

'... nothing in any provision of Part II, Part I of Schedule 8 or Schedule 10—

(a) applies to, or affects—
    (i) any decree granted before the coming into force of the provision;'

The effect of this is, therefore, that, if a petition has been filed before the appointed day, it may proceed and be dealt with under the law applicable before the 1996 Act came into effect. This is equally true in the case of a decree already granted; if a decree nisi had been granted, it could be made absolute.

10.3 Subparagraph (b) reinforces the point; nothing in the 1996 Act affects the operation of the 1973 Act, any other enactment, or any subordinate legislation in relation to any such proceedings or to any proceedings in connection with any proceedings or decree so begun or granted. Once a petition has been filed under the 'old law' therefore, any ancillary proceedings may continue to be dealt with under that law.

10.4 It was seen above that para 5(1) was subject to para 6 of the Schedule. Paragraph 6(1) provides that the MCA 1973, s 31 has effect, as amended by the 1996 Act, in relation to any other under Part II of the MCA 1973 made after the coming into force of the amendments. If, therefore, an order for ancillary relief were made after the appointed day in respect of a case in which the petition had been filed before the appointed day, the law applicable to any variation of such an order would be s 31 of the MCA 1973 as amended by the 1996 Act and not the unamended s 31.

Paragraph 6(2) goes further. It will be remembered that the 1996 Act amends s 31 of the MCA 1973 to insert new subsections (7) to (7F), the effect of which is to confer on the court new powers when discharging or varying an order for periodical payments; the court is now empowered to substitute a lump sum order or property adjustment order in place of the varied order (see Chapter Six, para **6.20**). Paragraph 6(2) provides that subsections (7) to (7F) have effect in relation to any order made before the coming into force of the amendments. This means that, once the amendments have been brought into force, they will have effect when the court is dealing with the variation of an order made under the 1973 Act. Some of the consequences of this have already been discussed at paras **6.29** et seq.

10.5   Paragraph 1 of Sch 9 appears to be designed to deal with the position of parties who were intending to petition for divorce or judicial separation under s 1(2)(d) or (e) of the 1973 Act (ie on the ground of two or five years' separation). The intention is that a period of separation which has accrued under the old law will not necessarily be 'lost', and may allow the person concerned to petition under the old law after the coming into force of the 1996 Act and during a transitional period. By para 1(3), ' "transitional period" means the period of two years beginning with the day on which section 3 [the section governing applications for divorce] is brought into force.'

This paragraph of the Schedule confers on the Lord Chancellor power to provide for these matters by order, and until the order is made it is only possible to speculate as to what the position will be. In the final debate, the Lord Chancellor said that, as a result of this provision, he would be able to modify the requirements of Part II of the Act in relation to people who had previously been living apart upon proof of such separation being produced to the court, for a transitional period of two years; he believed that the inclusion of this provision would avoid the difficulties which might otherwise have arisen in such cases.

One of the matters for which the order will have to provide is 'the evidence which a party who claims to have been living apart from the other party immediately before the beginning of the transitional period must produce to the court'.

The effect of this is that parties who, for example, have been separated for one year on the appointed day, may not have to proceed under the new Act if they do not wish to do so, and may have the option of proceeding under the 1973 Act.

APPENDIX ONE

Family Law Act 1996
(1996 c. 27)

ARRANGEMENT OF SECTIONS

PART I
PRINCIPLES OF PARTS II AND III

PART II
DIVORCE AND SEPARATION

Resolution of disputes

Financial provision

Jurisdiction and commencement of proceedings

Intestacy

Marriage support services

Interpretation

PART III
LEGAL AID FOR MEDIATION IN FAMILY MATTERS

PART IV
FAMILY HOMES AND DOMESTIC VIOLENCE

Rights to occupy matrimonial home

Occupation orders

PART V
SUPPLEMENTAL

An Act to make provision with respect to: divorce and separation; legal aid in connection with mediation in disputes relating to family matters; proceedings in cases where marriages have broken down; rights of occupation of certain domestic premises; prevention of molestation; the inclusion in certain orders under the Children Act 1989 of provisions about the occupation of a dwelling-house; the transfer of tenancies between spouses and persons who have lived together as husband and wife and for connected purposes.

[4th July 1996]

PART I
PRINCIPLES OF PARTS II AND III

1 The general principles underlying Parts II and III

The court and any person, in exercising functions under or in consequence of Parts II and III, shall have regard to the following general principles—

   (a)   that the institution of marriage is to be supported;

   (b)   that the parties to a marriage which may have broken down are to be encouraged to take all practicable steps, whether by marriage counselling or otherwise, to save the marriage;

   (c)   that a marriage which has irretrievably broken down and is being brought to an end should be brought to an end—

      (i)   with minimum distress to the parties and to the children affected;

(ii)   with questions dealt with in a manner designed to promote as good a continuing relationship between the parties and any children affected as is possible in the circumstances; and

(iii)   without costs being unreasonably incurred in connection with the procedures to be followed in bringing the marriage to an end; and

(d)   that any risk to one of the parties to a marriage, and to any children, of violence from the other party should, so far as reasonably practicable, be removed or diminished.

PART II
DIVORCE AND SEPARATION

Court orders

2 Divorce and separation

(1) The court may—

(a)   by making an order (to be known as a divorce order), dissolve a marriage; or

(b)   by making an order (to be known as a separation order), provide for the separation of the parties to a marriage.

(2) Any such order comes into force on being made.

(3) A separation order remains in force—

(a)   while the marriage continues; or

(b)   until cancelled by the court on the joint application of the parties.

3 Circumstances in which orders are made

(1) If an application for a divorce order or for a separation order is made to the court under this section by one or both of the parties to a marriage, the court shall make the order applied for if (but only if)—

(a)   the marriage has broken down irretrievably;

(b)   the requirements of section 8 about information meetings are satisfied;

(c)   the requirements of section 9 about the parties' arrangements for the future are satisfied; and

(d)   the application has not been withdrawn.

(2) A divorce order may not be made if an order preventing divorce is in force under section 10.

(3) If the court is considering an application for a divorce order and an application for a separation order in respect of the same marriage it shall proceed as if it were considering only the application for a divorce order unless—

(a)   an order preventing divorce is in force with respect to the marriage;

(b)   the court makes an order preventing divorce; or

(c)   section 7(6) or (13) applies.

4 Conversion of separation order into divorce order

(1) A separation order which is made before the second anniversary of the marriage may not be converted into a divorce order under this section until after that anniversary.

(2) A separation order may not be converted into a divorce order under this section at any time while—

(a)   an order preventing divorce is in force under section 10; or
(b)   subsection (4) applies.

(3) Otherwise, if a separation order is in force and an application for a divorce order—

(a)   is made under this section by either or both of the parties to the marriage, and
(b)   is not withdrawn,

the court shall grant the application once the requirements of section 11 have been satisfied.

(4) Subject to subsection (5), this subsection applies if—

(a)   there is a child of the family who is under the age of sixteen when the application under this section is made; or
(b)   the application under this section is made by one party and the other party applies to the court, before the end of such period as may be prescribed by rules of court, for time for further reflection.

(5) Subsection (4)—

(a)   does not apply if, at the time when the application under this section is made, there is an occupation order or a non-molestation order in force in favour of the applicant, or of a child of the family, made against the other party;
(b)   does not apply if the court is satisfied that delaying the making of a divorce order would be significantly detrimental to the welfare of any child of the family;
(c)   ceases to apply—
(i)   at the end of the period of six months beginning with the end of the period for reflection and consideration by reference to which the separation order was made; or
(ii)   if earlier, on there ceasing to be any children of the family to whom subsection (4)(a) applied.

Marital breakdown

5 Marital breakdown

(1) A marriage is to be taken to have broken down irretrievably if (but only if)—

(a)   a statement has been made by one (or both) of the parties that the maker of the statement (or each of them) believes that the marriage has broken down;
(b)   the statement complies with the requirements of section 6;
(c)   the period for reflection and consideration fixed by section 7 has ended; and
(d)   the application under section 3 is accompanied by a declaration by the party making the application that—
(i)   having reflected on the breakdown, and
(ii)   having considered the requirements of this Part as to the parties' arrangements for the future,
the applicant believes that the marriage cannot be saved.

(2) The statement and the application under section 3 do not have to be made by the same party.

(3) An application may not be made under section 3 by reference to a particular statement if—

(a) the parties have jointly given notice (in accordance with rules of court) withdrawing the statement; or

(b) a period of one year ('the specified period') has passed since the end of the period for reflection and consideration.

(4) Any period during which an order preventing divorce is in force is not to count towards the specified period mentioned in subsection (3)(b).

(5) Subsection (6) applies if, before the end of the specified period, the parties jointly give notice to the court that they are attempting reconciliation but require additional time.

(6) The specified period—

(a) stops running on the day on which the notice is received by the court; but

(b) resumes running on the day on which either of the parties gives notice to the court that the attempted reconciliation has been unsuccessful.

(7) If the specified period is interrupted by a continuous period of more than 18 months, any application by either of the parties for a divorce order or for a separation order must be by reference to a new statement received by the court at any time after the end of the 18 months.

(8) The Lord Chancellor may by order amend subsection (3)(b) by varying the specified period.

6 Statement of marital breakdown

(1) A statement under section 5(1)(a) is to be known as a statement of marital breakdown; but in this Part it is generally referred to as 'a statement'.

(2) If a statement is made by one party it must also state that that party—

(a) is aware of the purpose of the period for reflection and consideration as described in section 7; and

(b) wishes to make arrangements for the future.

(3) If a statement is made by both parties it must also state that each of them—

(a) is aware of the purpose of the period for reflection and consideration as described in section 7; and

(b) wishes to make arrangements for the future.

(4) A statement must be given to the court in accordance with the requirements of rules made under section 12.

(5) A statement must also satisfy any other requirements imposed by rules made under that section.

(6) A statement made at a time when the circumstances of the case include any of those mentioned in subsection (7) is ineffective for the purposes of this Part.

(7) The circumstances are—

(a) that a statement has previously been made with respect to the marriage and it is, or will become, possible—

  (i)   for an application for a divorce order, or
  (ii) for an application for a separation order,

  to be made by reference to the previous statement;

(b) that such an application has been made in relation to the marriage and has not been withdrawn;

(c) that a separation order is in force.

Reflection and consideration

7 Period for reflection and consideration

(1) Where a statement has been made, a period for the parties—

(a) to reflect on whether the marriage can be saved and to have an opportunity to effect a reconciliation, and

(b) to consider what arrangements should be made for the future,

must pass before an application for a divorce order or for a separation order may be made by reference to that statement.

(2) That period is to be known as the period for reflection and consideration.

(3) The period for reflection and consideration is nine months beginning with the fourteenth day after the day on which the statement is received by the court.

(4) Where—

(a) the statement has been made by one party,

(b) rules made under section 12 require the court to serve a copy of the statement on the other party, and

(c) failure to comply with the rules causes inordinate delay in service,

the court may, on the application of that other party, extend the period for reflection and consideration.

(5) An extension under subsection (4) may be for any period not exceeding the time between—

(a) the beginning of the period for reflection and consideration; and

(b) the time when service is effected.

(6) A statement which is made before the first anniversary of the marriage to which it relates is ineffective for the purposes of any application for a divorce order.

(7) Subsection (8) applies if, at any time during the period for reflection and consideration, the parties jointly give notice to the court that they are attempting a reconciliation but require additional time.

(8) The period for reflection and consideration—

(a) stops running on the day on which the notice is received by the court; but

(b) resumes running on the day on which either of the parties gives notice to the court that the attempted reconciliation has been unsuccessful.

(9) If the period for reflection and consideration is interrupted under subsection (8) by a continuous period of more than 18 months, any application by either of the parties

for a divorce order or for a separation order must be by reference to a new statement received by the court at any time after the end of the 18 months.

(10) Where an application for a divorce order is made by one party, subsection (13) applies if—

(a) the other party applies to the court, within the prescribed period, for time for further reflection; and

(b) the requirements of section 9 (except any imposed under section 9(3)) are satisfied.

(11) Where any application for a divorce order is made, subsection (13) also applies if there is a child of the family who is under the age of sixteen when the application is made.

(12) Subsection (13) does not apply if—

(a) at the time when the application for a divorce order is made, there is an occupation order or a non-molestation order in force in favour of the applicant, or of a child of the family, made against the other party; or

(b) the court is satisfied that delaying the making of a divorce order would be significantly detrimental to the welfare of any child of the family.

(13) If this subsection applies, the period for reflection and consideration is extended by a period of six months, but—

(a) only in relation to the application for a divorce order in respect of which the application under subsection (10) was made; and

(b) without invalidating that application for a divorce order.

(14) A period for reflection and consideration which is extended under subsection (13), and which has not otherwise come to an end, comes to an end on there ceasing to be any children of the family to whom subsection (11) applied.

8 Attendance at information meetings

(1) The requirements about information meetings are as follows.

(2) A party making a statement must (except in prescribed circumstances) have attended an information meeting not less than three months before making the statement.

(3) Different information meetings must be arranged with respect to different marriages.

(4) In the case of a statement made by both parties, the parties may attend separate meetings or the same meeting.

(5) Where one party has made a statement, the other party must (except in prescribed circumstances) attend an information meeting before—

(a) making any application to the court—

  (i) with respect to a child of the family; or

  (ii) of a prescribed description relating to property or financial matters; or

(b) contesting any such application.

(6) In this section 'information meeting' means a meeting organised, in accordance with prescribed provisions for the purpose—

(a)   of providing, in accordance with prescribed provisions, relevant information to the party or parties attending about matters which may arise in connection with the provisions of, or made under, this Part or Part III; and

(b)   of giving the party or parties attending the information meeting the opportunity of having a meeting with a marriage counsellor and of encouraging that party or those parties to attend that meeting.

(7) An information meeting must be conducted by a person who—

(a)   is qualified and appointed in accordance with prescribed provisions; and

(b)   will have no financial or other interest in any marital proceedings between the parties.

(8) Regulations made under this section may, in particular, make provision—

(a)   about the places and times at which information meetings are to be held;

(b)   for written information to be given to persons attending them;

(c)   for the giving of information to parties (otherwise than at information meetings) in cases in which the requirement to attend such meetings does not apply;

(d)   for information of a prescribed kind to be given only with the approval of the Lord Chancellor or only by a person or by persons approved by him; and

(e)   for information to be given, in prescribed circumstances, only with the approval of the Lord Chancellor or only by a person, or by persons, approved by him.

(9) Regulations made under subsection (6) must, in particular, make provision with respect to the giving of information about—

(a)   marriage counselling and other marriage support services;

(b)   the importance to be attached to the welfare, wishes and feelings of children;

(c)   how the parties may acquire a better understanding of the ways in which children can be helped to cope with the breakdown of a marriage;

(d)   the nature of the financial questions that may arise on divorce or separation, and services which are available to help the parties;

(e)   protection available against violence, and how to obtain support and assistance;

(f)   mediation;

(g)   the availability to each of the parties of independent legal advice and representation;

(h)   the principles of legal aid and where the parties can get advice about obtaining legal aid;

(i)   the divorce and separation process.

(10) Before making any regulations under subsection (6), the Lord Chancellor must consult such persons concerned with the provision of relevant information as he considers appropriate.

(11) A meeting with a marriage counsellor arranged under this section—

(a)   must be held in accordance with prescribed provisions; and

(b) must be with a person qualified and appointed in accordance with prescribed provisions.

(12) A person who would not be required to make any contribution towards mediation provided for him under Part IIIA of the Legal Aid Act 1988 shall not be required to make any contribution towards the cost of a meeting with a marriage counsellor arranged for him under this section.

(13) In this section 'prescribed' means prescribed by regulations made by the Lord Chancellor.

9 Arrangements for the future

(1) The requirements as to the parties' arrangements for the future are as follows.

(2) One of the following must be produced to the court—

(a) a court order (made by consent or otherwise) dealing with their financial arrangements;
(b) a negotiated agreement as to their financial arrangements;
(c) a declaration by both parties that they have made their financial arrangements;
(d) a declaration by one of the parties (to which no objection has been notified to the court by the other party) that—
    (i) he has no significant assets and does not intend to make an application for financial provision;
    (ii) he believes that the other party has no significant assets and does not intend to make an application for financial provision; and
    (iii) there are therefore no financial arrangements to be made.

(3) If the parties—

(a) were married to each other in accordance with usages of a kind mentioned in section 26(1) of the Marriage Act 1949 (marriages which may be solemnized on authority of superintendent registrar's certificate), and
(b) are required to co-operate if the marriage is to be dissolved in accordance with those usages,

the court may, on the application of either party, direct that there must also be produced to the court a declaration by both parties that they have taken such steps as are required to dissolve the marriage in accordance with those usages.

(4) A direction under subsection (3)—

(a) may be given only if the court is satisfied that in all the circumstances of the case it is just and reasonable to give it; and
(b) may be revoked by the court at any time.

(5) The requirements of section 11 must have been satisfied.

(6) Schedule 1 supplements the provisions of this section.

(7) If the court is satisfied, on an application made by one of the parties after the end of the period for reflection and consideration, that the circumstances of the case are—

(a) those set out in paragraph 1 of Schedule 1,
(b) those set out in paragraph 2 of that Schedule,
(c) those set out in paragraph 3 of that Schedule, or

(d)   those set out in paragraph 4 of that Schedule,

it may make a divorce order or a separation order even though the requirements of subsection (2) have not been satisfied.

(8) If the parties' arrangements for the future include a division of pension assets or rights under section 25B of the 1973 Act or section 10 of the Family Law (Scotland) Act 1985, any declaration under subsection (2) must be a statutory declaration.

Orders preventing divorce

10 Hardship: orders preventing divorce

(1) If an application for a divorce order has been made by one of the parties to a marriage, the court may, on the application of the other party, order that the marriage is not to be dissolved.

(2) Such an order (an 'order preventing divorce') may be made only if the court is satisfied—

(a)   that dissolution of the marriage would result in substantial financial or other hardship to the other party or to a child of the family; and

(b)   that it would be wrong, in all the circumstances (including the conduct of the parties and the interests of any child of the family), for the marriage to be dissolved.

(3) If an application for the cancellation of an order preventing divorce is made by one or both of the parties, the court shall cancel the order unless it is still satisfied—

(a)   that dissolution of the marriage would result in substantial financial or other hardship to the party in whose favour the order was made or to a child of the family; and

(b)   that it would be wrong, in all the circumstances (including the conduct of the parties and the interests of any child of the family), for the marriage to be dissolved.

(4) If an order preventing a divorce is cancelled, the court may make a divorce order in respect of the marriage only if an application is made under section 3 or 4(3) after the cancellation.

(5) An order preventing divorce may include conditions which must be satisfied before an application for cancellation may be made under subsection (3).

(6) In this section 'hardship' includes the loss of a chance to obtain a future benefit (as well as the loss of an existing benefit).

Welfare of children

11 Welfare of children

(1) In any proceedings for a divorce order or a separation order, the court shall consider—

(a)   whether there are any children of the family to whom this section applies; and

(b) where there are any such children, whether (in the light of the arrangements which have been, or are proposed to be, made for their upbringing and welfare) it should exercise any of its powers under the Children Act 1989 with respect to any of them.

(2) Where, in any case to which this section applies, it appears to the court that—

(a) the circumstances of the case required it, or are likely to require it, to exercise any of its powers under the Children Act 1989 with respect to any such child,

(b) it is not in a position to exercise the power, or (as the case may be) those powers, without giving further consideration to the case, and

(c) there are exceptional circumstances which make it desirable in the interests of the child that the court should give a direction under this section,

it may direct that the divorce order or separation order is not to be made until the court orders otherwise.

(3) In deciding whether the circumstances are as mentioned in subsection (2)(a), the court shall treat the welfare of the child as paramount.

(4) In making that decision, the court shall also have particular regard, on the evidence before it, to—

(a) the wishes and feelings of the child considered in the light of his age and understanding and the circumstances in which those wishes were expressed;

(b) the conduct of the parties in relation to the upbringing of the child;

(c) the general principle that, in the absence of evidence to the contrary, the welfare of the child will be best served by—

    (i) his having regular contact with those who have parental responsibility for him and with other members of his family; and

    (ii) the maintenance of as good a continuing relationship with his parents as is possible; and

(d) any risk to the child attributable to—

    (i) where the person with whom the child will reside is living or proposes to live;

    (ii) any person with whom that person is living or with whom he proposes to live; or

    (iii) any other arrangements for his care and upbringing.

(5) This section applies to—

(a) any child of the family who has not reached the age of sixteen at the date when the court considers the case in accordance with the requirements of this section; and

(b) any child of the family who has reached that age at that date and in relation to whom the court directs that this section shall apply.

Supplementary

12 Lord Chancellor's rules

(1) The Lord Chancellor may make rules—

(a) as to the form in which a statement is to be made and what information must accompany it;

(b) requiring the person making the statement to state whether or not, since satisfying the requirements of section 8, he has made any attempt at reconciliation;

(c) as to the way in which a statement is to be given to the court;

(d) requiring a copy of a statement made by one party to be served by the court on the other party;

(e) as to circumstances in which such service may be dispensed with or may be effected otherwise than by delivery to the party;

(f) requiring a party who has made a statement to provide the court with information about the arrangements that need to be made in consequence of the breakdown;

(g) as to the time, manner and (where attendance in person is required) place at which such information is to be given;

(h) where a statement has been made, requiring either or both of the parties—
    (i) to prepare and produce such other documents, and
    (ii) to attend in person at such places and for such purposes,
  as may be specified;

(i) as to the information and assistance which is to be given to the parties and the way in which it is to be given;

(j) requiring the parties to be given, in such manner as may be specified, copies of such statements and other documents as may be specified.

(2) The Lord Chancellor may make rules requiring a person who is the legal representative of a party to a marriage with respect to which a statement has been, or is proposed to be, made—

(a) to inform that party, at such time or times as may be specified—
    (i) about the availability to the parties of marriage support services;
    (ii) about the availability to them of mediation; and
    (iii) where there are children of the family, that in relation to the arrangements to be made for any child the parties should consider the child's welfare, wishes and feelings;

(b) to give that party, at such time or times as may be specified, names and addresses of persons qualified to help—
    (i) to effect a reconciliation; or
    (ii) in connection with mediation; and

(c) to certify, at such time or times as may be specified—
    (i) whether he has complied with the provision made in the rules by virtue of paragraphs (a) and (b);
    (ii) whether he has discussed with that party any of the matters mentioned in paragraph (a) or the possibility of reconciliation; and
    (iii) which, if any, of those matters they have discussed.

(3) In subsections (1) and (2) 'specified' means determined under or described in the rules.

(4) This section does not affect any power to make rules of court for the purposes of this Act.

Resolution of disputes

13 Directions with respect to mediation

(1) After the court has received a statement, it may give a direction requiring each party to attend a meeting arranged in accordance with the direction for the purpose—

(a) of enabling an explanation to be given of the facilities available to the parties for mediation in relation to disputes between them; and

(b) of providing an opportunity for each party to agree to take advantage of those facilities.

(2) A direction may be given at any time, including in the course of proceedings connected with the breakdown of the marriage (as to which see section 25).

(3) A direction may be given on the application of either of the parties or on the initiative of the court.

(4) The parties are to be required to attend the same meeting unless—

(a) one of them asks, or both of them ask, for separate meetings; or

(b) the court considers separate meetings to be more appropriate.

(5) A direction shall—

(a) specify a person chosen by the court (with that person's agreement) to arrange and conduct the meeting or meetings; and

(b) require such person as may be specified in the direction to produce to the court, at such time as the court may direct, a report stating—

(i) whether the parties have complied with the direction; and

(ii) if they have, whether they have agreed to take part in any mediation.

14 Adjournments

(1) The court's power to adjourn any proceedings connected with the breakdown of a marriage includes power to adjourn—

(a) for the purpose of allowing the parties to comply with a direction under section 13; or

(b) for the purpose of enabling disputes to be resolved amicably.

(2) In determining whether to adjourn for either purpose, the court shall have regard in particular to the need to protect the interests of any child of the family.

(3) If the court adjourns any proceedings connected with the breakdown of a marriage for either purpose, the period of the adjournment must not exceed the maximum period prescribed by rules of court.

(4) Unless the only purpose of the adjournment is to allow the parties to comply with a direction under section 13, the court shall order one or both of them to produce to the court a report as to—

(a) whether they have taken part in mediation during the adjournment;

(b) whether, as a result, any agreement has been reached between them;

(c) the extent to which any dispute between them has been resolved as a result of any such agreement;

(d) the need for further mediation; and

(e) how likely it is that further mediation will be successful.

Financial provision

15 Financial arrangements

(1) Schedule 2 amends the 1973 Act.

(2) The main object of Schedule 2 is—

(a) to provide that, in the case of divorce or separation, an order about financial provision may be made under that Act before a divorce order or separation order is made; but

(b) to retain (with minor changes) the position under that Act where marriages are annulled.

(3) Schedule 2 also makes minor and consequential amendments of the 1973 Act connected with the changes mentioned in subsection (1).

16 Division of pension rights: England and Wales

(1) The Matrimonial Causes Act 1973 is amended as follows.

(2) In section 25B (benefits under a pension scheme on divorce, etc.), in subsection (2), after paragraph (b), insert—

'(c) in particular, where the court determines to make such an order, whether the order should provide for the accrued rights of the party with pension rights ("the pension rights") to be divided between that party and the other party in such a way as to reduce the pension rights of the party with those rights and to create pension rights for the other party.'.

(3) After subsection (7) of that section, add—

(8) If a pensions adjustment order under subsection (2)(c) above is made, the pension rights shall be reduced and pension rights of the other party shall be created in the prescribed manner with benefits payable on prescribed conditions, except that the court shall not have the power—

(a) to require the trustees or managers of the scheme to provide benefits under their own scheme if they are able and willing to create the rights of the other party by making a transfer payment to another scheme and the trustees and managers of that other scheme are able and willing to accept such a payment and to create those rights; or

(b) to require the trustees or managers of the scheme to make a transfer to another scheme—

(i) if the scheme is an unfunded scheme (unless the trustees or managers are able and willing to make such a transfer payment); or

(ii) in prescribed circumstances.

(9) No pensions adjustment order may be made under subsection (2)(c) above—

(a) if the scheme is a scheme of a prescribed type, or

(b) in prescribed circumstances, or

(c) insofar as it would affect benefits of a prescribed type.'

(4) In section 25D (pensions: supplementary), insert—

(a) in subsection (2)—

    (i) at the end of paragraph (a), the words 'or prescribe the rights of the other party under the pension scheme,'; and

    (ii) after paragraph (a), the following paragraph—

'(aa) make such consequential modifications of any enactment or subordinate legislation as appear to the Lord Chancellor necessary or expedient to give effect to the provisions of section 25B; and an order under this paragraph may make provision applying generally in relation to enactments and subordinate legislation of a description specified in the order,';

(b) in subsection (4), in the appropriate place in alphabetical order, the following entries—

' "funded scheme' means a scheme under which the benefits are provided for by setting aside resources related to the value of the members' rights as they accrue (and "unfunded scheme" shall be construed accordingly);

"subordinate legislation" has the same meaning as in the Interpretation Act 1978;'; and

(c) after subsection (4), the following subsection—

'(4A) Other expressions used in section 25B above shall be construed in accordance with section 124 (interpretation of Part I) of the Pensions Act 1995.'

17 Division of pension assets: Scotland

Section 10 of the Family Law (Scotland) Act 1985 (sharing of value of matrimonial property), is amended as follows—

(a) in subsection (5) at the end of paragraph (b), insert ', and

    (c) in the assets in respect of which either party has accrued rights to benefits under a pension scheme'; and

(b) after subsection (5) insert—

'(5A) In the case of an unfunded pension scheme, the court may not make an order which would allow assets to be removed from the scheme earlier than would otherwise have been the case.'.

18 Grounds for financial provision orders in magistrates' courts

(1) In section 1 of the Domestic Proceedings and Magistrates' Courts Act 1978, omit paragraphs (c) and (d) (which provide for behaviour and desertion to be grounds on which an application for a financial provision order may be made).

(2) In section 7(1) of that Act (powers of magistrates' court where spouses are living apart by agreement), omit 'neither party having deserted the other'.

Jurisdiction and commencement of proceedings

19 Jurisdiction in relation to divorce and separation

(1) In this section 'the court's jurisdiction' means—

(a) the jurisdiction of the court under this Part to entertain marital proceedings; and

(b) any other jurisdiction conferred on the court under this Part, or any other enactment, in consequence of the making of a statement.

(2) The court's jurisdiction is exercisable only if—

    (a)   at least one of the parties was domiciled in England and Wales on the statement date;

    (b)   at least one of the parties was habitually resident in England and Wales throughout the period of one year ending with the statement date; or

    (c)   nullity proceedings are pending in relation to the marriage when the marital proceedings commence.

(3) Subsection (4) applies if—

    (a)   a separation order is in force; or

    (b)   an order preventing divorce has been cancelled.

(4) The court—

    (a)   continues to have jurisdiction to entertain an application made by reference to the order referred to in subsection (3); and

    (b)   may exercise any other jurisdiction which is conferred on it in consequence of such an application.

(5) Schedule 3 amends Schedule 1 to the Domicile and Matrimonial Proceedings Act 1973 (orders to stay proceedings where there are proceedings in other jurisdictions).

(6) The court's jurisdiction is exercisable subject to any order for a stay under Schedule 1 to that Act.

(7) In this section—

    'nullity proceedings' means proceedings in respect of which the court has jurisdiction under section 5(3) of the Domicile and Matrimonial Proceedings Act 1973; and

    'statement date' means the date on which the relevant statement was received by the court.

20 Time when proceedings for divorce or separation begin

(1) The receipt by the court of a statement is to be treated as the commencement of proceedings.

(2) The proceedings are to be known as marital proceedings.

(3) Marital proceedings are also—

    (a)   separation proceedings, if an application for a separation order has been made under section 3 by reference to the statement and not withdrawn;

    (b)   divorce proceedings, if an application for a divorce order has been made under section 3 by reference to the statement and not withdrawn.

(4) Marital proceedings are to be treated as being both divorce proceedings and separation proceedings at any time when no application by reference to the statement, either for a divorce order or for a separation order, is outstanding.

(5) Proceedings which are commenced by the making of an application under section 4(3) are also marital proceedings and divorce proceedings.

(6) Marital proceedings come to an end—

(a) on the making of a separation order;

(b) on the making of a divorce order;

(c) on the withdrawal of the statement by a notice in accordance with section 5(3)(a);

(d) at the end of the specified period mentioned in section 5(3)(b), if no application under section 3 by reference to the statement is outstanding;

(e) on the withdrawal of all such applications which are outstanding at the end of that period;

(f) on the withdrawal of an application under section 4(3).

Intestacy

21 Intestacy: effect of separation

Where—

(a) a separation order is in force, and

(b) while the parties to the marriage remain separated, one of them dies intestate as respects any real or personal property,

that property devolves as if the other had died before the intestacy occurred.

Marriage support services

22 Funding for marriage support services

(1) The Lord Chancellor may, with the approval of the Treasury, make grants in connection with—

(a) the provision of marriage support services;

(b) research into the causes of marital breakdown;

(c) research into ways of preventing marital breakdown.

(2) Any grant under this section may be made subject to such conditions as the Lord Chancellor considers appropriate.

(3) In exercising his power to make grants in connection with the provision of marriage support services, the Lord Chancellor is to have regard, in particular, to the desirability of services of that kind being available when they are first needed.

23 Provision of marriage counselling

(1) The Lord Chancellor or a person appointed by him may secure the provision, in accordance with regulations made by the Lord Chancellor, of marriage counselling.

(2) Marriage counselling may only be provided under this section at a time when a period for reflection and consideration—

(a) is running in relation to the marriage; or

(b) is interrupted under section 7(8) (but not for a continuous period of more than 18 months).

(3) Marriage counselling may only be provided under this section for persons who would not be required to make any contribution towards the cost of mediation provided for them under Part IIIA of the Legal Aid Act 1988.

(4) Persons for whom marriage counselling is provided under this section are not to be required to make any contribution towards the costs of the counselling.

(5) Marriage counselling is only to be provided under this section if it appears to the marriage counsellor to be suitable in all the circumstances.

(6) Regulations under subsection (1) may—

  (a)   make provision about the way in which marriage counselling is to be provided; and

  (b)   prescribe circumstances in which the provision of marriage counselling is to be subject to the approval of the Lord Chancellor.

(7) A contract entered into for the purposes of subsection (1) by a person appointed under that subsection must include such provision as the Lord Chancellor may direct.

(8) If a person appointed under subsection (1) is the Legal Aid Board, the powers conferred on the Board by or under the Legal Aid Act 1988 shall be exercisable for the purposes of this section as they are exercisable for the purposes of that Act.

(9) In section 15 of the Legal Aid Act 1988 (availability of, and payment for, representation under Part IV of the Act), after subsection (3H) insert—

  '(3I) A person may be refused representation for the purposes of any proceedings if—

  (a)   the proceedings are marital proceedings within the meaning of Part II of the Family Law Act 1996; and

  (b)   he is being provided with marriage counselling under section 23 of that Act in relation to the marriage.'

Interpretation

24 Interpretation of Part II etc

(1) In this Part—

  'the 1973 Act' means the Matrimonial Causes Act 1973;
  'child of the family' and 'the court' have the same meaning as in the 1973 Act;
  'divorce order' has the meaning given in section 2(1)(a);
  'divorce proceedings' is to be read with section 20;
  'marital proceedings' has the meaning given in section 20;
  'non-molestation order' has the meaning given by section 42(1);
  'occupation order' has the meaning given by section 39;
  'order preventing divorce' has the meaning given in section 10(2);
  'party', in relation to a marriage, means one of the parties to the marriage;
  'period for reflection and consideration' has the meaning given in section 7;
  'separation order' has the meaning given in section 2(1)(b);
  'separation proceedings' is to be read within section 20;
  'statement' means a statement of marital breakdown;
  'statement of marital breakdown' has the meaning given in section 6(1).

(2) For the purposes of this Part, references to the withdrawal of an application are references, in relation to an application made jointly by both parties, to its withdrawal by a notice given, in accordance with rules of court—

  (a)   jointly by both parties; or

(b) separately by each of them.

(3) Where only one party gives such a notice of withdrawal, in relation to a joint application, the application shall be treated as if it had been made by the other party alone.

25 Connected proceedings

(1) For the purposes of this Part, proceedings are connected with the breakdown of a marriage if they fall within subsection (2) and, at the time of the proceedings—

(a) a statement has been received by the court with respect to the marriage and it is or may become possible for an application for a divorce order or separation order to be made by reference to that statement;

(b) such an application in relation to the marriage has been made and not withdrawn; or

(c) a divorce order has been made, or a separation order is in force, in relation to the marriage.

(2) The proceedings are any under Parts I to V of the Child Act 1989 with respect to a child of the family or any proceedings resulting from an application—

(a) for, or for the cancellation of, an order preventing divorce in relation to the marriage;

(b) by either party to the marriage for an order under Part IV;

(c) for the exercise, in relation to a party to the marriage or child of the family, of any of the court's powers under Part II of the 1973 Act;

(d) made otherwise to the court with respect to, or in connection with, any proceedings connected with the breakdown of the marriage.

PART III
LEGAL AID FOR MEDIATION IN FAMILY MATTERS

26 Legal aid for mediation in family matters

(1) In the Legal Aid Act 1988 insert, after section 13—

'PART IIIA
MEDIATION

13A Scope of this Part

(1) This Part applies to mediation in disputes relating to family matters.

(2) "Family matters" means matters which are governed by English law and in relation to which any question has arisen, or may arise—

(a) under any provision of—
    (i) the 1973 Act;
    (ii) the Domestic Proceedings and Magistrates' Courts Act 1978;
    (iii) Parts I to V of the Children Act 1989;
    (iv) Parts II and IV of the Family Law Act 1996; or
    (v) any other enactment prescribed;
(b) under any prescribed jurisdiction of a prescribed court or tribunal; or
(c) under any prescribed rule of law.

(3) Regulations may restrict this Part to mediation in disputes of any prescribed description.

(4) The power to—

(a)   make regulations under subsection (2), or

(b)   revoke any regulations made under subsection (3),

is exercisable only with the consent of the Treasury.'

(2) In section 2 of the 1988 Act, after subsection (3), insert—

'(3A) "Mediation" means mediation to which Part IIIA of this Act applies; and includes steps taken by a mediator in any case—

(a)   in determining whether to embark on mediation;

(b)   in preparing for mediation; and

(c)   in making any assessment under that Part.'

(3) In section 43 of the 1988 Act, after the definition of 'legal representative' insert—

' "mediator" means a person with whom the Board contracts for the provision of mediation by any person.'

27 Provision and availability of mediation

After section 13A of the 1988 Act, insert—

'13B Provision and availability of mediation

(1) The Board may secure the provision of mediation under this Part.

(2) If mediation is provided under this Part, it is to be available to any person whose financial resources are such as, under regulations, make him eligible for mediation.

(3) A person is not to be granted mediation in relation to any dispute unless mediation appears to the mediator suitable to the dispute and the parties and all the circumstances.

(4) A grant of mediation under this Part may be amended, withdrawn or revoked.

(5) The power conferred by subsection (1) shall be exercised in accordance with any directions given by the Lord Chancellor.

(6) Any contract entered into by the Board for the provision of mediation under this Part must require the mediator to comply with a code of practice.

(7) The code must require the mediator to have arrangements designed to ensure—

(a)   that parties participate in mediation only if willing and not influenced by fear of violence or other harm;

(b)   that cases where either party may be influenced by fear of violence or other harm are identified as soon as possible;

(c)   that the possibility of reconciliation is kept under review throughout mediation; and

(d)   that each party is informed about the availability of independent legal advice.

(8) Where there are one or more children of the family, the code must also require the mediator to have arrangements designed to ensure that the parties are encouraged to consider—

(a) the welfare, wishes and feelings of each child; and
(b) whether and to what extent each child should be given the opportunity to express his or her wishes and feelings in the mediation.

(9) A contract entered into by the Board for the provision of mediation under this Part must also include such other provision as the Lord Chancellor may direct the Board to include.

(10) Directions under this section may apply generally to contracts, or to contracts of any description, entered into by the Board, but shall not be made with respect to any particular contract.'

28 Payment for mediation

(1) After section 13B of the 1988 Act, insert—

'13C Payment for mediation under this Part

(1) Except as provided by this section, the legally assisted person is not to be required to pay for mediation provided under this Part.

(2) Subsection (3) applies if the financial resources of a legally assisted person are such as, under regulations, make him liable to make a contribution.

(3) The legally assisted person is to pay to the Board in respect of the costs of providing the mediation, a contribution of such amount as is determined or fixed by or under the regulations.

(4) If the total contribution made by a person in respect of any mediation exceeds the Board's liability on his account, the excess shall be repaid to him.

(5) Regulations may provide that, where—

(a) mediation under this Part is made available to a legally assisted person, and
(b) property is recovered or preserved for the legally assisted person as a result of the mediation,

a sum equal to the Board's liability on the legally assisted person's account is, except so far as the regulations otherwise provide, to be a first charge on the property in favour of the Board.

(6) Regulations under subsection (5) may, in particular, make provision—

(a) as to circumstances in which property is to be taken to have been, or not to have been, recovered or preserved; and
(b) as to circumstances in which the recovery or preservation of property is to be taken to be, or not to be, the result of any mediation.

(7) For the purposes of subsection (5), the nature of the property and where it is situated is immaterial.

(8) The power to make regulations under section 34(2)(f) and (8) is exercisable in relation to any charge created under subsection (5) as it is exercisable in relation to the charge created by section 16.

(9) For the purposes of subsections (4) and (5), the Board's liability on any person's account in relation to any mediation is the aggregate amount of—

(a)   the sums paid or payable by the Board on his account for the mediation, determined in accordance with subsection (10);

(b)   any sums paid or payable in respect of its net liability on his account, determined in accordance with subsection (11) and the regulations—

   (i)   in respect of any proceedings, and

   (ii)   for any advice or assistance under Part III in connection with the proceedings or any matter to which the proceedings relate,

so far as the proceedings relate to any matter to which the mediation relates; and

(c)   any sums paid or payable in respect of its net liability on his account, determined in accordance with the regulations, for any other advice or assistance under Part III in connection with the mediation or any matter to which the mediation relates.

(10) For the purposes of subsection (9)(a), the sums paid or payable by the Board on any person's account for any mediation are—

(a)   sums determined under the contract between the Board and the mediator as payable by the Board on that person's account for the mediation; or

(b)   if the contract does not differentiate between such sums and sums payable on any other person's account or for any other mediation, such part of the remuneration payable under the contract as may be specified in writing by the Board.

(11) For the purposes of subsection (9)(b), the Board's net liability on any person's account in relation to any proceedings is its net liability on his account under section 16(9)(a) and (b) in relation to the proceedings.'

(2) In section 16(9), after paragraph (b) insert 'and

(c)   if and to the extent that regulations so provide, any sums paid or payable in respect of the Board's liability on the legally assisted person's account in relation to any mediation in connection with any matter to which those proceedings relate.'

(3) At the end of section 16, insert—

'(11) For the purposes of subsection (9)(c) above, the Board's liability on any person's account in relation to any mediation is its liability on his account under section 13C(9)(a) and (c) above in relation to the mediation.'

29 Mediation and civil legal aid

In section 15 of the 1988 Act, after subsection (3E) insert—

'(3F) A person shall not be granted representation for the purposes of proceedings relating to family matters, unless he has attended a meeting with a mediator—

(a)   to determine—

   (i)   whether mediation appears suitable to the dispute and the parties and all the circumstances, and

   (ii)   in particular, whether mediation could take place without either party being influenced by fear of violence or other harm; and

(b) if mediation does appear suitable, to help the person applying for representation to decide whether instead to apply for mediation.

(3G) Subsection (3F) does not apply—

(a) in relation to proceedings under—
   (i) Part IV of the Family Law Act 1996;
   (ii) section 37 of the Matrimonial Causes Act 1973;
   (iii) Part IV or V of the Children Act 1989;
(b) in relation to proceedings of any other description that may be prescribed; or
(c) in such circumstances as may be prescribed.

(3H) So far as proceedings relate to family matters, the Board, in determining under subsection (3)(a) whether, in relation to the proceedings, it is reasonable that a person should be granted representation under this Part—

(a) must have regard to whether and to what extent recourse to mediation would be a suitable alternative to taking the proceedings; and
(b) must for that purpose have regard to the outcome of the meeting held under subsection (3F) and to any assessment made for the purposes of section 13B(3).'

PART IV
FAMILY HOMES AND DOMESTIC VIOLENCE

Rights to occupy matrimonial home

30 Rights concerning matrimonial home where one spouse has no estate, etc.

(1) This section applies if—

(a) one spouse is entitled to occupy a dwelling-house by virtue of—
   (i) a beneficial estate or interest or contract; or
   (ii) any enactment giving that spouse the right to remain in occupation; and
(b) the other spouse is not so entitled.

(2) Subject to the provisions of this Part, the spouse not so entitled has the following rights ('matrimonial home rights')—

(a) if in occupation, a right not to be evicted or excluded from the dwelling-house or any part of it by the other spouse except with the leave of the court given by an order under section 33;
(b) if not in occupation, a right with the leave of the court so given to enter into and occupy the dwelling-house.

(3) If a spouse is entitled under this section to occupy a dwelling-house or any part of a dwelling-house, any payment or tender made or other thing done by that spouse in or towards satisfaction of any liability of the other spouse in respect of rent, mortgage payments or other outgoings affecting the dwelling-house shall, whether or not it is made or done in pursuance of an order under section 40, be as good as if made or done by the other spouse.

(4) A spouse's occupation by virtue of this section—

(a) is to be treated, for the purposes of the Rent (Agriculture) Act 1976 and the Rent Act 1977 (other than Part V and sections 103 to 106 of that Act), as occupation by the other spouse as the other spouse's residence, and

(b) if the spouse occupies the dwelling-house as that spouse's only or principal home, is to be treated, for the purposes of the Housing Act 1985 and Part I of the Housing Act 1988, as occupation by the other spouse as the other spouse's only or principal home.

(5) If a spouse ('the first spouse')—

(a) is entitled under this section to occupy a dwelling-house or any part of a dwelling-house, and

(b) makes any payment in or towards satisfaction of any liability of the other spouse ('the second spouse') in respect of mortgage payments affecting the dwelling-house,

the person to whom the payment is made may treat it as having been made by that other spouse, but the fact that that person has treated any such payment as having been so made does not affect any claim of the first spouse against the second spouse to an interest in the dwelling-house by virtue of the payment.

(6) If a spouse is entitled under this section to occupy a dwelling-house or part of a dwelling-house by reason of an interest of the other spouse under a trust, all the provisions of subsections (3) to (5) apply in relation to the trustees as they apply in relation to the other spouse.

(7) This section does not apply to a dwelling-house which has at no time been, and which was at no time intended by the spouses to be, a matrimonial home of theirs.

(8) A spouse's matrimonial home rights continue—

(a) only so long as the marriage subsists, except to the extent that an order under section 33(5) otherwise provides; and

(b) only so long as the other spouse is entitled as mentioned in subsection (1) to occupy the dwelling-house, except where provision is made by section 31 for those rights to be a charge on an estate or interest in the dwelling-house.

(9) It is hereby declared that a spouse—

(a) who has an equitable interest in a dwelling-house or in its proceeds of sale, but

(b) is not a spouse in whom there is vested (whether solely or as joint tenant) a legal estate in fee simple or a legal term of years absolute in the dwelling-house,

is to be treated, only for the purpose of determining whether he has matrimonial home rights, as not being entitled to occupy the dwelling-house by virtue of that interest.

31 Effect of matrimonial home rights as charge on dwelling-house

(1) Subsections (2) and (3) apply if, at any time during a marriage, one spouse is entitled to occupy a dwelling-house by virtue of a beneficial estate or interest.

(2) The other spouse's matrimonial home rights are a charge on the estate or interest.

(3) The charge created by subsection (2) has the same priority as if it were an equitable interest created at whichever is the latest of the following dates—

(a) the date on which the spouse so entitled acquires the estate or interest;

(b)   the date of the marriage; and

(c)   1st January 1968 (the commencement date of the Matrimonial Homes Act 1967).

(4) Subsections (5) and (6) apply if, at any time when a spouse's matrimonial home rights are a charge on an interest of the other spouse under a trust, there are, apart from either of the spouses, no persons, living or unborn, who are or could become beneficiaries under the trust.

(5) The rights are a charge also on the estate or interest of the trustees for the other spouse.

(6) The charge created by subsection (5) has the same priority as if it were an equitable interest created (under powers overriding the trusts) on the date when it arises.

(7) In determining for the purposes of subsection (4) whether there are any persons who are not, but could become, beneficiaries under the trust, there is to be disregarded any potential exercise of a general power of appointment exercisable by either or both of the spouses alone (whether or not the exercise of it requires the consent of another person).

(8) Even though a spouse's matrimonial home rights are a charge on an estate or interest in the dwelling-house, those rights are brought to an end by—

(a)   the death of the other spouse, or

(b)   the termination (otherwise than by death) of the marriage,

unless the court directs otherwise by an order made under section 33(5).

(9) If—

(a)   a spouse's matrimonial home rights are a charge on an estate or interest in the dwelling-house, and

(b)   that estate or interest is surrendered to merge in some other estate or interest expectant on it in such circumstances that, but for the merger, the person taking the estate or interest would be bound by the charge,

the surrender has effect subject to the charge and the persons thereafter entitled to the other estate or interest are, for so long as the estate or interest surrendered would have endured if not so surrendered, to be treated for all purposes of this Part as deriving title to the other estate or interest under the other spouse or, as the case may be, under the trustees for the other spouse, by virtue of the surrender.

(10) If the title to the legal estate by virtue of which a spouse is entitled to occupy a dwelling-house (including any legal estate held by trustees for that spouse) is registered under the Land Registration Act 1925 or any enactment replaced by that Act—

(a)   registration of a land charge affecting the dwelling-house by virtue of this Part is to be effected by registering a notice under that Act; and

(b)   a spouse's matrimonial home rights are not an overriding interest within the meaning of that Act affecting the dwelling-house even though the spouse is in actual occupation of the dwelling-house.

(11) A spouse's matrimonial home rights (whether or not constituting a charge) do not entitle that spouse to lodge a caution under section 54 of the Land Registration Act 1925.

(12) If—

    (a)   a spouse's matrimonial home rights are a charge on the estate of the other spouse or of trustees of the other spouse, and

    (b)   that estate is the subject of a mortgage,

then if, after the date of the creation of the mortgage ('the first mortgage'), the charge is registered under section 2 of the Land Charges Act 1972, the charge is, for the purposes of section 94 of the Law of Property Act 1925 (which regulates the rights of mortgagees to make further advances ranking in priority to subsequent mortgages), to be deemed to be a mortgage subsequent in date to the first mortgage.

(13) It is hereby declared that a charge under subsection (2) or (5) is not registrable under subsection 10 or under section 2 of the Land Charges Act 1972 unless it is a charge on a legal estate.

32 Further provisions relating to matrimonial home rights

Schedule 4 re-enacts with consequential amendments and minor modifications provisions of the Matrimonial Homes Act 1983.

Occupation orders

33 Occupation orders where applicant has estate or interest etc. or has matrimonial home rights

(1) If—

    (a)   a person ('the person entitled')—

        (i)   is entitled to occupy a dwelling-house by virtue of a beneficial estate or interest or contract or by virtue of any enactment giving him the right to remain in occupation, or

        (ii)   has matrimonial home rights in relation to a dwelling-house, and

    (b)   the dwelling-house—

        (i)   is or at any time has been the home of the person entitled and of another person with whom he is associated, or

        (ii)   was at any time intended by the person entitled and any such other person to be their home,

the person entitled may apply to the court for an order containing any of the provisions specified in subsections (3), (4) and (5).

(2) If an agreement to marry is terminated, no application under this section may be made by virtue of section 62(3)(e) by reference to that agreement after the end of the period of three years beginning with the date on which it is terminated.

(3) An order under this section may—

    (a)   enforce the applicant's entitlement to remain in occupation as against the other person ('the respondent');

    (b)   require the respondent to permit the applicant to enter and remain in the dwelling-house or part of the dwelling-house;

    (c)   regulate the occupation of the dwelling-house by either or both parties;

(d)   if the respondent is entitled as mentioned in subsection (1)(a)(i), prohibit, suspend or restrict the exercise by him of his right to occupy the dwelling-house;

(e)   if the respondent has matrimonial home rights in relation to the dwelling-house and the applicant is the other spouse, restrict or terminate those rights;

(f)   require the respondent to leave the dwelling-house or part of the dwelling-house; or

(g)   exclude the respondent from a defined area in which the dwelling-house is included.

(4) An order under this section may declare that the applicant is entitled as mentioned in subsection (1)(a)(i) or has matrimonial home rights.

(5) If the applicant has matrimonial home rights and the respondent is the other spouse, an order under this section made during the marriage may provide that those rights are not brought to an end by—

(a)   the death of the other spouse; or

(b)   the termination (otherwise than by death) of the marriage.

(6) In deciding whether to exercise its powers under subsection (3) and (if so) in what manner, the court shall have regard to all the circumstances including—

(a)   the housing needs and housing resources of each of the parties and of any relevant child;

(b)   the financial resources of the parties;

(c)   the likely effect of any order, or of any decision by the court not to exercise its powers under subsection (3), on the health, safety or well-being of the parties and of any relevant child; and

(d)   the conduct of the parties in relation to each other and otherwise.

(7) If it appears to the court that the applicant or any relevant child is likely to suffer significant harm attributable to conduct of the respondent if an order under this section containing one or more of the provisions mentioned in subsection (3) is not made, the court shall make the order unless it appears to the court that—

(a)   the respondent or any relevant child is likely to suffer significant harm if the order is made; and

(b)   the harm likely to be suffered by the respondent or child in that event is as great as, or greater than, the harm attributable to conduct of the respondent which is likely to be suffered by the applicant or child if the order is not made.

(8) The court may exercise its powers under subsection (5) in any case where it considers that in all the circumstances it is just and reasonable to do so.

(9) An order under this section—

(a)   may not be made after the death of either of the parties mentioned in subsection (1); and

(b)   except in the case of an order made by virtue of subsection (5)(a), ceases to have effect on the death of either party.

(10) An order under this section may, in so far as it has continuing effect, be made for a specified period, until the occurrence of a specified event or until further order.

34 Effect of order under s 33 where rights are charge on dwelling-house

(1) If a spouse's matrimonial home rights are a charge on the estate or interest of the other spouse or of trustees for the other spouse—

(a) any order under section 33 against the other spouse has, except so far as a contrary intention appears, the same effect against persons deriving title under the other spouse or under the trustees and affected by the charge, and

(b) subsections 33(1), (3), (4) and (10) and 30(3) to (6) apply in relation to any person deriving title under the other spouse or under the trustees and affected by the charge as they apply in relation to the other spouse.

(2) The court may make an order under section 33 by virtue of subsection (1)(b) if it considers that in all the circumstances it is just and reasonable to do so.

35 One former spouse with no existing right to occupy

(1) This section applies if—

(a) one former spouse is entitled to occupy a dwelling-house by virtue of a beneficial estate or interest or contract, or by virtue of any enactment giving him the right to remain in occupation;

(b) the other former spouse is not so entitled; and

(c) the dwelling-house was at any time their matrimonial home or was at any time intended by them to be their matrimonial home.

(2) The former spouse not so entitled may apply to the court for an order under this section against the other former spouse ('the respondent').

(3) If the applicant is in occupation, an order under this section must contain provision—

(a) giving the applicant the right not to be evicted or excluded from the dwelling-house or any part of it by the respondent for the period specified in the order; and

(b) prohibiting the respondent from evicting or excluding the applicant during that period.

(4) If the applicant is not in occupation, an order under this section must contain provision—

(a) giving the applicant the right to enter into and occupy the dwelling-house for the period specified in the order; and

(b) requiring the respondent to permit the exercise of that right.

(5) An order under this section may also—

(a) regulate the occupation of the dwelling-house by either or both of the parties;

(b) prohibit, suspend or restrict the exercise by the respondent of his right to occupy the dwelling-house;

(c) require the respondent to leave the dwelling-house or part of the dwelling-house; or

(d) exclude the respondent from a defined area in which the dwelling-house is included.

(6) In deciding whether to make an order under this section containing provision of the kind mentioned in subsection (3) or (4) and (if so) in what manner, the court shall have regard to all the circumstances including—

(a) the housing needs and housing resources of each of the parties and of any relevant child;

(b) the financial resources of each of the parties;

(c) the likely effect of any order, or of any decision by the court not to exercise its powers under subsection (3) or (4), on the health, safety or well-being of the parties and of any relevant child;

(d) the conduct of the parties in relation to each other and otherwise;

(e) the length of time that has elapsed since the parties ceased to live together;

(f) the length of time that has elapsed since the marriage was dissolved or annulled; and

(g) the existence of any pending proceedings between the parties—

   (i) for an order under section 23A or 24 of the Matrimonial Causes Act 1973 (property adjustment orders in connection with divorce proceedings etc.);

   (ii) for an order under paragraph 1(2)(d) or (e) of Schedule 1 to the Children Act 1989 (orders for financial relief against parents); or

   (iii) relating to the legal or beneficial ownership of the dwelling-house.

(7) In deciding whether to exercise its power to include one or more of the provisions referred to in subsection (5) ('a subsection (5) provision') and (if so) in what manner, the court shall have regard to all the circumstances including the matters mentioned in subsection (6)(a) to (e).

(8) If the court decides to make an order under this section and it appears to it that, if the order does not include a subsection (5) provision, the applicant or any relevant child is likely to suffer significant harm attributable to conduct of the respondent, the court shall include the subsection (5) provision in the order unless it appears to the court that—

(a) the respondent or any relevant child is likely to suffer significant harm if the provision is included in the order; and

(b) the harm likely to be suffered by the respondent or child in that event is as great as or greater than the harm attributable to conduct of the respondent which is likely to be suffered by the applicant or child if the provision is not included.

(9) An order under this section—

(a) may not be made after the death of either of the former spouses; and

(b) ceases to have effect on the death of either of them.

(10) An order under this section must be limited so as to have effect for a specified period not exceeding six months, but may be extended on one or more occasions for a further specified period not exceeding six months.

(11) A former spouse who has an equitable interest in the dwelling-house or in the proceeds of sale of the dwelling-house but in whom there is not vested (whether solely or as joint tenant) a legal estate in fee simple or a legal term of years absolute in the dwelling-house is to be treated (but only for the purpose of determining whether he is eligible to apply under this section) as not being entitled to occupy the dwelling-house by virtue of that interest.

(12) Subsection (11) does not prejudice any right of such a former spouse to apply for an order under section 33.

(13) So long as an order under this section remains in force, subsections (3) to (6) of section 30 apply in relation to the applicant—

  (a) as if he were the spouse entitled to occupy the dwelling-house by virtue of that section; and
  (b) as if the respondent were the other spouse.

36 One cohabitant or former cohabitant with no existing right to occupy

(1) This section applies if—

  (a) one cohabitant or former cohabitant is entitled to occupy a dwelling house by virtue of a beneficial estate or interest or contract or by virtue of any enactment giving him the right to remain in occupation;
  (b) the other cohabitant or former cohabitant is not so entitled; and
  (c) that dwelling-house is the home in which they live together as husband and wife or a home in which they at any time so lived together or intended so to live together.

(2) The cohabitant or former cohabitant not so entitled may apply to the court for an order under this section against the other cohabitant or former cohabitant ('the respondent').

(3) If the applicant is in occupation, an order under this section must contain provision—

  (a) giving the applicant the right not to be evicted or excluded from the dwelling-house or any part of it by the respondent for the period specified in the order, and
  (b) prohibiting the respondent from evicting or excluding the applicant during that period.

(4) If the applicant is not in occupation, an order under this section must contain provision—

  (a) giving the applicant the right to enter into and occupy the dwelling-house for the period specified in the order; and
  (b) requiring the respondent to permit the exercise of that right.

(5) An order under this section may also—

  (a) regulate the occupation of the dwelling-house by either or both of the parties;
  (b) prohibit, suspend or restrict the exercise by the respondent of his right to occupy the dwelling-house;
  (c) require the respondent to leave the dwelling-house or part of the dwelling-house; or
  (d) exclude the respondent from a defined area in which the dwelling-house is included.

(6) In deciding whether to make an order under this section containing provision of the kind mentioned in subsection (3) or (4) and (if so) in what manner, the court shall have regard to all the circumstances including—

(a) the housing needs and housing resources of each of the parties and of any relevant child;

(b) the financial resources of each of the parties;

(c) the likely effect of any order, or of any decision by the court not to exercise its powers under subsection (3) or (4), on the health, safety or well-being of the parties and of any relevant child;

(d) the conduct of the parties in relation to each other and otherwise;

(e) the nature of the parties' relationship;

(f) the length of time during which they have lived together as husband and wife;

(g) whether there are or have been any children who are children of both parties or for whom both parties have or have had parental responsibility;

(h) the length of time that has elapsed since the parties ceased to live together; and

(i) the existence of any pending proceedings between the parties—

    (i) for an order under paragraph 1(2)(d) or (e) of Schedule 1 to the Children Act 1989 (orders for financial relief against parents), or

    (ii) relating to the legal or beneficial ownership of the dwelling-house.

(7) In deciding whether to exercise its powers to include one or more of the provisions referred to in subsection (5) ('a subsection (5) provision') and (if so) in what manner, the court shall have regard to all the circumstances including—

(a) the matters mentioned in subsection (6)(a) to (d); and

(b) the questions mentioned in subsection (8).

(8) The questions are—

(a) whether the applicant or any relevant child is likely to suffer significant harm attributable to conduct of the respondent if the subsection (5) provision is not included in the order; and

(b) whether the harm likely to be suffered by the respondent or child if the provision is included is as great as or greater than the harm attributable to conduct of the respondent which is likely to be suffered by the applicant or child if the provision is not included.

(9) An order under this section—

(a) may not be made after the death of either of the parties; and

(b) ceases to have effect on the death of either of them.

(10) An order under this section must be limited so as to have effect for a specified period not exceeding six months, but may be extended on one occasion for a further specified period not exceeding six months.

(11) A person who has an equitable interest in the dwelling-house or in the proceeds of sale of the dwelling-house but in whom there is not vested (whether solely or as joint tenant) a legal estate in fee simple or a legal term of years absolute in the dwelling-house is to be treated (but only for the purpose of determining whether he is eligible to apply under this section) as not being entitled to occupy the dwelling-house by virtue of that interest.

(12) Subsection (11) does not prejudice any right of such a person to apply for an order under section 33.

(13) So long as the order remains in force, subsections (3) to (6) of section 30 apply in relation to the applicant—

(a)   as if he were a spouse entitled to occupy the dwelling-house by virtue of that section; and

(b)   as if the respondent were the other spouse.

37 Neither spouse entitled to occupy

(1) This section applies if—

(a)   one spouse or former spouse and the other spouse or former spouse occupy a dwelling-house which is or was the matrimonial home; but

(b)   neither of them is entitled to remain in occupation—

    (i)   by virtue of a beneficial estate or interest or contract; or

    (ii)   by virtue of any enactment giving him the right to remain in occupation.

(2) Either of the parties may apply to the court for an order against the other under this section.

(3) An order under this section may—

(a)   require the respondent to permit the applicant to enter and remain in the dwelling-house or part of the dwelling-house;

(b)   regulate the occupation of the dwelling-house by either or both of the spouses;

(c)   require the respondent to leave the dwelling-house or part of the dwelling-house; or

(d)   exclude the respondent from a defined area in which the dwelling-house is included.

(4) Subsections (6) and (7) of section 33 apply to the exercise by the court of its powers under this section as they apply to the exercise by the court of its powers under subsection (3) of that section.

(5) An order under this section must be limited so as to have effect for a specified period not exceeding six months, but may be extended on one or more occasions for a further specified period not exceeding six months.

38 Neither cohabitant or former cohabitant entitled to occupy

(1) This section applies if—

(a)   one cohabitant or former cohabitant and the other cohabitant or former cohabitant occupy a dwelling-house which is the home in which they live or lived together as husband and wife; but

(b)   neither of them is entitled to remain in occupation—

    (i)   by virtue of a beneficial estate or interest or contract; or

    (ii)   by virtue of any enactment giving him the right to remain in occupation.

(2) Either of the parties may apply to the court for an order against the other under this section.

(3) An order under this section may—

(a)   require the respondent to permit the applicant to enter and remain in the dwelling-house or part of the dwelling-house;

(b)   regulate the occupation of the dwelling-house by either or both of the parties;

(c)   require the respondent to leave the dwelling-house or part of the dwelling-house; or

(d)   exclude the respondent from a defined area in which the dwelling-house is included.

(4) In deciding whether to exercise its powers to include one or more of the provisions referred to in subsection (3) ('a subsection (3) provision') and (if so) in what manner, the court shall have regard to all the circumstances including—

(a)   the housing needs and housing resources of each of the parties and of any relevant child;

(b)   the financial resources of each of the parties;

(c)   the likely effect of any order, or of any decision by the court not to exercise its powers under subsection (3), on the health, safety or well-being of the parties and of any relevant child;

(d)   the conduct of the parties in relation to each other and otherwise; and

(e)   the questions mentioned in subsection (5).

(5) The questions are—

(a)   whether the applicant or any relevant child is likely to suffer significant harm attributable to conduct of the respondent if the subsection (3) provision is not included in the order; and

(b)   whether the harm likely to be suffered by the respondent or child if the provision is included is as great as or greater than the harm attributable to conduct of the respondent which is likely to be suffered by the applicant or child if the provision is not included.

(6) An order under this section shall be limited so as to have effect for a specified period not exceeding six months, but may be extended on one occasion for a further specified period not exceeding six months.

39 Supplementary provisions

(1) In this Part an 'occupation order' means an order under section 33, 35, 36, 37 or 38.

(2) An application for an occupation order may be made in other family proceedings or without any other family proceedings being instituted.

(3) If—

(a)   an application for an occupation order is made under section 33, 35, 36, 37 or 38, and

(b)   the court considers that it has no power to make the order under the section concerned, but that it has power to make an order under one of the other sections,

the court may make an order under that other section.

(4) The fact that a person has applied for an occupation order under sections 35 to 38, or that an occupation order has been made, does not affect the right of any person to claim a legal or equitable interest in any property in any subsequent proceedings (including subsequent proceedings under this Part).

40 Additional provisions that may be included in certain occupation orders

(1) The court may on, or at any time after, making an occupation order under section 33, 35 or 36—

- (a) impose on either party obligations as to—

  - (i) the repair and maintenance of the dwelling-house; or
  - (ii) the discharge of rent, mortgage payments or other outgoings affecting the dwelling-house;

- (b) order a party occupying the dwelling-house or any part of it (including a party who is entitled to do so by virtue of a beneficial estate or interest or contract or by virtue of any enactment giving him the right to remain in occupation) to make periodical payments to the other party in respect of the accommodation, if the other party would (but for the order) be entitled to occupy the dwelling-house by virtue of a beneficial estate or interest or contract or by virtue of any such enactment;

- (c) grant either party possession or use of furniture or other contents of the dwelling-house;

- (d) order either party to take reasonable care of any furniture or other contents of the dwelling-house;

- (e) order either party to take reasonable steps to keep the dwelling-house and any furniture or other contents secure.

(2) In deciding whether and, if so, how to exercise its powers under this section, the court shall have regard to all the circumstances of the case including—

- (a) the financial needs and financial resources of the parties; and
- (b) the financial obligations which they have, or are likely to have in the foreseeable future, including financial obligations to each other and to any relevant child.

(3) An order under this section ceases to have effect when the occupation order to which it relates ceases to have effect.

41 Additional considerations if parties are cohabitants or former cohabitants

(1) This section applies if the parties are cohabitants or former cohabitants.

(2) Where the court is required to consider the nature of the parties' relationship, it is to have regard to the fact that they have not given each other the commitment involved in marriage.

Non-molestation orders

42 Non-molestation orders

(1) In this Part a 'non-molestation order' means an order containing either or both of the following provisions—

- (a) provision prohibiting a person ('the respondent') from molesting another person who is associated with the respondent;
- (b) provision prohibiting the respondent from molesting a relevant child.

(2) The court may make a non-molestation order—

(a) if an application for the order has been made (whether in other family proceedings or without any other family proceedings being instituted) by a person who is associated with the respondent; or

(b) if in any family proceedings to which the respondent is a party the court considers that the order should be made for the benefit of any other party to the proceedings or any relevant child even though no such application has been made.

(3) In subsection (2) 'family proceedings' includes proceedings in which the court has made an emergency protection order under section 44 of the Children Act 1989 which includes an exclusion requirement (as defined in section 44A(3) of that Act).

(4) Where an agreement to marry is terminated, no application under subsection (2)(a) may be made by virtue of section 62(3)(e) by reference to that agreement after the end of the period of three years beginning with the day on which it is terminated.

(5) In deciding whether to exercise its powers under this section and, if so, in what manner, the court shall have regard to all the circumstances including the need to secure the health, safety and well-being—

(a) of the applicant or, in a case falling within subsection (2)(b), the person for whose benefit the order would be made; and

(b) of any relevant child.

(6) A non-molestation order may be expressed so as to refer to molestation in general, to particular acts of molestation, or to both.

(7) A non-molestation order may be made for a specified period or until further order.

(8) A non-molestation order which is made in other family proceedings ceases to have effect if those proceedings are withdrawn or dismissed.

Further provisions relating to occupation and non-molestation orders

43 Leave of court required for applications by children under sixteen

(1) A child under the age of sixteen may not apply for an occupation order or a non-molestation order except with the leave of the court.

(2) The court may grant leave for the purposes of subsection (1) only if it is satisfied that the child has sufficient understanding to make the proposed application for the occupation order or non-molestation order.

44 Evidence of agreement to marry

(1) Subject to subsection (2) the court shall not make an order under section 33 or 42 by virtue of section 62(3)(e) unless there is produced to it evidence in writing of the existence of the agreement to marry.

(2) Subsection (1) does not apply if the court is satisfied that the agreement to marry was evidenced by—

(a) the gift of an engagement ring by one party to the agreement to the other in contemplation of their marriage, or

(b)   a ceremony entered into by the parties in the presence of one or more other persons assembled for the purpose of witnessing the ceremony.

45 Ex parte orders

(1) The court may, in any case where it considers that it is just and convenient to do so, make an occupation order or a non-molestation order even though the respondent has not been given such notice of the proceedings as would otherwise be required by rules of court.

(2) In determining whether to exercise its powers under subsection (1), the court shall have regard to all the circumstances including—

(a)   any risk of significant harm to the applicant or a relevant child, attributable to conduct of the respondent, if the order is not made immediately;
(b)   whether it is likely that the applicant will be deterred or prevented from pursuing the application if an order is not made immediately; and
(c)   whether there is reason to believe that the respondent is aware of the proceedings but is deliberately evading service and that the applicant or a relevant child will be seriously prejudiced by the delay involved—

　　(i)   where the court is a magistrates' court, in effecting service of proceedings; or
　　(ii)   in any other case, in effecting substituted service.

(3) If the court makes an order by virtue of subsection (1) it must afford the respondent an opportunity to make representations relating to the order as soon as just and convenient at a full hearing.

(4) If, at a full hearing, the court makes an occupation order ('the full order'), then—

(a)   for the purposes of calculating the maximum period for which the full order may be made to have effect, the relevant section is to apply as if the period for which the full order will have effect began on the date on which the initial order first had effect; and
(b)   the provisions of section 36(10) or 38(6) as to the extension of orders are to apply as if the full order and the initial order were a single order.

(5) In this section—

'full hearing' means a hearing of which notice has been given to all the parties in accordance with rules of court;
'initial order' means an occupation order made by virtue of subsection (1); and
'relevant section' means section 33(10), 35(10), 36(10), 37(5) or 38(6).

46 Undertakings

(1) In any case where the court has power to make an occupation order or non-molestation order, the court may accept an undertaking from any party to the proceedings.

(2) No power of arrest may be attached to any undertaking given under subsection (1).

(3) The court shall not accept an undertaking under subsection (1) in any case where apart from this section a power of arrest would be attached to the order.

(4) An undertaking given to a court under subsection (1) is enforceable as if it were an order of the court.

(5) This section has effect without prejudice to the powers of the High Court and the county court apart from this section.

47 Arrest for breach of order

(1) In this section 'a relevant order' means an occupation order or a non-molestation order.

(2) If—

    (a)   the court makes a relevant order; and

    (b)   it appears to the court that the respondent has used or threatened violence against the applicant or a relevant child,

it shall attach a power of arrest to one or more provisions of the order unless the court is satisfied that in all the circumstances of the case the applicant or child will be adequately protected without such a power of arrest.

(3) Subsection (2) does not apply in any case where the relevant order is made by virtue of section 45(1), but in such a case the court may attach a power of arrest to one or more provisions of the order if it appears to it—

    (a)   that the respondent has used or threatened violence against the applicant or a relevant child; and

    (b)   that there is a risk of significant harm to the applicant or child, attributable to conduct of the respondent, if the power of arrest is not attached to those provisions immediately.

(4) If, by virtue of subsection (3), the court attaches a power of arrest to any provisions of a relevant order, it may provide that the power of arrest is to have effect for a shorter period than the other provisions of the order.

(5) Any period specified for the purposes of subsection (4) may be extended by the court (on one or more occasions) on an application to vary or discharge the relevant order.

(6) If, by virtue of subsection (2) or (3), a power of arrest is attached to certain provisions of an order, a constable may arrest without warrant a person whom he has reasonable cause for suspecting to be in breach of any such provision.

(7) If a power of arrest is attached under subsection (2) or (3) to certain provisions of the order and the respondent is arrested under subsection (6)—

    (a)   he must be brought before the relevant judicial authority within the period of 24 hours beginning at the time of his arrest; and

    (b)   if the matter is not then disposed of forthwith, the relevant judicial authority before whom he is brought may remand him.

In reckoning for the purposes of this subsection any period of 24 hours, no account is to be taken of Christmas Day, Good Friday or any Sunday.

(8) If the court has made a relevant order but—

    (a)   has not attached a power of arrest under subsection (2) or (3) above to any provisions of the order, or

(b)   has attached that power only to certain provisions of the order,

then, if at any time the applicant considers that the respondent has failed to comply with the order, he may apply to the relevant judicial authority for the issue of a warrant for the arrest of the respondent.

(9) The relevant judicial authority shall not issue a warrant on an application under subsection (8) unless—

(a)   the application is substantiated on oath; and
(b)   the relevant judicial authority has reasonable grounds for believing that the respondent has failed to comply with the order.

(10) If a person is brought before a court by virtue of a warrant issued under subsection (9) and the court does not dispose of the matter forthwith, the court may remand him.

(11) Schedule 5 (which makes provision corresponding to that applying in magistrates' courts in civil cases under sections 128 and 129 of the Magistrates' Courts Act 1980) has effect in relation to the powers of the High Court and a county court to remand a person by virtue of this section.

(12) If a person remanded under this section is granted bail (whether in the High Court or a county court under Schedule 5 or in a magistrates' court under section 128 or 129 of the Magistrates' Courts Act 1980), he may be required by the relevant judicial authority to comply, before release on bail or later, with such requirements as appear to that authority to be necessary to secure that he does not interfere with witnesses or otherwise obstruct the course of justice.

48 Remand for medical examination and report

(1) If the relevant judicial authority has reason to consider that a medical report will be required, any power to remand a person under section 47(7)(b) or (10) may be exercised for the purpose of enabling a medical examination and report to be made.

(2) If such a power is so exercised, the adjournment must not be for more than 4 weeks at a time unless the relevant judicial authority remands the accused in custody.

(3) If the relevant judicial authority so remands the accused, the adjournment must not be for more than 3 weeks at a time.

(4) If there is reason to suspect that a person who has been arrested—

(a)   under section 47(6), or
(b)   under a warrant issued on an application made under section 47(8),

is suffering from mental illness or severe mental impairment, the relevant judicial authority has the same power to make an order under section 35 of the Mental Health Act 1983 (remand for report on accused's mental condition) as the Crown Court has under section 35 of the Act of 1983 in the case of an accused person within the meaning of that section.

49 Variation and discharge of orders

(1) An occupation order or non-molestation order may be varied or discharged by the court on an application by—

(a)   the respondent, or

(b)   the person on whose application the order was made.

(2) In the case of a non-molestation order made by virtue of section 42(2)(b), the order may be varied or discharged by the court even though no such application has been made.

(3) If a spouse's matrimonial home rights are a charge on the estate or interest of the other spouse or of trustees for the other spouse, an order under section 33 against the other spouse may also be varied or discharged by the court on an application by any person deriving title under the other spouse or under the trustees and affected by the charge.

(4) If, by virtue of section 47(3), a power of arrest has been attached to certain provisions of an occupation order or non-molestation order, the court may vary or discharge the order under subsection (1) in so far as it confers a power of arrest (whether or not any application has been made to vary or discharge any other provision of the order).

Enforcement powers of magistrates' courts

50 Power of magistrates' court to suspend execution of committal order

(1) If, under section 63(3) of the Magistrates' Courts Act 1980, a magistrates' court has power to commit a person to custody for breach of a relevant requirement, the court may by order direct that the execution of the order of committal is to be suspended for such period or on such terms and conditions as it may specify.

(2) In subsection (1) 'a relevant requirement' means—

(a)   an occupation order or non-molestation order;
(b)   an exclusion requirement included by virtue of section 38A of the Children Act 1989 in an interim care order made under section 38 of that Act; or
(c)   an exclusion requirement included by virtue of section 44A of the Children Act 1989 in an emergency protection order under section 44 of that Act.

51 Power of magistrates' court to order hospital admission or guardianship

(1) A magistrates' court shall have the same power to make a hospital order or guardianship order under section 37 of the Mental Health Act 1983 or an interim hospital order under section 38 of that Act in the case of a person suffering from mental illness or severe mental impairment who could otherwise be committed to custody for breach of a relevant requirement as a magistrates' court has under those sections in the case of a person convicted of an offence punishable on summary conviction with imprisonment.

(2) In subsection (1) 'a relevant requirement' has the meaning given by section 50(2).

Interim care orders and emergency protection orders

52 Amendments of Children Act 1989

Schedule 6 makes amendments of the provisions of the Children Act 1989 relating to interim care orders and emergency protection orders.

Transfer of tenancies

53 Transfer of certain tenancies

Schedule 7 makes provision in relation to the transfer of certain tenancies on divorce etc. or on separation of cohabitants.

Dwelling-house subject to mortgage

54 Dwelling-house subject to mortgage

(1) In determining for the purposes of this Part whether a person is entitled to occupy a dwelling-house by virtue of an estate or interest, any right to possession of the dwelling-house conferred on a mortgagee of the dwelling-house under or by virtue of his mortgage is to be disregarded.

(2) Subsection (1) applies whether or not the mortgagee is in possession.

(3) Where a person ('A') is entitled to occupy a dwelling-house by virtue of an estate or interest, a connected person does not by virtue of—

    (a)   any matrimonial home rights conferred by section 30, or
    (b)   any rights conferred by an order under section 35 or 36,

have any larger right against the mortgagee to occupy the dwelling-house than A has by virtue of his estate or interest and of any contract with the mortgagee.

(4) Subsection (3) does not apply, in the case of matrimonial home rights, if under section 31 those rights are a charge, affecting the mortgagee, on the estate or interest mortgaged.

(5) In this section 'connected person', in relation to any person, means that person's spouse, former spouse, cohabitant or former cohabitant.

55 Actions by mortgagees: joining connected persons as parties

(1) This section applies if a mortgagee of land which consists of or includes a dwelling-house brings an action in any court for the enforcement of his security.

(2) A connected person who is not already a party to the action is entitled to be made a party in the circumstances mentioned in subsection (3).

(3) The circumstances are that—

    (a)   the connected person is enabled by section 30(3) or (6) (or by section 30(3) or (6) as applied by section 35(13) or 36(13)), to meet the mortgagor's liabilities under the mortgage;
    (b)   he has applied to the court before the action is finally disposed of in that court; and
    (c)   the court sees no special reason against his being made a party to the action and is satisfied—

        (i)   that he may be expected to make such payments or do such other things in or towards satisfaction of the mortgagor's liabilities or obligations as might affect the outcome of the proceedings; or
        (ii)   that the expectation of it should be considered under section 36 of the Administration of Justice Act 1970.

(4) In this section 'connected person' has the same meaning as in section 54.

56 Actions by mortgagees: service of notice on certain persons

(1) This section applies if a mortgagee of land which consists, or substantially consists, of a dwelling-house brings an action for the enforcement of his security, and at the relevant time there is—

(a) in the case of unregistered land, a land charge of Class F registered against the person who is the estate owner at the relevant time or any person who, where the estate owner is a trustee, preceded him as trustee during the subsistence of the mortgage; or

(b) in the case of registered land, a subsisting registration of—

    (i) a notice under section 31(10);

    (ii) a notice under section 2(8) of the Matrimonial Homes Act 1983; or

    (iii) a notice or caution under section 2(7) of the Matrimonial Homes Act 1967.

(2) If the person on whose behalf—

(a) the land charge is registered, or

(b) the notice or caution is entered,

is not a party to the action, the mortgagee must serve notice of the action on him.

(3) If—

(a) an official search has been made on behalf of the mortgagee which would disclose any land charge of Class F, notice or caution within subsection (1)(a) or (b),

(b) a certificate of the result of the search has been issued, and

(c) the action is commenced within the priority period,

the relevant time is the date of the certificate.

(4) In any other case the relevant time is the time when the action is commenced.

(5) The priority period is, for both registered and unregistered land, the period for which, in accordance with section 11(5) and (6) of the Land Charges Act 1972, a certificate on an official search operates in favour of a purchaser.

Jurisdiction and procedure etc.

57 Jurisdiction of courts

(1) For the purposes of this Act 'the court' means the High Court, a county court or a magistrates' court.

(2) Subsection (1) above is subject to the provision made by or under the following provisions of this section, to section 59 and to any express provision as to the jurisdiction of any court made by any other provision of this Part.

(3) The Lord Chancellor may by order specify proceedings under this Act which may only be commenced in—

(a) a specified level of court;

(b) a court which falls within a specified class of court; or

(c)   a particular court determined in accordance with, or specified in, the order.

(4) The Lord Chancellor may by order specify circumstances in which specified proceedings under this Part may only be commenced in—

(a)   a specified level of court;
(b)   a court which falls within a specified class of court; or
(c)   a particular court determined in accordance with, or specified in, the order.

(5) The Lord Chancellor may by order provide that in specified circumstances the whole, or any specified part of any specified proceedings under this Part shall be transferred to—

(a)   a specified level of court;
(b)   a court which falls within a specified class of court; or
(c)   a particular court determined in accordance with, or specified in, the order.

(6) An order under subsection (5) may provide for the transfer to be made at any stage, or specified stage, of the proceedings and whether or not the proceedings, or any part of them, have already been transferred.

(7) An order under subsection (5) may make provision as the Lord Chancellor thinks appropriate for excluding specified proceedings from the operation of section 38 or 39 of the Matrimonial and Family Proceedings Act 1984 (transfer of family proceedings) or any other enactment which would otherwise govern the transfer of those proceedings, or any part of them.

(8) For the purposes of subsections (3), (4) and (5), there are three levels of court—

(a)   the High Court;
(b)   any county court; and
(c)   any magistrates' court.

(9) The Lord Chancellor may by order make provision for the principal registry of the Family Division of the High Court to be treated as if it were a county court for specified purposes of this Part, or of any provision made under this Part.

(10) Any order under subsection (9) may make such provision as the Lord Chancellor thinks expedient for the purpose of applying (with or without modifications) provisions which apply in relation to the procedure in county courts to the principal registry when it acts as if it were a county court.

(11) In this section 'specified' means specified by an order under this section.

58 Contempt proceedings

The powers of the court in relation to contempt of court arising out of a person's failure to comply with an order under this Part may be exercised by the relevant judicial authority.

59 Magistrates' courts

(1) A magistrates' court shall not be competent to entertain any application, or make any order, involving any disputed question as to a party's entitlement to occupy any

property by virtue of a beneficial estate or interest or contract or by virtue of any enactment giving him the right to remain in occupation, unless it is unnecessary to determine the question in order to deal with the application or make the order.

(2) A magistrates' court may decline jurisdiction in any proceedings under this Part if it considers that the case can more conveniently be dealt with by another court.

(3) The powers of a magistrates' court under section 63(2) of the Magistrates' Courts Act 1980 to suspend or rescind orders shall not apply in relation to any order made under this Part.

60 Provision for third parties to act on behalf of victims of domestic violence

(1) Rules of court may provide for a prescribed person, or any person in a prescribed category, ('a representative') to act on behalf of another in relation to proceedings to which this Part applies.

(2) Rules made under this section may, in particular, authorise a representative to apply for an occupation order or for a non-molestation order for which the person on whose behalf the representative is acting could have applied.

(3) Rules made under this section may prescribe—

(a) conditions to be satisfied before a representative may make an application to the court on behalf of another; and

(b) considerations to be taken into account by the court in determining whether, and if so how, to exercise any of its powers under this Part when a representative is acting on behalf of another.

(4) Any rules made under this section may be made so as to have effect for a specified period and may make consequential or transitional provision with respect to the expiry of the specified period.

(5) Any such rules may be replaced by further rules made under this section.

61 Appeals

(1) An appeal shall lie to the High Court against—

(a) the making by a magistrates' court of any order under this Part, or

(b) any refusal by a magistrates' court to make such an order,

but no appeal shall lie against any exercise by a magistrates' court of the power conferred by section 59(2) of this Act.

(2) On an appeal under this section, the High Court may make such orders as may be necessary to give effect to its determination of the appeal.

(3) Where an order is made under subsection (2), the High Court may also make such incidental or consequential orders as appear to it to be just.

(4) Any order of the High Court made on an appeal under this section (other than one directing that an application be re-heard by a magistrates' court) shall, for the purposes—

(a) of the enforcement of the order, and

(b) of any power to vary, revive or discharge orders,

be treated as if it were an order of the magistrates' court from which the appeal was brought and not an order of the High Court.

(5) The Lord Chancellor may by order make provision as to the circumstances in which appeals may be made against decisions taken by courts on questions arising in connection with the transfer, or proposed transfer, of proceedings by virtue of any order under section 57(5).

(6) Except to the extent provided for in any order made under subsection (5), no appeal may be made against any decision of a kind mentioned in that subsection.

General

62 Meaning of 'cohabitants', 'relevant child' and 'associated persons'

(1) For the purposes of this Part—

  (a)   'cohabitants' are a man and a woman who, although not married to each other, are living together as husband and wife; and
  (b)   'former cohabitants' is to be read accordingly, but does not include cohabitants who have subsequently married each other.

(2) In this Part, 'relevant child', in relation to any proceedings under this Part, means—

  (a)   any child who is living with or might reasonably be expected to live with either party to the proceedings;
  (b)   any child in relation to whom an order under the Adoption Act 1976 or the Children Act 1989 is in question in the proceedings; and
  (c)   any other child whose interests the court considers relevant.

(3) For the purposes of this Part, a person is associated with another person if—

  (a)   they are or have been married to each other;
  (b)   they are cohabitants or former cohabitants;
  (c)   they live or have lived in the same household, otherwise than merely by reason of one of them being the other's employee, tenant, lodger or boarder;
  (d)   they are relatives;
  (e)   they have agreed to marry one another (whether or not that agreement has been terminated);
  (f)   in relation to any child, they are both persons falling within subsection (4); or
  (g)   they are parties to the same family proceedings (other than proceedings under this Part).

(4) A person falls within this subsection in relation to a child if—

  (a)   he is a parent of the child; or
  (b)   he has or has had parental responsibility for the child.

(5) If a child has been adopted or has been freed for adoption by virtue of any of the enactments mentioned in section 16(1) of the Adoption Act 1976, two persons are also associated with each other for the purpose of this Part if—

  (a)   one is a natural parent of the child or a parent of such a natural parent, and
  (b)   the other is the child or any person—
    (i)   who had become a parent of the child by virtue of an adoption order or has applied for an adoption order, or
    (ii)   with whom the child has at any time been placed for adoption.

(6) A body corporate and another person are not, by virtue of subsection (3)(f) or (g), to be regarded for the purposes of this Part as associated with each other.

63 Interpretation of Part IV

(1) In this Part—

'adoption order' has the meaning given by section 72(1) of the Adoption Act 1976;

'associated', in relation to a person, is to be read with section 62(3) to (6);

'child' means a person under the age of eighteen years;

'cohabitant' and 'former cohabitant' have the meaning given by section 62(1);

'the court' is to be read with section 57;

'development' means physical, intellectual, emotional, social or behavioural development;

'dwelling-house' includes (subject to subsection (4))—

    (a) any building or part of a building which is occupied as a dwelling,

    (b) any caravan, house-boat or structure which is occupied as a dwelling,

and any yard, garden, garage or outhouse belonging to it and occupied with it;

'family proceedings' means any proceedings—

    (a) under the inherent jurisdiction of the High Court in relation to children; or

    (b) under the enactments mentioned in subsection (2),

'harm'—

    (a) in relation to a person who has reached the age of eighteen years, means ill-treatment or the impairment of health; and

    (b) in relation to a child, means ill-treatment or the impairment of health or development;

'health' includes physical or mental health;

'ill-treatment' includes forms of ill-treatment which are not physical and, in relation to a child, includes sexual abuse;

'matrimonial home rights' has the meaning given by section 30;

'mortgage', 'mortgagor' and 'mortgagee' have the same meaning as in the Law of Property Act 1925;

'mortgage payments' includes any payments which, under the terms of the mortgage, the mortgagor is required to make to any person;

'non-molestation order' has the meaning given by section 42(1);

'occupation order' has the meaning given by section 39;

'parental responsibility' has the same meaning as in the Children Act 1989;

'relative', in relation to a person, means—

    (a) the father, mother, stepfather, stepmother, son, daughter, stepson, step-daughter, grandmother, grandfather, grandson or granddaughter of that person or of that person's spouse or former spouse, or

    (b) the brother, sister, uncle, aunt, niece or nephew (whether of the full blood or of the half blood or by affinity) of that person or of that person's spouse or former spouse,

and includes, in relation to a person who is living or has lived with another person as husband or wife, any person who would fall within paragraph (a) or (b) if the parties were married to each other;

'relevant child', in relation to any proceedings under this Part, has the meaning given by section 62(2);

'the relevant judicial authority', in relation to any order under this Part, means—

(a) where the order was made by the High Court, a judge of that court;
(b) where the order was made by a county court, a judge or district judge of that or any other county court; or
(c) where the order was made by a magistrates' court, any magistrates' court.

(2) The enactments referred to in the definition of 'family proceedings' are—

(a) Part II;
(b) this Part;
(c) the Matrimonial Causes Act 1973;
(c) the Adoption Act 1976;
(e) the Domestic Proceedings and Magistrates' Court Act 1978;
(f) Part III of the Matrimonial and Family Proceedings Act 1984;
(g) Parts I, II and IV of the Children Act 1989;
(h) section 30 of the Human Fertilisation and Embryology Act 1990.

(3) Where the question of whether harm suffered by a child is significant turns on the child's health or development, his health or development shall be compared with that which could reasonably be expected of a similar child.

(4) For the purposes of sections 31, 32, 53 and 54 and such other provisions of this Part (if any) as may be prescribed, this Part is to have effect as if paragraph (b) of the definition of "dwelling-house" were omitted.

(5) It is hereby declared that this Part applies as between the parties to a marriage even though either of them is, or has at any time during the marriage been, married to more than one person.

PART V
SUPPLEMENTAL

64 Provision for separate representation for children

(1) The Lord Chancellor may by regulations provide for the separate representation of children in proceedings in England and Wales which relate to any matter in respect of which a question has arisen, or may arise, under—

(a) Part II;
(b) Part IV;
(c) the 1973 Act; or
(d) the Domestic Proceedings and Magistrates' Courts Act 1978.

(2) The regulations may provide for such representation only in specified circumstances.

65 Rules, regulations and orders

(1) Any power to make rules, orders or regulations which is conferred by this Act is exercisable by statutory instrument.

(2) Any statutory instrument made under this Act may—

(a) contain such incidental, supplemental, consequential and transitional provision as the Lord Chancellor considers appropriate; and

(b) make different provision for different purposes.

(3) Any statutory instrument containing an order, rules or regulations made under this Act, other than an order made under section 5(8) or 67(3), shall be subject to annulment by a resolution of either House of Parliament.

(4) No order shall be made under section 5(8) unless a draft of the order has been laid before, and approved by a resolution of, each House of Parliament.

(5) This section does not apply to rules of court made, or any power to make rules of court, for the purposes of this Act.

66 Consequential amendments, transitional provisions and repeals

(1) Schedule 8 makes minor and consequential amendments.

(2) Schedule 9 provides for the making of other modifications consequential on provisions of this Act, makes transitional provisions and provides for savings.

(3) Schedule 10 repeals certain enactments.

67 Short title, commencement and extent

(1) This Act may be cited as the Family Law Act 1996.

(2) Section 65 and this section come into force on the passing of this Act.

(3) The other provisions of this Act come into force on such day as the Lord Chancellor may by order appoint; and different days may be appointed for different purposes.

(4) This Act, other than section 17, extends only to England and Wales, except that—

(a) in Schedule 8—
   (i)   the amendments of section 38 of the Family Law Act 1986 extend also to Northern Ireland;
   (ii) the amendments of the Judicial Proceedings (Regulation of Reports) Act 1926 extend also to Scotland; and
   (iii) the amendments of the Maintenance Orders Act 1950, the Civil Jurisdiction and Judgments Act 1982, the Finance Act 1985 and sections 42 and 51 of the Family Law Act 1986 extend also to both Northern Ireland and Scotland; and
(b) in Schedule 10, the repeal of section 2(1)(b) of the Domestic and Appellate Proceedings (Restriction of Publicity) Act 1968 extends also to Scotland.

SCHEDULES

SCHEDULE 1

ARRANGEMENTS FOR THE FUTURE

Section 9(6)

The first exemption

1   The circumstances referred to in section 9(7)(a) are that—

(a)   the requirements of section 11 have been satisfied;

(b)   the applicant has, during the period for reflection and consideration, taken such steps as are reasonably practicable to try to reach agreement about the parties' financial arrangements; and

(c)   the applicant has made an application to the court for financial relief and has complied with all requirements of the court in relation to proceedings for financial relief but—

(i)   the other party had delayed in complying with requirements of the court or has otherwise been obstructive; or

(ii)   for reasons which are beyond the control of the applicant, or of the other party, the court has been prevented from obtaining the information which it requires to determine the financial position of the parties.

The second exemption

2   The circumstances referred to in section 9(7)(b) are that—

(a)   the requirements of section 11 have been satisfied;

(b)   the applicant has, during the period for reflection and consideration, taken such steps as are reasonably practicable to try to reach agreement about the parties' financial arrangements;

(c)   because of—

(i)   the ill health or disability of the applicant, the other party or a child of the family (whether physical or mental), or

(ii)   an injury sufferd by the applicant, the other party or a child of the family, the applicant has not been able to reach agreement with the other party about those arrangements and is unlikely to be able to do so in the foreseeable future; and

(d)   a delay in making the order applied for under section 3—

(i)   would be significantly detrimental to the welfare of any child of the family; or

(ii)   would be seriously prejudicial to the applicant.

The third exemption

3   The circumstances referred to in section 9(7)(c) are that—

(a)   the requirements of section 11 have been satisfied;

(b)   the applicant has found it impossible to contact the other party; and

(c)   as a result, it had been impossible for the applicant to reach agreement with the other party about their financial arrangements.

The fourth exemption

4 The circumstances referred to in section 9(7)(d) are that—

(a) the requirements of section 11 have been satisfied;

(b) an occupation order or a non-molestation order is in force in favour of the applicant or a child of the family, made against the other party;

(c) the applicant has, during the period for reflection and consideration, taken such steps as are reasonably practicable to try to reach agreement about the parties' financial arrangements;

(d) the agreement has not been able to reach agreement with the other party about those arrangements and is unlikely to be able to do so in the foreseeable future; and

(e) a delay in making the order applied for under section 3—

(i) would be significantly detrimental to the welfare of any child of the family; or

(ii) would be seriously prejudicial to the applicant.

Court orders and agreements

5 (1) Section 9 is not to be read as requiring any order or agreement to have been carried into effect at the time when the court is considering whether arrangements for the future have been made by the parties.

(2) The fact that an appeal is pending against an order of the kind mentioned in section 9(2)(a) is to be disregarded.

Financial arrangements

6 In section 9 and this Schedule 'financial arrangements' has the same meaning as in section 34(2) of the 1973 Act.

Negotiated agreements

7 In section 9(2)(b) 'negotiated agreement' means a written agreement between the parties as to future arrangements—

(a) which has been reached as the result of mediation or any other form of negotiation involving a third party; and

(b) which satisfies such requirements as may be imposed by rules of court.

Declarations

8 (1) Any declaration of a kind mentioned in section 9—

(a) must be in a prescribed form;

(b) must, in prescribed cases, be accompanied by such documents as may be prescribed; and

(c) must, in prescribed cases, satisfy such other requirements as may be prescribed.

(2) The validity of a divorce order or separation order made by reference to such a declaration is not to be affected by any inaccuracy in the declaration.

9 In this Schedule—

'financial relief' has such meaning as may be prescribed; and
'prescribed' means prescribed by rules of court.

SCHEDULE 2

FINANCIAL PROVISION

Section 15

Introductory

1 Part II of the 1973 Act (financial provision and property adjustment orders) is amended as follows.

The orders

2 For section 21 (definitions) substitute—

'21 Financial provision and property adjustment orders

(1) For the purposes of this Act, a financial provision order is—

    (a)   an order that a party must make in favour of another person such periodical payments, for such term, as may be specified (a "periodical payments order");

    (b)   an order that a party must, to the satisfaction of the court, secure in favour of another person such periodical payments, for such term, as may be specified (a "secured periodical payments order");

    (c)   an order that a party must make a payment in favour of another person of such lump sum or sums as may be specified (an "order for the payment of a lump sum").

(2) For the purposes of this Act, a property adjustment order is—

    (a)   an order that a party must transfer such of his or her property as may be specified in favour of the other party or a child of the family;

    (b)   an order that a settlement of such property of a party as may be specified must be made, to the satisfaction of the court, for the benefit of the other party and of the children of the family, or either or any of them;

    (c)   an order varying, for the benefit of the parties and of the children of the family, or either or any of them, any marriage settlement;

    (d)   an order extinguishing or reducing the interest of either of the parties under any marriage settlement.

(3) Subject to section 40 below, where an order of the court under this Part of this Act requires a party to make or secure a payment in favour of another person or to transfer property in favour of any person, that payment must be made or secured or that property transferred—

    (a)   if that other person is the other party to the marriage, to that other party; and

    (b)   if that other person is a child of the family, according to the terms of the order—

(i)   to the child; or

(ii)   to such other person as may be specified, for the benefit of that child.

(4) References in this section to the property of a party are references to any property to which that party is entitled either in possession or in reversion.

(5) Any power of the court under this Part of this Act to make such an order as is mentioned in subsection (2)(b) to (d) above is exercisable even though there are no children of the family.

(6) In this section—

"marriage settlement" means an ante-nuptial or post-nuptial settlement made on the parties (including one made by will or codicil);
"party" means a party to a marriage; and
"specified" means specified in the order in question.'

Financial provision: divorce and separation

3   Insert, before section 23—

'22A Financial provision orders: divorce and separation

(1) On an application made under this section, the court may at the appropriate time make one or more financial provision orders in favour of—

(a)   a party to the marriage to which the application relates; or

(b)   any of the children of the family.

(2) The "appropriate time" is any time—

(a)   after a statement of marital breakdown has been received by the court and before any application for a divorce order or for a separation order is made to the court by reference to that statement;

(b)   when an application for a divorce order or separation order has been made under section 3 of the 1996 Act and has not been withdrawn;

(c)   when an application for a divorce order has been made under section 4 of the 1996 Act and has not been withdrawn;

(d)   after a divorce order has been made;

(e)   when a separation order is in force.

(3) The court may make—

(a)   a combined order against the parties on one occasion,

(b)   separate orders on different occasions,

(c)   different orders in favour of different children,

(d)   different orders from time to time in favour of the same child,

but may not make, in favour of the same party, more than one periodical payments order, or more than one order for payment of a lump sum, in relation to any marital proceedings, whether in the course of the proceedings or by reference to a divorce order or separation order made in the proceedings.

(4) If it would not otherwise be in a position to make a financial provision order in favour of a party or child of the family, the court may make an interim periodical

payments order, an interim order for the payment of a lump sum or a series of such orders, in favour of that party or child.

(5) Any order for the payment of a lump sum made under this section may—

    (a)   provide for the payment of the lump sum by instalments of such amounts as may be specified in the order; and

    (b)   require the payment of the instalments to be secured to the satisfaction of the court.

(6) Nothing in subsection (5) above affects—

    (a)   the power of the court under this section to make an order for the payment of a lump sum; or

    (b)   the provisions of this Part of this Act as to the beginning of the term specified in any periodical payments order or secured periodical payments order.

(7) Subsection (8) below applies where the court—

    (a)   makes an order under this section ("the main order") for the payment of a lump sum; and

    (b)   directs—

        (i)   that payment of that sum, or any part of it, is to be deferred; or

        (ii)   that that sum, or any part of it, is to be paid by instalments.

(8) In such a case, the court may, on or at any time after making the main order, make an order ("the order for interest") for the amount deferred, or the instalments, to carry interest (at such rate as may be specified in the order for interest)—

    (a)   from such date, not earlier than the date of the main order, as may be so specified;

    (b)   until the date when the payment is due.

(9) This section is to be read subject to any restrictions imposed by this Act and to section 19 of the 1996 Act.

22B Restrictions affecting section 22A

(1) No financial provision order, other than an interim order, may be made under section 22A above so as to take effect before the making of a divorce order or separation order in relation to the marriage, unless the court is satisfied—

    (a)   that the circumstances of the case are exceptional; and

    (b)   that it would be just and reasonable for the order to be so made.

(2) Except in the case of an interim periodical payments order, the court may not make a financial provision order under section 22A above at any time while the period for reflection and consideration is interrupted under section 7(8) of the 1996 Act.

(3) No financial provision order may be made under section 22A above by reference to the making of a statement of marital breakdown if, by virtue of section 5(3) or 7(9) of the 1996 Act (lapse of divorce or separation process), it has ceased to be possible—

    (a)   for an application to be made by reference to that statement; or

    (b)   for an order to be made on such an application.

(4) No financial provision order may be made under section 22A after a divorce order has been made, or while a separation order is in force, except—

(a)   in response to an application made before the divorce order or separation order was made; or

(b)   on a subsequent application made with the leave of the court.'

(5) In this section, "period for reflection and consideration" means the period fixed by section 7 of the 1996 Act.'

Financial provision: nullity of marriage

4   For section 23 substitute—

'23 Financial provision orders: nullity

(1) On or after granting a decree of nullity of marriage (whether before or after the decree is made absolute), the court may, on an application made under this section, make one or more financial provision orders in favour of—

(a)   either party to the marriage; or

(b)   any child of the family.

(2) Before granting a decree in any proceedings for nullity of marriage, the court may make against either or each of the parties to the marriage—

(a)   an interim periodical payments order, an interim order for the payment of a lump sum, or a series of such orders, in favour of the other party;

(b)   an interim periodical payments order, an interim order for the payment of a lump sum, a series of such orders or any one or more other financial provision orders in favour of each child of the family.

(3) Where any such proceedings are dismissed, the court may (either immediately or within a reasonable period after the dismissal) make any one or more financial provision orders in favour of each child of the family.

(4) An order under this section that a party to a marriage must pay a lump sum to the other party may be made for the purpose of enabling that other party to meet any liabilities or expenses reasonably incurred by him or her in maintaining himself or herself or any child of the family before making an application for an order under this section in his or her favour.

(5) An order under this section for the payment of a lump sum to or for the benefit of a child of the family may be made for the purpose of enabling any liabilities or expenses reasonably incurred by or for the benefit of that child before the making of an application for an order under this section in his favour to be met.

(6) An order under this section for the payment of a lump sum may—

(a)   provide for the payment of that sum by instalments of such amount as may be specified in the order; and

(b)   require the payment of the instalments to be secured to the satisfaction of the court.

(7) Nothing in subsections (4) to (6) above affects—

(a)   the power under subsection (1) above to make an order for the payment of a lump sum; or

(b)   the provisions of this Act as to the beginning of the term specified in any periodical payments order or secured periodical payments order.

(8) The powers of the court under this section to make one or more financial provision orders are exercisable against each party to the marriage by the making of—

(a)   a combined order on one occasion, or

(b)   separate orders on different occasions,

but the court may not make more than one periodical payments order, or more than one order for payment of a lump sum, in favour of the same party.

(9) The powers of the court under this section so far as they consist in power to make one or more orders in favour of the children of the family—

(a)   may be exercised differently in favour of different children; and

(b)   except in the case of the power conferred by subsection (3) above, may be exercised from time to time in favour of the same child; and

(c)   in the case of the power conferred by that subsection, if it is exercised by the making of a financial provision order of any kind in favour of a child, shall include power to make, from time to time, further financial provision orders of that or any other kind in favour of that child.

(10) Where an order is made under subsection (1) above in favour of a party to the marriage on or after the granting of a degree of nullity of marriage, neither the order nor any settlement made in pursuance of the order takes effect unless the decree has been made absolute.

(11) Subsection (10) above does not affect the power to give a direction under section 30 below for the settlement of an instrument by conveyancing counsel.

(12) Where the court—

(a)   makes an order under this section ("the main order") for the payment of a lump sum; and

(b)   directs—

    (i)   that payment of that sum or any part of it is to be deferred; or

    (ii)   that that sum or any part of it is to be paid by instalments,

it may, on or at any time after making the main order, make an order ("the order for interest") for the amount deferred or the instalments to carry interest at such rate as may be specified by the order for interest from such date, not earlier than the date of the main order, as may be so specified, until the date when payment of it is due.

(13) This section is to be read subject to any restrictions imposed by this Act.'

Property adjustment orders: divorce and separation

5   Insert, before section 24—

'23A Property adjustment orders: divorce and separation

(1) On an application made under this section, the court may, at any time mentioned in section 22A(2) above, make one or more property adjustment orders.

(2) If the court makes, in favour of the same party to the marriage, more than one property adjustment order in relation to any marital proceedings, whether in the course of the proceedings or by reference to a divorce order or separation order made in the proceedings, each order must fall within a different paragraph of section 21(2) above.

(3) The court shall exercise its powers under this section, so far as is practicable, by making on one occasion all such provision as can be made by way of one or more property adjustment orders in relation to the marriage as it thinks fit.

(4) Subsection (3) above does not affect section 31 or 31A below.

(5) This section is to be read subject to any restrictions imposed by this Act and to section 19 of the 1996 Act.

23B Restrictions affecting section 23A

(1) No property adjustment order may be made under section 23A above so as to take effect before the making of a divorce order or separation order in relation to the marriage unless the court is satisfied—

(a)   that the circumstances of the case are exceptional; and
(b)   that it would be just and reasonable for the order to be so made.

(2) The court may not make a property adjustment order under section 23A above at any time while the period for reflection and consideration is interrupted under section 7(8) of the 1996 Act.

(3) No property adjustment order may be made under section 23A above by virtue of the making of a statement of marital breakdown if, by virtue of section 5(3) or 7(5) of the 1996 Act (lapse of divorce or separation process), it has ceased to be possible—

(a)   for an application to be made by reference to that statement; or
(b)   for an order to be made on such an application.

(4) No property adjustment order may be made under section 23A above after a divorce order had been made, or while a separation order is in force, except—

(a)   in response to an application made before the divorce order or separation order was made; or
(b)   on a subsequent application made with the leave of the court.

(5) In this section, "period for reflection and consideration" means the period fixed by section 7 of the 1996 Act.'

Property adjustment orders: nullity

6   For section 24, substitute—

'24 Property adjustment orders: nullity of marriage

(1) On or after granting a decree of nullity of marriage (whether before or after the decree is made absolute), the court may, on an application made under this section, make one or more property adjustment orders in relation to the marriage.

(2) The court shall exercise its powers under this section, so far as is practicable, by making on one occasion all such provision as can be made by way of one or more property adjustment orders in relation to the marriage as it thinks fit.

(3) Subsection (2) above does not affect section 31 or 31A below.

(4) Where a property adjustment order is made under this section on or after the granting of a decree of nullity of marriage, neither the order nor any settlement made in pursuance of the order is to take effect unless the decree has been made absolute.

(5) That does not affect the power to give a direction under section 30 below for the settlement of an instrument by conveyancing counsel.

(6) This section is to be read subject to any restrictions imposed by this Act.'

Period of secured and unsecured payments orders

7   (1) In section 28(1) (duration of a continuing financial provision order in favour of a party to a marriage), for paragraphs (a) and (b) substitute—

'(a)   a term specified in the order which is to begin before the making of the order shall begin no earlier—

   (i)   where the order is made by virtue of section 22A(2)(a) or (b) above, unless sub-paragraph (ii) below applies, than the beginning of the day on which the statement of marital breakdown in question was received by the court;

   (ii)   where the order is made by virtue of section 22A(2)(b) above and the application for the divorce order was made following cancellation of an order preventing divorce under section 10 of the 1996 Act, than the date of the making of that application;

   (iii)   where the order is made by virtue of section 22A(2)(c) above, than the date of the making of the application for the divorce order; or

   (iv)   in any other case, than the date of the making of the application on which the order is made;

 (b)   a term specified in a periodical payments order or secured periodical payments order shall be so defined as not to extend beyond—

   (i)   in the case of a periodical payments order, the death of the party by whom the payments are to be made; or

   (ii)   in either case, the death of the party in whose favour the order was made or the remarriage of that party following the making of a divorce order or decree of nullity.'

(2) In section 29 (duration of continuing financial provision order in favour of a child of the family) insert after subsection (1)—

'(1A) The term specified in a periodical payments order or secured peridical payments order made in favour of a child shall be such term as the court thinks fit.

(1B) If that term is to begin before the making of the order, it may do so no earlier than—

   (a)   in the case of an order made by virtue of section 22A(2)(a) or (b) above, except where paragraph (b) below applies, the beginning of the day on which the statement of marital breakdown in question was received by the court;

(b)   in the case of an order made by virtue of section 22A(2)(b) above where the application for the divorce order was made following cancellation of an order preventing divorce under section 10 of the 1996 Act, the date of the making of that application;

(c)   in the case of an order made by virtue of section 22A(2)(c) above, the date of the making of the application for the divorce order; or

(d)   in any other case, the date of the making of the application on which the order is made.'

Variations etc. following reconciliations

8   Insert after section 31—

'31A Variation etc. following reconciliations

(1) Where, at a time before the making of a divorce order—

(a)   an order ("a paragraph (a) order") for the payment of a lump sum has been made under section 22A above in favour of a party,

(b)   such an order had been made in favour of a child of the family but the payment has not yet been made, or

(c)   a property adjustment order ("a paragraph (c) order") has been made under section 23A above,

the court may, on an application made jointly by the parties to the marriage, vary or discharge the order.

(2) Where the court varies or discharges a paragraph (a) order, it may order the repayment of an amount equal to the whole or any part of the lump sum.

(3) Where the court varies or discharges a paragraph (c) order, it may (if the order has taken effect)—

(a)   order any person to whom property was transferred in pursuance of the paragraph (c) order to transfer—

   (i)   the whole or any part of that property, or

   (ii)   the whole or any part of any property appearing to the court to represent that property,

   in favour of a party to the marriage or a child of the family; or

(b)   vary any settlement to which the order relates in favour of any person or extinguish or reduce any person's interest under that settlement.

(4) Where the court acts under subsection (3) it may make such supplemental provision (including a further property adjustment order or an order for the payment of a lump sum) as it thinks appropriate in consequence of any transfer, variation, extinguishment or reduction to be made under paragraph (a) or (b) of that subsection.

(5) Sections 24A and 30 above apply for the purposes of this section as they apply where the court makes a property adjustment order under section 23A or 24 above.

(6) The court shall not make an order under subsection (2), (3) or (4) above unless it appears to it that there has been a reconciliation between the parties to the marriage.

(7) The court shall also not make an order under subsection (3) or (4) above unless it appears to it that the order will not prejudice the interests of—

(a) any child of the family; or

(b) any person who has acquired any right or interest in consequence of the paragraph (c) order and is not a party to the marriage or a child of the family.'

SCHEDULE 3

STAY OF PROCEEDINGS

Section 19(5)

Introductory

1 Schedule 1 to the Domicile and Matrimonial Proceedings Act 1973 (which relates to the staying of matrimonial proceedings) is amended as follows.

Interpretation

2 In paragraph 1, for 'The following five paragraphs' substitute 'Paragraphs 2 to 6 below'.

3 For paragraph 2 substitute—

'**2** (1) "Matrimonial proceedings" means—

(a) marital proceedings;

(b) proceedings for nullity of marriage;

(c) proceedings for a declaration as to the validity of a marriage of the petitioner; or

(d) proceedings for a declaration as to the subsistence of such a marriage.

(2) "Marital proceedings" has the meaning given by section 20 of the Family Law Act 1996.

(3) "Divorce proceedings" means marital proceedings that are divorce proceedings by virtue of that section.'

4 Insert, after paragraph 4—

'4A(1) "Statement of marital breakdown" has the same meaning as in the Family Law Act 1996.

(2) "Relevant statement" in relation to any marital proceedings, means—

(a) the statement of marital breakdown with which the proceedings commenced; or

(b) if the proceedings are for the conversion of a separation order into a divorce order under section 4 of the Family Law Act 1996, the statement of marital breakdown by reference to which the separation order was made.'

Duty to furnish particulars of concurrent proceedings

5 For paragraph 7 substitute—

'7(1) While marital proceedings are pending in the court with respect to a marriage, this paragraph applies—

(a) to the party or parties to the marriage who made the relevant statement; and

(b)   in prescribed circumstances where the statement was made by only one
party, to the other party.

(2) While matrimonial proceedings of any other kind are pending in the court with
respect to a marriage and the trial or first trial in those proceedings has not begun,
this paragraph applies—

(a)   to the petitioner; and
(b)   if the respondent has included a prayer for relief in his answer, to the
respondent.

(3) A person to whom this paragraph applies must give prescribed information
about any proceedings which—

(a)   he knows to be continuing in another jurisdiction; and
(b)   are in respect of the marriage or capable of affecting its validity or
subsistence.

(4) The information must be given in such manner, to such persons and on such
occasions as may be prescribed.'

Obligatory stays in divorce cases

6   (1) Paragraph 8 is amended as follows.

(2) For the words before paragraph (a) of sub-paragraph (1) substitute—

'(1) This paragraph applies where divorce proceedings are continuing in the court
with respect to a marriage.
(2) Where it appears to the court, on the application of a party to the marriage—'.

(3) In sub-paragraph (1), in the words after paragraph (d), for 'proceedings' substitute
'divorce proceedings'.

(4) For sub-paragraph (2) substitute—

'(3) The effect of such an order is that, while it is in force—
(a)   no application for a divorce order in relation to the marriage may be made
either by reference to the relevant statement or by reference to any
subsequent statement of marital breakdown; and
(b)   if such an application has been made, no divorce order may be made on that
application.'

Discretionary stays

7   (1) Paragraph 9 is amended as follows.

(2) For sub-paragraph (1), substitute—

'(1) Sub-paragraph (1A) below applies where—

(a)   marital proceedings are continuing in the court; or
(b)   matrimonial proceedings of any other kind are continuing in the court, if the
trial or first trial in the proceedings has not begun.

(1A) The court may make an order staying the proceedings if it appears to the
court—

(a)   that proceedings in respect of the marriage, or capable of affecting its validity or subsistence, are continuing in another jurisdiction; and

(b)   that the balance of fairness (including convenience) as between the parties to the marriage is such that it is appropriate for proceedings in that jurisdiction to be disposed of before further steps are taken in the proceedings to which the order relates.'

(3) For sub-paragraph (3) substitute—

'(3) Where an application for a stay is pending under paragraph 8 above, the court shall not make an order under sub-paragraph (1A) staying marital proceedings in relation to the marriage.'

(4) In sub-paragraph 4, after 'pending in the court,' insert 'other than marital proceedings,'.

(5) After sub-paragraph (4), insert—

'(5) The effect of an order under sub-paragraph (1A) for a stay of marital proceedings is that, while it is in force—

(a)   no application for a divorce order or separation order in relation to the marriage may be made either by reference to the relevant statement or by reference to any subsequent statement of marital breakdown; and

(b)   if such an application has been made, no divorce order or separation order shall be made on that application.'

Discharge of orders

8   In paragraph 10, for sub-paragraph (2), substitute—

'(1A) Where the court discharges an order staying any proceedings, it may direct that the whole or a specified part of any period while the order has been in force—

(a)   is not to count towards any period specified in section 5(3) or 7(9) of the Family Law Act 1996; or

(b)   is to count towards any such period only for specified purposes.

(2) Where the court discharges an order under paragraph 8 above, it shall not again make such an order in relation to the marriage except in a case where the obligation to do so arises under that paragraph following receipt by the court of a statement of marital breakdown after the discharge of the order.'

Ancillary matters

9   (1)Paragraph 11 is amended as follows.

(2) For sub-paragraph (1) substitute—

'(1) Sub-paragraphs (2) and (3) below apply where a stay of marital proceedings or proceedings for nullity of marriage—

(a)   has been imposed by reference to proceedings in a related jurisdiction for divorce, separation or nullity of marriage, and

(b)   is in force.

(1A) In this paragraph—

"lump sum order", in relation to a stay, means an order—

(a) under section 22A or 23, 31 or 31A of the Matrimonial Causes Act 1973 which is an order for the payment of a lump sum for the purposes of Part II of that Act, or

(b) made in any equivalent circumstances under Schedule 1 to the Children Act 1989 and of a kind mentioned in paragraph 1(2)(a) or (b) of that Schedule,

so far as it satisfies the condition mentioned in sub-paragraph (1C) below;
"the other proceedings", in relation to a stay, means the proceedings in another jurisdiction by reference to which the stay was imposed;
"relevant order", in relation to a stay, means—

(a) any financial provision order (including an interim order), other than a lump sum order;

(b) any order made in equivalent circumstances under Schedule 1 to the Children Act 1989 and of a kind mentioned in paragraph 1(2)(a) or (b) of that Schedule;

(c) any section 8 order under the Act of 1989; and

(d) except for the purposes of sub-paragraph (3) below, any order restraining a person from removing a child out of England and Wales or out of the care of another person,

so far as it satisfies the condition mentioned in sub-paragraph (1C) below.

(1C) The condition is that the order is, or (apart from this paragraph) could be, made in connection with the proceedings to which the stay applies.'

(3) In sub-paragraph (2)—

(a) for 'any proceedings are stayed' substitute 'this paragraph applies in relation to a stay';

(b) in paragraph (a), and in the first place in paragraph (c), omit 'in connection with the stayed proceedings'; and

(c) in paragraphs (b) and (c), for 'made in connection with the stayed proceedings' substitute 'already made'.

(4) In sub-paragraph (3)—

(a) for 'any proceedings are stayed' substitute 'this paragraph applies in relation to a stay';

(b) in paragraph (a), for 'made in connection with the stayed proceedings' substitute 'already made';

(c) in paragraphs (b) and (c), omit 'in connection with the stayed proceedings'.

(5) In sub-paragraph (3A), for the words before 'any order made' substitute—

'Where a secured periodical payments order within the meaning of the Matrimonial Causes Act 1973—

(a) has been made under section 22A(1)(b) or 23(1)(b) or (2)(b) of that Act, but

(b) ceases to have effect by virtue of sub-paragraph (2) or (3) above,'.

(6) For sub-paragraph (4), substitute—

'(4) Nothing in sub-paragraphs (2) and (3) above affects any relevant order or lump sum order or any power to make such an order in so far as—

    (a)   where the stay applies to matrimonial proceedings other than marital proceedings, the order has been made or the power may be exercised following the receipt by the court of a statement of marital breakdown;

    (b)   where the stay is of marital proceedings, the order has been made or the power may be exercised in matrimonial proceedings of any other kind; or

    (c)   where the stay is of divorce proceedings only, the order has been made or the power may be exercised—

        (i)   in matrimonial proceedings which are not marital proceedings, or

        (ii)   in marital proceedings in which an application has been made for a separation order.'

(7) In sub-paragraph (5)(c), for the words from 'in connection' onwards substitute 'where a stay no longer applies'.

SCHEDULE 4

PROVISIONS SUPPLEMENTARY TO SECTIONS 30 AND 31

Section 32

Interpretation

1   (1) In this Schedule—

    (a)   any reference to a solicitor includes a reference to a licensed conveyancer or a recognised body, and

    (b)   any reference to a person's solicitor includes a reference to a licensed conveyancer or recognised body acting for that person.

(2) In sub-paragraph (1)—

    'licensed conveyancer' has the meaning given by section 11(2) of the Administration of Justice Act 1985;

    'recognised body' means a body corporate for the time being recognised under section 9 (incorporated practices) or section 32 (provision of conveyancing by recognised bodies) of that Act.

Restriction on registration where spouse entitled to more than one charge

2   Where one spouse is entitled by virtue of section 31 to a registrable charge in respect of each of two or more dwelling-houses, only one of the charges to which that spouse is so entitled shall be registered under section 31(10) or under section 2 of the Land Charges Act 1972 at any one time, and if any of those charges is registered under either of those provisions the Chief Land Registrar, on being satisfied that any other of them is so registered, shall cancel the registration of the charge first registered.

Contract for sale of house affected by registered charge to include term requiring cancellation of registration before completion

3   (1) Where one spouse is entitled by virtue of section 31 to a charge on an estate in a dwelling-house and the charge is registered under section 31(10) or section 2 of the Land Charges Act 1972, it shall be a term of any contract for the sale of that estate whereby the vendor agrees to give vacant possession of the dwelling-house on completion of the contract that the vendor will before such completion procure the cancellation of the registration of the charge at his expense.

(2) Sub-paragraph (1) shall not apply to any such contract made by a vendor who is entitled to sell the estate in the dwelling-house freed from any such charge.

(3) If, on the completion of such a contract as is referred to in sub-paragraph (1), there is delivered to the purchaser or his solicitor an application by the spouse entitled to the charge for the cancellation of the registration of that charge, the term of the contract for which sub-paragraph (1) provides shall be deemed to have been performed.

(4) This paragraph applies only if and so far as a contrary intention is not expressed in the contract.

(5) This paragraph shall apply to a contract for exchange as it applies to a contract for sale.

(6) This paragraph shall, with the necessary modifications, apply to a contract for the grant of a lease or underlease of a dwelling-house as it applies to a contract for the sale of an estate in a dwelling-house.

Cancellation of registration after termination of marriage, etc.

4 (1) Where a spouse's matrimonial home rights are a charge on an estate in the dwelling-house and the charge is registered under section 31(10) or under section 2 of the Land Charges Act 1972, the Chief Land Registrar shall, subject to sub-paragraph (2), cancel the registration of the charge if he is satisfied—

   (a)   by the production of a certificate or other sufficient evidence, that either spouse is dead, or

   (b)   by the production of an official copy of a decree or order of a court, that the marriage in question has been terminated otherwise than by death, or

   (c)   by the production of an order of the court, that the spouse's matrimonial home rights constituting the charge have been terminated by the order.

(2) Where—

   (a)   the marriage in question has been terminated by the death of the spouse entitled to an estate in the dwelling-house or otherwise than by death, and

   (b)   an order affecting the charge of the spouse not so entitled had been made under section 35(5),

then if, after the making of the order, registration of the charge was renewed or the charge registered in pursuance of sub-paragraph (3), the Chief Land Registrar shall not cancel the registration of the charge in accordance with sub-paragraph (1) unless he is also satisfied that the order has ceased to have effect.

(3) Where such an order has been made, then, for the purposes of sub-paragraph (2), the spouse entitled to the charge affected by the order may—

   (a)   if before the date of the order the charge was registered under section 31(10) or under section 2 of the Land Charges Act 1972, renew the registration of the charge, and

   (b)   if before the said date the charge was not so registered, register the charge under section 31(10) or under section 2 of the Land Charges Act 1972.

(4) Renewal of the registration of a charge in pursuance of sub-paragraph (3) shall be effected in such manner as may be prescribed, and an application for such renewal or for registration of a charge in pursuance of that sub-paragraph shall contain such particulars of any order affecting the charge made under section 33(5) as may be prescribed.

(5) The renewal in pursuance of sub-paragraph (3) of the registration of a charge shall not affect the priority of the charge.

(6) In this paragraph 'prescribed' means prescribed by rules made under section 16 of the Land Charges Act 1972 or section 144 of the Land Registration Act 1925, as the circumstances of the case require.

Release of matrimonial home rights

5 (1) A spouse entitled to matrimonial home rights may by a release in writing release those rights or release them as respects part only of the dwelling-house affected by them.

(2) Where a contract is made for the sale of an estate or interest in a dwelling-house, or for the grant of a lease or underlease of a dwelling-house, being (in either case) a dwelling-house affected by a charge registered under section 31(10) or under section 2 of the Land Charges Act 1972, then, without prejudice to sub-paragraph (1), the matrimonial home rights constituting the charge shall be deemed to have been released on the happening of whichever of the following events first occurs—

(a) the delivery to the purchaser or lessee, as the case may be, or his solicitor on completion of the contract of an application by the spouse entitled to the charge for the cancellation of the registration of the charge; or

(b) the lodging of such an application at Her Majesty's Land Registry.

Postponement of priority of charge

6 A spouse entitled by virtue of section 31 to a charge on an estate or interest may agree in writing that any other charge on, or interest in, that estate or interest shall rank in priority to the charge to which that spouse is so entitled.

SCHEDULE 5

POWERS OF HIGH COURT AND COUNTY COURT TO REMAND

Section 47(11)

Interpretation

1 In this Schedule 'the court' means the High Court or a county court and includes—

(a) in relation to the High Court, a judge of that court, and

(b) in relation to a county court, a judge or district judge of that court.

Remand in custody or on bail

2 (1) Where a court has power to remand a person under section 47, the court may—

(a) remand him in custody, that is to say, commit him to custody to be brought before the court at the end of the period of remand or at such earlier time as the court may require, or

  (b)   remand him on bail—

      (i)   by taking from him a recognizance (with or without sureties) conditioned as provided in sub-paragraph (3), or

     (ii)   by fixing the amount of the recognizances with a view to their being taken subsequently in accordance with paragraph 4 and in the meantime committing the person to custody in accordance with paragraph (a).

(2) Where a person is brought before the court after remand, the court may further remand him.

(3) Where a person is remanded on bail under sub-paragraph (1), the court may direct that his recognizance be conditioned for his appearance—

  (a)   before that court at the end of the period of remand, or

  (b)   at every time and place to which during the course of the proceedings the hearing may from time to time be adjourned.

(4) Where a recognizance is conditioned for a person's appearance in accordance with sub-paragraph (1)(b), the fixing of any time for him next to appear shall be deemed to be a remand; but nothing in this sub-paragraph or sub-paragraph (3) shall deprive the court of power at any subsequent hearing to remand him afresh.

(5) Subject to paragraph 3, the court shall not remand a person under this paragraph for a period exceeding 8 clear days, except that—

  (a)   if the court remands him on bail, it may remand him for a longer period if he and the other party consent, and

  (b)   if the court adjourns a case under section 48(1), the court may remand him for the period of the adjournment.

(6) Where the court has power under this paragraph to remand a person in custody it may, if the remand for a period not exceeding 3 clear days, commit him to the custody of a constable.

Further remand

3 (1) If the court is satisfied that any person who has been remanded under paragraph 2 is unable by reason of illness or accident to appear or be brought before the court at the expiration of the period for which he was remanded, the court may, in his absence, remand him for a further time; and paragraph 2(5) shall not apply.

(2) Notwithstanding anything in paragraph 2(1), the power of the court under sub-paragraph (1) to remand a person on bail for a further time may be exercised by enlarging his recognizance and those of any sureties for him to a later time.

(3) Where a person remanded on bail under paragraph 2 is bound to appear before the court at any time and the court has no power to remand him under sub-paragraph (1), the court may in his absence enlarge his recognizance and those of any sureties for him to a later time; and the enlargement of his recognizance shall be deemed to be a further remand.

Postponement of taking of recognizance

4 Where under paragraph 2(1)(b)(ii) the court fixes the amount in which the principal and his sureties, if any, are to be bound, the recognizance may thereafter be taken by such person as may be prescribed by rules of court, and the same consequences shall follow as if it had been entered into before the court.

SCHEDULE 6

AMENDMENTS OF CHILDREN ACT 1989

Section 52

1   After section 38 of the Children Act 1989 insert—

'38A Power to include exclusion requirement in interim care order

(1) Where—

  (a)   on being satisfied that there are reasonable grounds for believing that the circumstances with respect to a child are as mentioned in section 31(2)(a) and (b)(i), the court makes an interim care order with respect to a child, and
  (b)   the conditions mentioned in subsection (2) are satisfied,

the court may include an exclusion requirement in the interim care order.

(2) The conditions are—

  (a)   that there is reasonable cause to believe that, if a person ("the relevant person") is excluded from a dwelling-house in which the child lives, the child will cease to suffer, or cease to be likely to suffer, significant harm, and
  (b)   that another person living in the dwelling-house (whether a parent of the child or some other person)—

      (i)   is able and willing to give to the child the care which it would be reasonable to expect a parent to give him, and
      (ii)   consents to the inclusion of the exclusion requirement.

(3) For the purposes of this section an exclusion requirement is any one or more of the following—

  (a)   a provision requiring the relevant person to leave a dwelling-house in which he is living with the child,
  (b)   a provision prohibiting the relevant person from entering a dwelling-house in which the child lives, and
  (c)   a provision excluding the relevant person from a defined area in which a dwelling-house in which the child lives is situated.

(4) The court may provide that the exclusion requirement is to have effect for a shorter period than the other provisions of the interim care order.

(5) Where the court makes an interim care order containing an exclusion requirement, the court may attach a power of arrest to the exclusion requirement.

(6) Where the court attaches a power of arrest to an exclusion requirement of an interim care order, it may provide that the power of arrest is to have effect for a shorter period than the exclusion requirement.

(7) Any period specified for the purposes of subsection (4) or (6) may be extended by the court (on one or more occasions) on an application to vary or discharge the interim care order.

(8) Where a power of arrest is attached to an exclusion requirement of an interim care order by virtue of subsection (5), a constable may arrest without warrant any person whom he has reasonable cause to believe to be in breach of the requirement.

(9) Sections 47(7), (11) and (12) and 48 of, and Schedule 5 to, the Family Law Act 1996 shall have effect in relation to a person arrested under subsection (8) of this section as they have effect in relation to a person arrested under section 47(6) of that Act.

(10) If, while an interim care order containing an exclusion requirement is in force, the local authority have removed the child from the dwelling-house from which the relevant person is excluded to other accommodation for a continuous period of more than 24 hours, the interim care order shall cease to have effect in so far as it imposes the exclusion requirement.

38B Undertakings relating to interim care orders

(1) In any case where the court has power to include an exclusion requirement in an interim care order, the court may accept an undertaking from the relevant person.

(2) No power of arrest may be attached to any undertaking given under subsection (1).

(3) An undertaking given to a court under subsection (1)—

  (a) shall be enforceable as if it were an order of the court, and
  (b) shall cease to have effect if, while it is in force, the local authority have removed the child from the dwelling-house from which the relevant person is excluded to other accommodation for a continuous period of more than 24 hours.

(4) This section has effect without prejudice to the powers of the High Court and county court apart from this section.

(5) In this section "exclusion requirement" and "relevant person" have the same meaning as in section 38A.'

2   In section 39 of the Children Act 1989 (discharge and variation etc. of care orders and supervision orders) after subsection (3) insert—

'(3A) On the application of a person who is not entitled to apply for the order to be discharged, but who is a person to whom an exclusion requirement contained in the order applies, an interim care order may be varied or discharged by the court in so far as it imposes the exclusion requirement.

(3B) Where a power of arrest has been attached to an exclusion requirement of an interim care order, the court may, on the application of any person entitled to apply for the discharge of the order so far as it imposes the exclusion requirement, vary or discharge the order in so far as it confers a power of arrest (whether or not any application has been made to vary or discharge any other provision of the order).'

3 After section 44 of the Children Act 1989 insert—

'44A Power to include exclusion requirement in emergency protection order

(1) Where—

> (a) on being satisfied as mentioned in section 44(1)(a), (b) or (c), the court makes an emergency protection order with respect to a child, and
>
> (b) the conditions mentioned in subsection (2) are satisfied,

the court may include an exclusion requirement in the emergency protection order.

(2) The conditions are—

> (a) that there is reasonable cause to believe that, if a person ("the relevant person") is excluded from a dwelling-house in which the child lives, then—
>
>> (i) in the case of an order made on the ground mentioned in section 44(1)(a), the child will not be likely to suffer significant harm, even though the child is not removed as mentioned in section 44(1)(a)(i) or does not remain as mentioned in section 44(1)(a)(ii), or
>>
>> (ii) in the case of an order made on the ground mentioned in paragraph (b) or (c) of section 44(1), the enquiries referred to in that paragraph will cease to be frustrated, and
>
> (b) that another person living in the dwelling-house (whether a parent of the child or some other person)—
>
>> (i) is able and willing to give to the child the care which it would be reasonable to expect a parent to give him, and
>>
>> (ii) consents to the inclusion of the exclusion requirement.

(3) For the purposes of this section an exclusion requirement is any one or more of the following—

> (a) a provision requiring the relevant person to leave a dwelling-house in which he is living with the child,
>
> (b) a provision prohibiting the relevant person from entering a dwelling-house in which the child lives, and
>
> (c) a provision excluding the relevant person from a defined area in which a dwelling-house in which the child lives is situated.

(4) The court may provide that the exclusion requirement is to have effect for a shorter period than the other provisions of the order.

(5) Where the court makes an emergency protection order containing an exclusion requirement, the court may attach a power of arrest to the exclusion requirement.

(6) Where the court attaches a power of arrest to an exclusion requirement of an emergency protection order, it may provide that the power of arrest is to have effect for a shorter period than the exclusion requirement.

(7) Any period specified for the purposes of subsection (4) or (6) may be extended by the court (on one or more occasions) on an application to vary or discharge the emergency protection order.

(8) Where a power of arrest is attached to an exclusion requirement of an emergency protection order by virtue of subsection (5), a constable may arrest without warrant any person whom he has reasonable cause to believe to be in breach of the requirement.

(9) Sections 47(7), (11) and (12) and 48 of, and Schedule 5 to, the Family Law Act 1996 shall have effect in relation to a person arrested under subsection (8) of this section as they have effect in relation to a person arrested under section 47(6) of that Act.

(10) If, while an emergency protection order containing an exclusion requirement is in force, the applicant has removed the child from the dwelling-house from which the relevant person is excluded to other accommodation for a continuous period of more than 24 hours, the order shall cease to have effect in so far as it imposes the exclusion requirement.

44B Undertakings relating to emergency protection orders

(1) In any case where the court has power to include an exclusion requirement in an emergency protection order, the court may accept an undertaking from the relevant person.

(2) No power of arrest may be attached to any undertaking given under subsection (1).

(3) An undertaking given to a court under subsection (1)—

(a) shall be enforceable as if it were an order of the court, and
(b) shall cease to have effect if, while it is in force, the applicant has removed the child from the dwelling-house from which the relevant person is excluded to other accommodation for a continuous period of more than 24 hours.

(4) This section has effect without prejudice to the powers of the High Court and county court apart from this section.

(5) In this section "exclusion requirement" and "relevant person" have the same meaning as in section 44A.'

4 In section 45 of the Children Act 1989 (duration of emergency protection orders and other supplemental provisions), after subsection (8) insert—

'(8A) On the application of a person who is not entitled to apply for the order to be discharged, but who is a person to whom an exclusion requirement contained in the order applies, an emergency protection order may be varied or discharged by the court in so far as it imposes the exclusion requirement.

(8B) Where a power of arrest has been attached to an exclusion requirement of an emergency protection order, the court may, on the application of any person entitled to apply for the discharge of the order so far as it imposes the exclusion requirement, vary or discharge the order in so far as it confers a power of arrest (whether or not any application has been made to vary or discharge any other provision of the order).'

5 In section 105(1) of the Children Act 1989 (interpretation), after the definition of "domestic premises", insert—

"dwelling-house" includes—

(a) any building or part of a building which is occupied as a dwelling;

(b) any caravan, house-boat or structure which is occupied as a dwelling;

and any yard, garden, garage or outhouse belonging to it and occupied with it;".

SCHEDULE 7

TRANSFER OF CERTAIN TENANCIES ON DIVORCE ETC OR ON SEPARATION OF COHABITANTS

PART I

Section 53   GENERAL

Interpretation

1   In this Schedule—

'cohabitant', except in paragraph 3, includes (where the context requires) former cohabitant,
'the court' does not include a magistrates' court,
'landlord' includes—

(a) any person from time to time deriving title under the original landlord; and

(b) in relation to any dwelling-house, any person other than the tenant who is, or (but for Part VII of the Rent Act 1977 or Part II of the Rent (Agriculture) Act 1976) would be, entitled to possession of the dwelling-house;

'Part II order' means an order under Part II of this Schedule;
'a relevant tenancy' means—

(a) a protected tenancy or statutory tenancy within the meaning of the Rent Act 1977;

(b) a statutory tenancy within the meaning of the Rent (Agriculture) Act 1976;

(c) a secure tenancy within the meaning of section 79 of the Housing Act 1985; or

(d) an assured tenancy or assured agricultural occupancy within the meaning of Part I of the Housing Act 1988;

'spouse', except in paragraph 2, includes (where the context requires) former spouse; and
'tenancy' includes sub-tenancy.

Cases in which court may make order

2   (1) This paragraph applies if one spouse is entitled, either in his own right or jointly with the other spouse, to occupy a dwelling-house by virtue of a relevant tenancy.

(2) At any time when it has power to make a property adjustment order under section 23A (divorce or separation) or 24 (nullity) of the Matrimonial Causes Act 1973 with respect to the marriage, the court may make a Part II order.

3   (1) This paragraph applies if one cohabitant is entitled, either in his own right or jointly with the other cohabitant, to occupy a dwelling-house by virtue of a relevant tenancy.

(2) If the cohabitants cease to live together as husband and wife, the court may make a Part II order.

4 The court shall not make a Part II order unless the dwelling-house is or was—

(a) in the case of spouses, a matrimonial home; or

(b) in the case of cohabitants, a home in which they lived together as husband and wife.

Matters to which the court must have regard

5 In determining whether to exercise its powers under Part II of this Schedule and, if so, in what manner, the court shall have regard to all the circumstances of the case including—

(a) the circumstances in which the tenancy was granted to either or both of the spouses or cohabitants or, as the case requires, the circumstances in which either or both of them became tenant under the tenancy;

(b) the matters mentioned in section 33(6)(a), (b) and (c) and, where the parties are cohabitants and only one of them is entitled to occupy the dwelling-house by virtue of the relevant tenancy, the further matters mentioned in section 36(6)(e), (f), (g) and (h); and

(c) the suitability of the parties as tenants.

PART II
ORDERS THAT MAY BE MADE

References to entitlement to occupy

6 References in this Part of this Schedule to a spouse or a cohabitant being entitled to occupy a dwelling-house by virtue of a relevant tenancy apply whether that entitlement is in his own right or jointly with the other spouse or cohabitant.

Protected, secure or assured tenancy or assured agricultural occupancy

7 (1) If a spouse or cohabitant is entitled to occupy the dwelling-house by virtue of a protected tenancy within the meaning of the Rent Act 1977, a secure tenancy within the meaning of the Housing Act 1985 or an assured tenancy or assured agricultural occupancy within the meaning of Part I of the Housing Act 1988, the court may by order direct that, as from such date as may be specified in the order, there shall, by virtue of the order and without further assurance, be transferred to, and vested in, the other spouse or cohabitant—

(a) the estate or interest which the spouse or cohabitant so entitled had in the dwelling-house immediately before that date by virtue of the lease or agreement creating the tenancy and any assignment of that lease or agreement, with all rights, privileges and appurtenances attaching to that estate or interest but subject to all covenants, obligations, liabilities and incumbrances to which it is subject; and

(b) where the spouse or cohabitant so entitled is an assignee of such lease or agreement, the liability of that spouse or cohabitant under any covenant of indemnity by the assignee express or implied in the assignment of the lease or agreement to that spouse or cohabitant.

(2) If an order is made under this paragraph, any liability or obligation to which the spouse or cohabitant so entitled is subject under any covenant having reference to the dwelling-house in the lease or agreement, being a liability or obligation falling due to be discharged or performed on or after the date so specified, shall not be enforceable against that spouse or cohabitant.

(3) If the spouse so entitled is a successor within the meaning of Part IV of the Housing Act 1985, his former spouse or former cohabitant (or, if a separation order is in force, his spouse) shall be deemed also to be a successor within the meaning of that Part.

(4) If the spouse or cohabitant so entitled is for the purpose of section 17 of the Housing Act 1988 a successor in relation to the tenancy or occupancy, his former spouse or former cohabitant (or, if a separation order is in force, his spouse) is to be deemed to be a successor in relation to the tenancy or occupation for the purposes of that section.

(5) If the transfer under sub-paragraph (1) is of an assured agricultural occupancy, then, for the purposes of Chapter III of Part I of the Housing Act 1988—

(a)   the agricultural worker condition is fulfilled with respect to the dwelling-house while the spouse or cohabitant to whom the assured agricultural occupancy is transferred continues to be the occupier under that occupancy, and

(b)   that condition shall be treated as so fulfilled by virtue of the same paragraph of Schedule 3 to the Housing Act 1988 as was applicable before the transfer.

(6) In this paragraph, references to a separation order being in force include references to there being a judicial separation in force.

Statutory tenancy within the meaning of the Rent Act 1977

8 (1) This paragraph applies if the spouse or cohabitant is entitled to occupy the dwelling-house by virtue of a statutory tenancy within the meaning of the Rent Act 1977.

(2) The court may by order direct that, as from the date specified in the order—

(a)   that spouse or cohabitant is to cease to be entitled to occupy the dwelling-house; and

(b)   the other spouse or cohabitant is to be deemed to be the tenant or, as the case may be, the sole tenant under that statutory tenancy.

(3) The question whether the provisions of paragraphs 1 to 3, or (as the case may be) paragraphs 5 to 7 of Schedule 1 to the Rent Act 1977, as to the succession by the surviving spouse of a deceased tenant, or by a member of the deceased tenant's family, to the right to retain possession are capable of having effect in the event of the death of the person deemed by an order under this paragraph to be the tenant or sole tenant under the statutory tenancy is to be determined according as those provisions have or have not already had effect in relation to the statutory tenancy.

Statutory tenancy within the meaning of the Rent (Agriculture) Act 1976

9 (1) This paragraph applies if the spouse or cohabitant is entitled to occupy the dwelling-house by virtue of a statutory tenancy within the meaning of the Rent (Agriculture) Act 1976.

(2) The court may by order direct that, as from such date as may be specified in the order—

(a) that spouse or cohabitant is to cease to be entitled to occupy the dwelling-house; and

(b) the other spouse or cohabitant is to be deemed to be the tenant or, as the case may be, the sole tenant under that statutory tenancy.

(3) A spouse or cohabitant who is deemed under this paragraph to be the tenant under a statutory tenancy is (within the meaning of that Act) a statutory tenant in his own right, or a statutory tenant by succession, according as the other spouse or cohabitant was a statutory tenant in his own right or a statutory tenant by succession.

PART III
SUPPLEMENTARY PROVISIONS

Compensation

10 (1) If the court makes a Part II order, it may by the order direct the making of a payment by the spouse or cohabitant to whom the tenancy is transferred ('the transferee') to the other spouse or cohabitant ('the transferor').

(2) Without prejudice to that, the court may, on making an order by virtue of sub-paragraph (1) for the payment of a sum—

(a) direct that payment of that sum or any part of it is to be deferred until a specified date or until the occurrence of a specified event, or

(b) direct that that sum or any part of it is to be paid by instalments.

(3) Where an order has been made by virtue of sub-paragraph (1), the court may, on the application of the transferee or the transferor—

(a) exercise its powers under sub-paragraph (2), or

(b) vary any direction previously given under that sub-paragraph,

at any time before the sum whose payment is required by the order is paid in full.

(4) In deciding whether to exercise its powers under this paragraph and, if so, in what manner, the court shall have regard to all the circumstances including—

(a) the financial loss that would otherwise be suffered by the transferor as a result of the order;

(b) the financial needs and financial resources of the parties; and

(c) the financial obligations which the parties have, or are likely to have in the foreseeable future, including financial obligations to each other and to any relevant child.

(5) The court shall not give any direction under sub-paragraph (2) unless it appears to it that immediate payment of the sum required by the order would cause the transferee financial hardship which is greater than any financial hardship that would be caused to the transferor if the direction were given.

Liabilities and obligations in respect of the dwelling-house

11 (1) If the court makes a Part II order, it may by the order direct that both spouses or cohabitants are to be jointly and severally liable to discharge or perform any or all of the liabilities and obligations in respect of the dwelling-house (whether arising under the tenancy or otherwise) which—

(a) have at the date of the order fallen due to be discharged or performed by one only of them; or

(b) but for the direction, would before the date specified as the date on which the order is to take effect fall due to be discharged or performed by one only of them.

(2) If the court gives such a direction, it may further direct that either spouse or cohabitant is to be liable to indemnify the other in whole or in part against any payment made or expenses incurred by the other in discharging or performing any such liability or obligation.

Date when order made between spouses is to take effect

12 (1) In the case of a decree of nullity of marriage, the date specified in a Part II order as the date on which the order is to take effect must not be earlier than the date on which the decree is made absolute.

(2) In the case of divorce proceedings or separation proceedings, the date specified in a Part II order as the date on which the order is to take effect is to be determined as if the court were making a property adjustment order under section 23A of the Matrimonial Causes Act 1973 (regard being had to the restrictions imposed by section 23B of that Act).

Remarriage of either spouse

13 (1) If after the making of a divorce order or the grant of a decree annulling a marriage either spouse remarries, that spouse is not entitled to apply, by reference to the making of that order or the grant of that decree, for a Part II order.

(2) For the avoidance of doubt it is hereby declared that the reference in sub-paragraph (1) to remarriage includes a reference to a marriage which is by law void or voidable.

Rules of court

14 (1) Rules of court shall be made requiring the court, before it makes an order under this Schedule, to give the landlord of the dwelling-house to which the order will relate an opportunity of being heard.

(2) Rules of court may provide that an application for a Part II order by reference to an order or decree may not, without the leave of the court by which that order was made or decree was granted, be made after the expiration of such period from the order or grant as may be prescribed by the rules.

Saving for other provisions of Act

15 (1) If a spouse is entitled to occupy a dwelling-house by virtue of a tenancy, this Schedule does not affect the operation of sections 30 and 31 in relation to the other spouse's matrimonial home rights.

(2) If a spouse or cohabitant is entitled to occupy a dwelling-house by virtue of a tenancy, the court's powers to make orders under this Schedule are additional to those conferred by sections 33, 35 and 36.

SCHEDULE 8

MINOR AND CONSEQUENTIAL AMENDMENTS

Section 66(1)

PART I
AMENDMENTS CONNECTED WITH PART II

The Wills Act 1837 (c. 26)

1 In section 18A(1) of the Wills Act 1837 (effect of dissolution or annulment of marriage on wills), for 'a decree' substitute 'an order or decree'.

The Judicial Proceedings (Regulation of Reports) Act 1926 (c. 61)

2 In section 1(1)(b) of the Judicial Proceedings (Regulation of Reports) Act 1926 (restriction on reporting) after 'in relation to' insert 'any proceedings under Part II of the Family Law Act 1996 or otherwise in relation to'.

The Maintenance Orders Act 1950 (c. 37)

3 In section 16 of the Maintenance Orders Act 1950 (orders to which Part II of that Act applies)—

(a) in subsection (2)(a)(i), for '23(1), (2) and (4)' substitute '22A, 23'; and
(b) in subsection (2)(c)(v), after 'Matrimonial Causes Act 1973' insert '(as that Act had effect immediately before the passing of the Family Law Act 1996)'.

The Matrimonial Causes Act 1973 (c. 18)

4 The 1973 Act is amended as follows.

5 In section 8 (intervention of Queen's Proctor)—

(a) for 'a petition for divorce' substitute 'proceedings for a divorce order';
(b) in subsection (1)(b), omit 'or before the decree nisi is made absolute'; and
(c) in subsection (2), for 'a decree nisi in any proceedings for divorce' substitute 'the making of a divorce order'.

6 For section 15 (application of provisions relating to divorce to nullity proceedings) substitute—

'15 Decrees of nullity to be decrees nisi

Every decree of nullity of marriage shall in the first instance be a decree nisi and shall not be made absolute before the end of six weeks from its grant unless—

(a) the High Court by general order from time to time fixes a shorter period; or
(b) in any particular case, the court in which the proceedings are for the time being pending from time to time by special order fixes a shorter period than the period otherwise applicable for the time being by virtue of this section.

15A Intervention of Queen's Proctor

(1) In the case of a petition for nullity of marriage—

(a) the court may, if it thinks fit, direct all necessary papers in the matter to be sent to the Queen's Proctor, who shall under the directions of the Attorney-General instruct counsel to argue before the court any question in relation to the matter which the court considers it necessary or expedient to have fully argued;

(b) any person may at any time during the progress of the proceedings or before the decree nisi is made absolute give information to the Queen's Proctor on any matter material to the due decision of the case, and the Queen's Proctor may thereupon take such steps as the Attorney-General considers necessary or expedient.

(2) If the Queen's Proctor intervenes or shows cause against a decree nisi in any proceedings for nullity of marriage, the court may make such order as may be just as to the payment by other parties to the proceedings of the costs incurred by him in so doing or as to the payment by him of any costs incurred by any of those parties by reason of his so doing.

(3) Subsection (3) of section 8 above applies in relation to this section as it applies in relation to that section.

15B Proceedings after decree nisi: general powers of court

(1) Where a decree of nullity of marriage has been granted under this Act but not made absolute, then, without prejudice to section 15A above, any person (excluding a party to the proceedings other than the Queen's Proctor) may show cause why the decree should not be made absolute by reason of material facts not having been brought before the court; and in such a case the court may—

(a) notwithstanding anything in section 15 above (but subject to secction 41 below) make the decree absolute; or

(b) rescind the decree; or

(c) require further inquiry; or

(d) otherwise deal with the case as it thinks fit.

(2) Where a decree of nullity of marriage has been granted under this Act and no application for it to be made absolute has been made by the party to whom it was granted, then, at any time after the expiration of three months from the earliest date on which that party could have made such an application, the party against whom it was granted may make an application to the court, and on that application the court may exercise any of the powers mentioned in paragraphs (a) to (d) of subsection (1) above.'

7   In section 19(4) (application of provisions relating to divorce to proceedings under section 19)—

(a) for '1(5), 8 and 9' substitute '15, 15A and 15B'; and

(b) for 'divorce' in both places substitute 'nullity of marriage'.

8   In section 24A(1) (orders for sale of property), for 'section 23 or 24 of this Act' substitute 'any of sections 22A to 24 above'.

9 (1) Section 25 (matters to which the court is to have regard) is amended as follows.

(2) In subsection (1), for 'section 23, 24 or 24A' substitute 'any of sections 22A to 24A'.

(3) In subsection (2)—

    (a)   for 'section 23(1)(a), (b) or (c)' substitute 'section 22A or 23 above to make a financial provision order in favour of a party to a marriage or the exercise of its powers under section 23A,';

    (b)   in paragraph (g), after 'parties' insert ', whatever the nature of the conduct and whether it occurred during the marriage or after the separation of the parties or (as the case may be) dissolution or annulment of the marriage,'; and

    (c)   in paragraph (h), omit 'in the case of proceedings for divorce or nullity of marriage,'.

(4) In subsection (3), for 'section 23(1)(d), (e) or (f), (2) or (4)' substitute 'section 22A or 23 above to make a financial provision order in favour of a child of the family or the exercise of its powers under section 23A,'.

(5) In subsection (4), for 'section 23(1)(d), (e) or (f), (2) or (4), 24 or 24A' substitute 'any of sections 22A to 24A'.

(6) After subsection (4) insert—

'(5) In relation to any power of the court to make an interim periodical payments order or an interim order for the payment of a lump sum, the preceding provisions of this section, in imposing any obligation on the court with respect to the matters to which it is to have regard, shall not require the court to do anything which would cause such a delay as would, in the opinion of the court, be inappropriate having regard—

    (a)   to any immediate need for an interim order;

    (b)   to the matters in relation to which it is practicable for the court to inquire before making an interim order; and

    (c)   to the ability of the court to have regard to any matter and to make appropriate adjustments when subsequently making a financial provision order which is not interim.'

10 (1) Section 25A (requirement to consider need to provide for 'a clean break') is amended as follows.

(2) In subsection (1), for the words from the beginning to 'the marriage' substitute—

'If the court decides to exercise any of its powers under any of sections 22A to 24A above in favour of a party to a marriage (other than its power to make an interim periodical payments order or an interim order for the payment of a lump sum)'.

(3) In subsection (1), for 'the decree' substitute 'a divorce order or decree of nullity'.

(4) For subsection (3) substitute—

'(3) If the court—

    (a)   would have power under section 22A or 23 above to make a financial provision order in favour of a party to a marriage ("the first party"), but

(b)   considers that no continuing obligation should be imposed on the other party to the marriage ("the second party") to make or secure periodical payments in favour of the first party,

it may direct that the first party may not at any time after the direction takes effect, apply to the court for the making against the second party of any periodical payments order or secured periodical payments order and, if the first party has already applied to the court for the making of such an order, it may dismiss the application.

(3A) If the court—

(a)   exercises, or has exercised, its power under section 22A at any time before making a divorce order, and

(b)   gives a direction under subsection (3) above in respect of a periodical payments order or a secured periodical payments order,

it shall provide for the direction not to take effect until a divorce order is made.'

11   In each of sections 25B(2) and (3), 25C(1) and (3) and 25D(1)(a), (2)(a), (c) and (e) (benefits under a pension scheme on divorce, etc.) for 'section 23' substitute 'section 22A or 23'.

12   In section 26(1) (commencement of proceedings for ancillary relief), for the words from the beginning to '22 above' substitute—

'(1) If a petition for nullity of marriage has been presented, then, subject to subsection (2) below, proceedings'.

13   (1) Section 27 (financial provision orders etc. in case of failure to provide proper maintenance) is amended as follows.

(2) In subsection (5)—

(a)   after 'an order requiring the respondent' insert '—
      (a)   '; and

(b)   at the end insert ', or
      (b)   to pay to the applicant such lump sum or sums as the court thinks reasonable.'

(3) For subsection (6) substitute—

'(6) Subject to the restrictions imposed by the following provisions of this Act, if on an application under this section the applicant satisfies the court of any ground mentioned in subsection (1) above, the court may make one or more financial provision orders against the respondent in favour of the applicant or a child of the family.'

(4) In subsection (7), for '(6)(c) or (f)' substitute '(6)'.

14   (1) Section 28 (duration of continuing financial provision order in favour of a party to a marriage) is amended as follows.

(2) In subsection (1A), for the words from the beginning to 'nullity of marriage' substitute—

'(1A) At any time when—

    (a)   the court exercises, or has exercised, its power under section 22A or 23 above to make a financial provision order in favour of a party to a marriage,

    (b)   but for having exercised that power, the court would have power under one of those sections to make such an order, and

    (c)   an application for a divorce order or a petition for a decree of nullity of marriage is outstanding or has been granted in relation to the marriage,'.

(3) Insert, after subsection (1A)—

'(1B) If the court—

    (a)   exercises, or has exercised, its power under section 22A at any time before making a divorce order, and

    (b)   gives a direction under subsection (1A) above in respect of a periodical payments order or a secured periodical payments order,

it shall provide for the direction not to take effect until a divorce order is made.'

(4) In subsection (2), for the words from 'on or after' to 'nullity of marriage' substitute 'at such a time as is mentioned in subsection (1A)(c) above'.

(5) In subsection (3)—

    (a)   for 'a decree' substitute 'an order or decree'; and

    (b)   for 'that decree' substitute 'that order or decree'.

15   In section 29(1) (duration of a continuing financial provision order in favour of a child of the family), for 'under section 24(1)(a)' substitute 'such as is mentioned in section 21(2)(a)'.

16   (1) Section 31 (variation etc. of orders) is amended as follows.

(2) In subsection (2)—

    (a)   after 'following orders' insert 'under this Part of this Act';

    (b)   for paragraph (d) substitute—

        '(d)   an order for the payment of a lump sum in a case in which the payment is to be by instalments;';

    (c)   in paragraph (dd), for '23(1)(c)' substitute '21(1)(c)';

    (d)   after paragraph (dd) insert—

        '(de)   any other order for the payment of a lump sum, if it is made at a time when no divorce order has been made, and no separation order is in force, in relation to the marriage;';

    (e)   for paragraph (e) substitute—

        '(e)   any order under section 23A of a kind referred to in section 21(2)(b), (c) or (d) which is made on or after the making of a separation order;

        (ea)   any order under section 23A which is made at a time when no divorce order has been made, and no separation order is in force, in relation to the marriage;'.

(3) In subsection (4)—

    (a)   for the words from 'for a settlement' to '24(1)(c) or (d)', substitute 'referred to in subsection (2)(e)'; and

    (b)   for paragraphs (a) and (b) substitute 'on an application for a divorce order in relation to the marriage'.

(4) After subsection (4) insert—

'(4A) In relation to an order which falls within subsection (2)(de) or (ea) above ("the subsection (2) order")—

(a)   the powers conferred by this section may be exercised—
      (i)   only on an application made before the subsection (2) order has or, but for paragraph (b) below, would have taken effect; and
      (ii)   only if, at the time when the application is made, no divorce order has been made in relation to the marriage and no separation order has been so made since the subsection (2) order was made; and
(b)   an application made in accordance with paragraph (a) above prevents the subsection (2) order from taking effect before the application has been dealt with.

(4B) No variation—

(a)   of a financial provision order made under section 22A above, other than an interim order, or
(b)   of a property adjustment order made under section 23A above,

made so as to take effect before the making of a divorce order or separation order in relation to the marriage, unless the court is satisfied that the circumstances of the case are exceptional, and that it would be just and reasonable for the variation to be so made.'

(5) In subsection (5)—

(a)   insert, at the beginning, 'Subject to subsections (7A) to (7F) below and without prejudice to any power exercisable by virtue of subsection (2)(d), (dd) or (e) above or otherwise than by virtue of this section,'; and
(b)   for 'section 23', in each place, substitute 'section 22A or 23'.

(6) In subsection (7)(a)—

(a)   for 'on or after' to 'consider' substitute 'in favour of a party to a marriage, the court shall, if the marriage has been dissolved or annulled, consider'; and
(b)   after 'sufficient' insert '(in the light of any proposed exercise by the court, where the marriage has been dissolved, of its powers under subsection (7B) below)'.

(7) After subsection (7), insert—

'(7A) Subsection (7B) below applies where, after the dissolution of a marriage, the court—

(a)   discharges a periodical payments order or secured periodical payments order made in favour of a party to the marriage; or
(b)   varies such an order so that payments under the order are required to be made or secured only for such further period as is determined by the court.

(7B) The court has power, in addition to any power it has apart from this subsection, to make supplemental provision consisting of any of—

(a)   an order for the payment of a lump sum in favour of a party to the marriage;
(b)   one or more property adjustment orders in favour of a party to the marriage;

(c)   a direction that the party in whose favour the original order discharged or varied was made is not entitled to make any further application for—
    (i)   a periodical payments or secured periodical payments order, or
    (ii)   an extension of the period to which the original order is limited by any variation made by the court.

(7C) An order for the payment of a lump sum made under subsection (7B) above may—
    (a)   provide for the payment of that sum by instalments of such amount as may be specified in the order; and
    (b)   require the payment of the instalments to be secured to the satisfaction of the court.

(7D) Subsections (7) and (8) of section 22A above apply where the court makes an order for the payment of a lump sum under subsection (7B) above as they apply where it makes such an order under section 22A above.

(7E) If under subsection (7B) above the court makes more than one property adjustment order in favour of the same party to the marriage, each of those orders must fall within a different paragraph of section 21(2) above.

(7F) Sections 24A and 30 above apply where the court makes a property adjustment order under subsection (7B) above as they apply where it makes such an order under section 23A above.'

17   In section 32(1) (payment of certain arrears to be unenforceable), for the words from 'an order' to 'financial provision order' substitute 'any financial provision order under this Part of this Act or any interim order for maintenance'.

18   For section 33(2) (repayment of sums paid under certain orders) substitute—

'(2) This section applies to the following orders under this Part of this Act—

    (a)   any periodical payments order;
    (b)   any secured periodical payments order; and
    (c)   any interim order for maintenance, so far as it requires the making of periodical payments.'

19   (1) Section 33A (consent orders) is amended as follows.

(2) In subsection (2), after 'applies', in the first place, insert '(subject, in the case of the powers of the court under section 31A above, to subsections (6) and (7) of that section)'.

(3) In subsection (3), in the definition of 'order for financial relief', for 'an order under any of sections 23, 24, 24A or 27 above' substitute 'any of the following orders under this Part of this Act, that is to say, any financial provision order, any property adjustment order, any order for the sale of property or any interim order for maintenance'.

20   In section 35 (alteration of maintenance agreements), after subsection (6), insert—

'(7) Subject to subsection (5) above, references in this Act to any such order as is mentioned in section 21 above shall not include references to any order under this section.'

21 In section 37(1) (avoidance of transactions intended to prevent or reduce financial relief), for '22, 23, 24, 27, 31 (except subsection (6))' substitute '22A to 24, 27, 31 (except subsection (6)), 31A'.

22 In section 47(2) (relief in cases of polygamous marriages)—

  (a) in paragraph (a), after 'any' insert the words 'divorce order, any separation order under the 1996 Act or any'; and
  (b) in paragraph (d), after 'this Act' insert 'or the 1996 Act' and for 'such decree or order' substitute 'a statement of marital breakdown or any such order or decree'.

23 Omit section 49 (under which a person who is alleged to have committed adultery with a party to a marriage is required to be made a party to certain proceedings).

24 (1) Section 52(1) (interpretation) is amended as follows.

(2) After 'In this Act', insert—

' "the 1996 Act" means the Family Law Act 1996;'.

(3) After the definition of 'maintenance assessment' insert—

' "statement of marital breakdown" has the same meaning as in the Family Law Act 1996.'

25 In section 52(2)(a), for 'with section 21 above' substitute '(subject to section 35(7) above) with section 21 above and—

  (i)   in the case of a financial provision order or periodical payments order, as including (except where the context otherwise requires) references to an interim periodical payments order under section 22A or 23 above; and
  (ii) in the case of a financial provision order or order for the payment of a lump sum, as including (except where the context otherwise requires) references to an interim order for the payment of a lump sum under section 22A or 23 above;'.

The Domicile and Matrimonial Proceedings Act 1973 (c. 45)

26 For section 5(5) of the Domicile and Matrimonial Proceedings Act 1973 (jurisdiction in cases of change of domicile or habitual residence) substitute—

'(5) The court shall have jurisdiction to entertain proceedings for nullity of marriage (even though it would not otherwise have jurisdiction) at any time when marital proceedings, as defined by section 20 of the Family Law Act 1996, are pending in relation to the marriage.'

The Inheritance (Provision for Family and Dependants) Act 1975 (c. 63)

27 (1) The Inheritance (Provision for Family and Dependants) Act 1975 (meaning of reasonable financial provision) is amended as follows.

(2) In section 1(2)(a), for the words from 'the marriage' to 'in force' substitute ', at the date of death, a separation order under the Family Law Act 1996 was in force in relation to the marriage'.

(3) In section 3(2) (matters to which the court is to have regard)—

(a) for 'decree of judicial separation' substitute 'separation order under the Family Law Act 1996'; and

(b) for 'a decree of divorce' substitute 'a divorce order'.

(4) In section 14 (provision where no financial relief was granted on divorce)—

(a) in subsection (1), for the words from 'a decree' to 'first granted' substitute 'a divorce order or separation order has been made under the Family Law Act 1996 in relation to a marriage or a decree of nullity of marriage has been made absolute';

(b) in subsection (1)(a), for 'section 23' and 'section 24' substitute, respectively, 'section 22A or 23' and 'section 23A or 24';

(c) after paragraph (b), for the words from 'the decree of divorce' to the end substitute ', as the case may be, the divorce order or separation order had not been made or the decree of nullity had not been made absolute'; and

(d) in subsection (2), for 'decree of judicial separation' and 'the decree' substitute, respectively, 'separation order' and 'the order'.

(5) In section 15(1) (restriction imposed in divorce proceedings on applications under that Act), for the words from the beginning to 'thereafter' substitute—

'At any time when the court—

(a) has jurisdiction under section 23A or 24 of the Matrimonial Causes Act 1973 to make a property adjustment order in relation to a marriage; or

(b) would have such jurisdiction if either the jurisdiction had not already been exercised or an application for such an order were made with the leave of the court,'.

(6) In section 15, for subsections (2) to (4) substitute—

'(2) An order made under subsection (1) above with respect to any party to a marriage has effect in accordance with subsection (3) below at any time—

(a) after the marriage has been dissolved;

(b) after a decree of nullity has been made absolute in relation to the marriage; and

(c) while a separation order under the Family Law Act 1996 is in force in relation to the marriage and the separation is continuing.

(3) If at any time when an order made under subsection (1) above with respect to any party to a marriage has effect the other party to the marriage dies, the court shall not entertain any application made by the surviving party to the marriage for an order under section 2 of this Act.'

(7) In section 19(2)(b) (effect and duration of certain orders), for the words from 'the marriage' to 'in force' substitute ', at the date of death, a separation order under the Family Law Act 1996 was in force in relation to the marriage with the deceased'.

(8) In section 25 (interpretation), in the definition of 'former wife' and 'former husband', for 'a decree', in the first place, substitute 'an order or decree'.

The Domestic Proceedings and Magistrates' Courts Act 1978 (c. 22)

28 (1) Section 28(1) of the Domestic Proceedings and Magistrates' Courts Act 1978 (power of High Court in respect of orders under Part I) is amended as follows.

(2) After 'this Act' insert—

'(a)   a statement of marital breakdown under section 5 of the Family Law Act 1996
       with respect to the marriage has been received by the court but no application
       has been made under that Act by reference to that statement, or
(b)   '.

(3) For the words from 'then' to 'lump sum' substitute 'then, except in the case of an
order for the payment of a lump sum, any court to which an application may be made
under that Act by reference to that statement or, as the case may be,'.

The Housing Act 1980 (c. 51)

29   In section 54(2) of the Housing Act 1980 (prohibition of assignment of shorthold
tenancy under that section) for 'section 24' substitute 'sections 23A or 24'.

The Supreme Court Act 1981 (c. 54)

30   In section 18 of the Supreme Court Act 1981 (restrictions on appeals to Court of
Appeal), in paragraph (d) of subsection (1) omit 'divorce or' and after that paragraph
insert—

'(dd) from a divorce order;'.

The Civil Jurisdiction and Judgments Act 1982 (c. 27)

31   In section 18(6)(a) of the Civil Jurisdiction and Judgments Act 1982 (decrees of
judicial separation), for 'a decree' substitute 'an order or decree'.

The Matrimonial and Family Proceedings Act 1984 (c. 42)

32   (1) The Matrimonial and Family Proceedings Act 1984 is amended as follows.

(2) In section 17(1) (financial relief in the case of overseas divorces etc.), for the words
from 'any' where it first occurs to the end substitute 'one or more orders each of which
would, within the meaning of Part II of the 1973 Act, be a financial provision order in
favour of a party to the marriage or child of the family or a property adjustment order in
relation to the marriage.'

(3) For section 21(a) (provisions of the 1973 Act applied for the purposes of the
powers to give relief in the case of overseas divorces etc.) substitute—

'(a)   section 22A(5) (provisions about lump sums in relation to divorce or
       separation);
(aa)   section 23(4), (5) and (6) (provisions about lump sums in relation to
       annulment);'.

(4) In section 27 (interpretation), for the definition of 'property adjustment order',
substitute—

' "property adjustment order" and "secured periodical payments order" mean any
order which would be a property adjustment order or, as the case may be, secured
periodical payments order within the meaning of Part II of the 1973 Act;'

(5) In section 32 (meaning of 'family business'), for the definition of 'matrimonial
cause' substitute—

' "matrimonial cause" means an action for nullity of marriage or any marital proceedings under the Family Law Act 1996;'.

The Finance Act 1985 (c. 54)

33 In section 83(1) of the Finance Act 1985 (stamp duty for transfers of property in connection with divorce etc.)—

(a) after paragraph (b), insert—

'(bb) is executed in pursuance of an order of a court which is made at any time under section 22A, 23A or 24A of the Matrimonial Causes Act 1973, or'; and

(b) in paragraph (c), for 'or their judicial separation' substitute ', their judicial separation or the making of a separation order in respect of them'.

The Housing Act 1985 (c. 68)

34 In each of sections 39(1)(c), 88(2), 89(3), 90(3)(a), 91(3)(b), 99B(2)(e), 101(3)(c), 160(1)(c), 171B(4)(b)(i) of, and paragraph 1(2)(c) to, Schedule 6A of the Housing Act 1985 (which refers to the 1973 Act), for 'section 24' substitute 'section 23A or 24'.

The Housing Associations Act 1985 (c. 69)

35 In paragraph 5(1)(c) of Schedule 2 to the Housing Associations Act 1985 (which refers to the 1973 Act), for 'section 24' substitute 'section 23A or 24'.

The Agricultural Holdings Act 1986 (c. 5)

36 In paragraph 1(3) of Schedule 6 to the Agricultural Holdings Act 1986 (spouse of close relative not to be treated as such when marriage subject to decree nisi etc.), for the words from 'when' to the end substitute 'when a separation order or a divorce order under the Family Law Act 1996 is in force in relation to the relative's marriage or that marriage is the subject of a decree nisi of nullity.'

The Family Law Act 1986 (c. 55)

37 (1) The Family Law Act 1986 is amended as follows.

(2) For section 2(1) and (2) (jurisdiction to make orders under section 1) substitute—

'(1) A court in England and Wales shall not have jurisdiction to make a section 1(1)(a) order with respect to a child unless—

(a) the case falls within section 2A below; or

(b) in any other case, the condition in section 3 below is satisfied.'

(3) For section 2A(1) (jurisdiction in or in connection with matrimonial proceedings), substitute—

'(1) Subject to subsections (2) to (4) below, a case falls within this section for the purposes of the making of a section 1(1)(a) order if that order is made—

(a) at a time when—

(i) a statement of marital breakdown under section 5 of the Family Law Act 1996 with respect to the marriage of the parents of the child concerned has been received by the court; and

(ii)   it is or may become possible for an application for a divorce order or for a separation order to be made by reference to that statement; or

(b)   at a time when an application in relation to that marriage for a divorce order, or for a separation order under the Act of 1996, has been made and not withdrawn.

(1A) A case also falls within this section for the purposes of the making of a section 1(1)(a) order if that order is made in or in connection with any proceedings for the nullity of the marriage of the parents of the child concerned and—

(a)   those proceedings are continuing; or
(b)   the order is made—
  (i)   immediately on the dismissal, after the beginning of the trial, of the proceedings; and
  (ii)   on an application made before the dismissal.'

(4) In section 2A(2), for the words from the beginning to 'judicial separation' substitute 'A case does not fall within this section if a separation order under the Family Law Act 1996 is in force in relation to the marriage of the parents of the child concerned if,'.

(5) In section 2A(3), for 'in which the other proceedings there referred to' substitute 'in Scotland, Northern Ireland or a specified dependent territory in which the proceedings for divorce or nullity'.

(6) In section 2A(4)—

(a)   for 'in or in connection with matrimonial proceedings' substitute 'by virtue of the case falling within this section'; and
(b)   for 'in or in connection with those proceedings' substitute 'by virtue of section 2(1)(a) of this Act'.

(7) In section 3 (child habitually resident or present in England and Wales), for 'section 2(2)' substitute 'section 2(1)(b)'.

(8) In section 6 (duration and variation of Part I orders), for subsections (3A) and (3B) substitute—

'(3A) Subsection (3) above does not apply if the Part I order was made in a case falling within section 2A of this Act.'

(9) In section 38 (restriction on removal of wards of court from the jurisdiction), insert after subsection (3)—

'(4) The reference in subsection (2) above to a time when proceedings for divorce or judicial separation are continuing in respect of a marriage in another part of the United Kingdom includes, in relation to any case in which England and Wales would be another part of the United Kingdom, any time when—

(a)   a statement of marital breakdown under section 5 of the Family Law Act 1996 with respect to that marriage has been received by the court and it is or may become possible for an application for a divorce order or for a separation order to be made by reference to that statement; or
(b)   an application in relation to that marriage for a divorce order, or for a separation order under the Act of 1996, has been made and not withdrawn.'

(10) In section 42(2) (times when divorce etc. proceedings are to be treated as continuing for the purposes of certain restrictions on the removal of children from the jurisdiction), for the words from 'unless' to the end substitute 'be treated as continuing (irrespective of whether a divorce order, separation order or decree of nullity has been made)—

(a) from the time when a statement of marital breakdown under section 5 of the Family Law Act 1996 with respect to the marriage is received by the court in England and Wales until such time as the court may designate or, if earlier, until the time when—
  (i) the child concerned attains the age of eighteen; or
  (ii) it ceases, by virtue of section 5(3) or 7(9) or that Act (lapse of divorce or separation process) to be possible for an application for a divorce order, or for a separation order, to be made by reference to that statement; and
(b) from the time when a petition for nullity is presented in relation to the marriage in England and Wales or a petition for divorce, judicial separation or nullity is presented in relation to the marriage in Northern Ireland or a specified dependent territory, until the time when—
  (i) the child concerned attains the age of eighteen; or
  (ii) if earlier, proceedings on the petition are dismissed.'

(11) In section 51(4) (definitions), after the definition of 'the relevant date' insert—

' "judicial separation" includes a separation order under the Family Law Act 1996;'.

The Landlord and Tenant Act 1987 (c. 31)

38 In section 4(2)(c) of the Landlord and Tenant Act 1987 (which refers to the 1973 Act), for 'section 24' substitute 'section 23A, 24'.

The Legal Aid Act 1988 (c. 34)

39 In paragraph 5A of Part II of Schedule 2 to the Legal Aid Act 1988 (excepted proceedings)—

(a) for 'decree of divorce or judicial separation' substitute 'a divorce order or a separation order'; and
(b) in sub-paragraph (b) of that paragraph, for 'petition' substitute 'application'.

The Housing Act 1988 (c. 50)

40 In paragraph 4(1)(c) of Schedule 11 (which refers to the 1973 Act), for 'section 24' substitute 'section 23A or 24'.

The Children Act 1989 (c. 41)

41 (1) The Children Act 1989 is amended as follows.

(2) In section 6(3A) (revocation or appointment of guardian) for paragraph (a) substitute—

'(a) a court of civil jurisdiction in England and Wales by order dissolves, or by decree annuls, a marriage, or'.

(3) In section 8(3) after 'means' insert '(subject to subsection (5))'.

(4) In section 8, insert after subsection (4)—

'(5) For the purposes of any reference in this Act to family proceedings, powers which under this Act are exercisable in family proceedings shall also be exercisable in relation to a child, without any such proceedings having been commenced or any application having been made to the court under this Act, if—

    (a)   a statement of marital breakdown under section 5 of the Family Law Act 1996 with respect to the marriage in relation to which that child is a child of the family has been received by the court; and

    (b)   it may, in due course, become possible for an application for a divorce order or for a separation order to be made by reference to that statement.'

The Local Government and Housing Act 1989 (c. 42)

42 In section 124(3)(c) of the Local Government and Housing Act 1989 (which refers to the 1973 Act), for 'section 24' substitute 'section 23A or 24'.

Pensions Act 1995 (c. 26)

43 In section 166(4) of the Pensions Act 1995 (jurisdiction of the court under the Matrimonial Causes Act 1973 in respect of pensions to which that section applies) for 'section 23' substitute 'section 22A or 23'.

PART II
AMENDMENTS CONNECTED WITH PART III

The Legal Aid Act 1988 (c. 34)

44 (1) The 1988 Act is amended as follows.

(2) In section 1, after 'III' insert 'IIIA'.

(3) In sections 1, 2(11), 3(2), 4(1), (2) and (4), 5(1) and (6), 6(2)(a) and (3)(a), 34(2)(c) and (d) and (11), 38(1) and (6) and 39(1) and (4)(a), after 'assistance', in each place, insert ', mediation'.

(4) In section 3(9), after paragraph (a) insert—

'(aa) the provision of mediation;'.

(5) In section 6, after subsection (3)(c) insert—

'(ca) any sum which is to be paid out of property on which it is charged under regulations under section 13C(5) below'.

(6) In section 15—

    (a)   in subsection (1), after '(3D)' insert 'and (3F)'; and
    (b)   in subsection (3D), after '(3)' insert 'and (3F)'.

(7) In section 16(9), leave out 'and' at the end of paragraph (a).

(8) In section 38—

    (a)   in subsection (1)(f), after 'legal representatives' insert 'or mediators'; and
    (b)   in subsection (6), after 'legal representative' insert 'or mediator'.

(9) In section 43—

(a) after ' "assistance" ' insert ', "mediation" ';

(b) after '(3)' insert ', (3A)'; and

(c) after the definition of 'financial resources' insert—

' "family matters" has the meaning assigned by section 13A(2);'.

PART III
AMENDMENTS CONNECTED WITH PART IV

The Land Registration Act 1925 (c. 21)

45 In section 64 of the Land Registration Act 1925 (certificates to be produced and noted on dealings) in subsection (5) for 'section 2(8) of the Matrimonial Homes Act 1983' substitute 'section 31(10) of the Family Law Act 1996 and for 'rights of occupation' substitute 'matrimonial home rights'.

The Land Charges Act 1972 (c. 61)

46 In section 1(6A) of the Land Charges Act 1972 (cases where county court has jurisdiction to vacate registration) in paragraph (d)—

(a) after 'section 1 of the Matrimonial Homes Act 1983' insert 'or section 33 of the Family Law Act 1996'; and

(b) for 'that section' substitute 'either of those sections'.

47 In section 2(7) of that Act (Class F land charge) for 'Matrimonial Homes Act 1983' substitute 'Part IV of the Family Law Act 1996'.

The Land Compensation Act 1973 (c. 26)

48 (1) Section 29A of the Land Compensation Act 1973 (spouses having statutory rights of occupation) is amended as follows.

(2) In subsection (1), for 'rights of occupation (within the meaning of the Matrimonial Homes Act 1983)' substitute 'matrimonial home rights (within the meaning of Part IV of the Family Law Act 1996)'.

(3) In subsection (2)(a), for 'rights of occupation' substitute 'matrimonial home rights'.

The Magistrates' Courts Act 1980 (c. 43)

49 In section 65(1) of the Magistrates' Courts Act 1980 (meaning of family proceedings) after paragraph (o) insert—

'(p) Part IV of the Family Law Act 1996;'.

The Contempt of Court Act 1981 (c. 49)

50 In Schedule 3 to the Contempt of Court Act 1981 (application of Magistrates' Courts Act 1980 to civil contempt proceedings), in paragraph 3 for the words from ' "or, having been arrested" onwards substitute—

' "or, having been arrested under section 47 of the Family Law Act 1996 in connection with the matter of the complaint, is at large after being remanded under subsection (7)(b) or (10) of that section." '

The Supreme Court Act 1981 (c. 54)

51   In Schedule 1 to the Supreme Court Act 1981 (distribution of business in High Court), in paragraph 3 (Family Division)—

(a)   in paragraph (d), after 'matrimonial proceedings' insert 'or proceedings under Part IV of the Family Law Act 1996', and

(b)   in paragraph (f)(i), for 'Domestic Violence and Matrimonial Proceedings Act 1976' substitute 'Part IV of the Family Law Act 1996'.

The Matrimonial and Family Proceedings Act 1984 (c. 42)

52   For section 22 of the Matrimonial and Family Proceedings Act 1984 substitute—

'22 Powers of court in relation to certain tenancies of dwelling-houses

(1) This section applies if—

(a)   an application is made by a party to a marriage for an order for financial relief; and

(b)   one of the parties is entitled, either in his own right or jointly with the other party, to occupy a dwelling-house situated in England or Wales by virtue of a tenancy which is a relevant tenancy within the meaning of Schedule 7 to the Family Law Act 1996 (certain statutory tenancies).

(2) The court may make in relation to that dwelling-house any order which it could make under Part II of that Schedule if—

(a)   a divorce order,

(b)   a separation order, or

(c)   a decree of nullity of marriage,

had been made or granted in England and Wales in respect of the marriage.

(3) The provisions of paragraphs 10, 11 and 14(1) in Part III of that Schedule apply in relation to any order under this section as they apply to any order under Part II of that Schedule.'

The Housing Act 1985 (c. 68)

53   (1) Section 85 of the Housing Act 1985 (extended discretion of court in certain proceedings for possession) is amended as follows.

(2) In subsection (5)—

(a)   in paragraph (a), for 'rights of occupation under the Matrimonial Homes Act 1983' substitute 'matrimonial home rights under Part IV of the Family Law Act 1996'; and

(b)   for 'those rights of occupation' substitute 'those matrimonial home rights'.

(3) After subsection (5) insert—

'(5A) If proceedings are brought for possession of a dwelling-house which is let under a secure tenancy and—

(a) an order is in force under section 35 of the Family Law Act 1996 conferring rights on the former spouse of the tenant or an order is in force under section 36 of that Act conferring rights on a cohabitant or former cohabitant (within the meaning of that Act) of the tenant,

(b) the former spouse, cohabitant or former cohabitant is then in occupation of the dwelling-house, and

(c) the tenancy is terminated as a result of those proceedings,

the former spouse, cohabitant or former cohabitant shall, so long as he or she remains in occupation, have the same rights in relation to, or in connection with, any adjournment, stay, suspension or postponement in pursuance of this section as he or she would have if the rights conferred by the order referred to in paragraph (a) were not affected by the termination of the tenancy.'

54. In section 99B of that Act (persons qualifying for compensation for improvements) in subsection (2) for paragraph (f) substitute—

'(f) a spouse, former spouse, cohabitant or former cohabitant of the improving tenant to wom the tenancy has been transferred by an order made under Schedule 1 to the Matrimonial Homes Act 1983 or Schedule 7 to the Family Law Act 1996.'

55 In section 101 of that Act (rent not to be increased on account of tenant's improvements) in subsection (3) for paragraph (d) substitute—

'(d) a spouse, former spouse, cohabitant or former cohabitant of the tenant to whom the tenancy has been transferred by an order made under Schedule 1 to the Matrimonial Homes Act 1983 or Schedule 7 to the Family Law Act 1996.'

56 In section 171B of that Act (extent of preserved right to buy: qualifying persons and dwelling-houses) in subsection (4)(b)(ii) after 'Schedule 1 to the Matrimonial Homes Act 1983' insert 'or Schedule 7 to the Family Law Act 1996'.

The Insolvency Act 1986 (c. 45)

57 (1) Section 336 of the Insolvency Act 1986 (rights of occupation etc. of bankrupt's spouse) is amended as follows.

(2) In subsection (1), for 'rights of occupation under the Matrimonial Homes Act 1983' substitute 'matrimonial home rights under Part IV of the Family Law Act 1996'.

(3) In subsection (2)—

(a) for 'rights of occupation under the Act of 1983' substitute 'matrimonial home rights under the Act of 1996', and

(b) in paragraph (b), for 'under section 1 of that Act' substitute 'under section 33 of that Act'.

(4) In subsection (4), for 'section 1 of the Act of 1983' substitute 'section 33 of the Act of 1996'.

58 (1) Section 337 of that Act is amended as follows.

(2) In subsection (2), for 'rights of occupation under the Matrimonial Homes Act 1983' substitute 'matrimonial home rights under Part IV of the Family Law Act 1996'.

(3) For subsection (3) substitute—

'(3) The Act of 1996 has effect, with the necessary modifications, as if—

(a)   the rights conferred by paragraph (a) of subsection (2) were matrimonial home rights under that Act,

(b)   any application for such leave as is mentioned in that paragraph were an application for an order under section 33 of that Act, and

(c)   any charge under paragraph (b) of that subsection on the estate or interest of the trustee were a charge under that Act on the estate or interest of a spouse.'

(4) In subsections (4) and (5) for 'section 1 of the Act of 1983' substitute 'section 33 of the Act of 1996'.

The Housing Act 1988 (c. 50)

59   (1) Section 9 of the Housing Act 1988 (extended discretion of court in possession claims) is amended as follows.

(2) In subsection (5)—

(a)   in paragraph (a), for 'rights of occupation under the Matrimonial Homes Act 1983' substitute 'matrimonial home rights under Part IV of the Family Law Act 1996', and

(b)   for 'those rights of occupation' substitute 'those matrimonial home rights',

(3) After subsection (5) insert—

'(5A) In any case where—

(a)   at a time when proceedings are brought for possession of a dwelling-house let on an assured tenancy—

(i)   an order is in force under section 35 of the Family Law Act 1996 conferring rights on the former spouse of the tenant, or

(ii)   an order is in force under section 36 of that Act conferring rights on a cohabitant or former cohabitant (within the meaning of that Act) of the tenant,

(b)   that cohabitant, former cohabitant or former spouse is then in occupation of the dwelling-house, and

(c)   the assured tenancy is terminated as a result of those proceedings,

the cohabitant, former cohabitant or former spouse shall have the same rights in relation to, or in connection with, any such adjournment as is referred to in subsection (1) above or any such stay, suspension or postponement as is referred to in subsection (2) above as he or she would have if the rights conferred by the order referred to in paragraph (a) above were not affected by the termination of the tenancy.'

The Children Act 1989 (c. 41)

60   (1) In section 8(4) of the Children Act 1989 (meaning of 'family proceedings' for purposes of that Act), omit paragraphs (c) and (f) and after paragraph (g) insert—

'(h) the Family Law Act 1996.'

(2) In Schedule 11 to that Act, in paragraph 6(a) (amendment of the Domestic Proceedings and Magistrates' Courts Act 1978), for 'sections 16(5)(c) and' substitute 'section'.

The Courts and Legal Services Act 1990 (c. 41)

61   In section 58 of the Courts and Legal Services Act 1990 (conditional fee agreements) in subsection (10), omit paragraphs (b) and (e) and immediately before the 'or' following paragraph (g) insert—

'(gg) Part IV of the Family Law Act 1996'.

SCHEDULE 9

MODIFICATIONS, SAVING AND TRANSITIONAL

Section 66(2)

Transitional arrangements for those who have been living apart

1   (1) The Lord Chancellor may by order provide for the application of Part II to marital proceedings which—

(a)   are begun during the transitional period, and

(b)   relate to parties to a marriage who immediately before the beginning of that period were living apart,

subject to such modifications (which may include omissions) as may be prescribed.

(2) An order made under this paragraph may, in particular, make provision as to the evidence which a party who claims to have been living apart from the other party immediately before the beginning of the transitional period must produce to the court.

(3) In this paragraph—

'marital proceedings' has the same meaning as in section 24;

'prescribed' means prescribed by the order; and

'transitional period' means the period of two years beginning with the day on which section 3 is brought into force.

Modifications of enactments etc.

2   (1) The Lord Chancellor may by order make such consequential modifications of any enactment or subordinate legislation as appear to him necessary or expedient in consequence of Part II in respect of any reference (in whatever terms) to—

(a)   a petition;

(b)   the presentation of a petition;

(c)   the petitioner or respondent in proceedings on a petition;

(d)   proceedings on a petition;

(e)   proceedings in connection with any proceedings on a petition;

(f)   any other matrimonial proceedings;

(g)   a decree; or

(h)   findings of adultery in any proceedings.

(2) An order under sub-paragraph (1) may, in particular—

(a)   make provision applying generally in relation to enactments and subordinate legislation of a description specified in the order;

(b)   modify the effect of sub-paragraph (3) in relation to documents and agreements of a description so specified.

(3) Otherwise a reference (in whatever terms) in any instrument or agreement to the presentation of a petition or to a decree has effect, in relation to any time after the coming into force of this paragraph—

    (a)   in the case of a reference to the presentation of a petition, as if it included a reference to the making of a statement; and

    (b)   in the case of a reference to a decree, as if it included a reference to a divorce order or (as the case may be) a separation order.

3   If an Act or subordinate legislation—

    (a)   refers to an enactment repealed or amended by or under this Act, and

    (b)   was passed or made before the repeal or amendment came into force,

the Lord Chancellor may by order make such consequential modifications of any provision contained in the Act or subordinate legislation as appears to him necessary or expedient in respect of the reference.

Expressions used in paragraphs 2 and 3

4   In paragraphs 2 and 3—

    'decree' means a decree of divorce (whether a decree nisi or a decree which has been made absolute) or a decree of judicial separation;

    'instrument' includes any deed, will or other instrument or document

    'petition' means a petition for a decree of divorce or a petition for a decree of judicial separation; and

    'subordinate legislation' has the same meaning as in the Interpretation Act 1978.

Proceedings under way

5   (1) Except for paragraph 6 of this Schedule, nothing in any provision of Part II, Part I of Schedule 8 or Schedule 10—

    (a)   applies to, or affects—

        (i)   any decree granted before the coming into force of the provision;

        (ii)   any proceedings begun, by petition or otherwise, before that time; or

        (iii) any decree granted in any such proceedings;

    (b)   affects the operation of—

        (i)   the 1973 Act,

        (ii)   any other enactment, or

        (iii) any subordinate legislation,

        in relation to any such proceedings or decree or to any proceedings in connection with any such proceedings or decree; or

    (c)   without prejudice to paragraph (b), affects any transitional provision having effect under Schedule 1 to the 1973 Act.

(2) In this paragraph, 'subordinate legislation' has the same meaning as in the Interpretation Act 1978.

6   (1) Section 31 of the 1973 Act has effect as amended by this Act in relation to any order under Part II of the 1973 Act made after the coming into force of the amendments.

(2) Subsections (7) to (7F) of that section also have effect as amended by this Act in relation to any order made before the coming into force of the amendments.

Interpretation

7   In paragraphs 8 to 15 'the 1983 Act' means the Matrimonial Homes Act 1983.

Pending applications for orders relating to occupation and molestation

8   (1) In this paragraph and paragraph 10 'the existing enactments' means—

(a)   the Domestic Violence and Matrimonial Proceedings Act 1976;
(b)   sections 16 to 18 of the Domestic Proceedings and Magistrates' Courts Act 1978; and
(c)   sections 1 and 9 of the 1983 Act.

(2) Nothing in Part IV, Part III of Schedule 8 or Schedule 10 affects any application for an order or injunction under any of the existing enactments which is pending immediately before the commencement of the repeal of that enactment.

Pending applications under Schedule 1 to the Matrimonial Homes Act 1983

9   Nothing in Part IV, Part III of Schedule 8 or Schedule 10 affects any application for an order under Schedule 1 to the 1983 Act which is pending immediately before the commencement of the repeal of that Schedule.

Existing orders relating to occupation and molestation

10   (1) In this paragraph 'an existing order' means any order or injunction under any of the existing enactments which—

(a)   is in force immediately before the commencement of the repeal of that enactment; or
(b)   was made or granted after that commencement in proceedings brought before that commencement.

(2) Subject to sub-paragraphs (3) and (4), nothing in Part IV, Part III of Schedule 8 or Schedule 10—

(a)   prevents an existing order from remaining in force; or
(b)   affects the enforcement of an existing order.

(3) Nothing in Part IV, Part III of Schedule 8 or Schedule 10 affects any application to extend, vary or discharge an existing order, but the court may, if it thinks it just and reasonable to do so, treat the application as an application for an order under Part IV.

(4) The making of an order under Part IV between parties with respect to whom an existing order is in force discharges the existing order.

Matrimonial home rights

11   (1) Any reference (however expressed) in any enactment, instrument or document (whether passed or made before or after the passing of this Act) to rights of occupation under, or within the meaning of, the 1983 Act shall be construed, so far as is required for continuing the effect of the instrument or document, as being or as the case requires including a reference to matrimonial home rights under, or within the meaning of, Part IV.

(2) Any reference (however expressed) in this Act or in any other enactment, instrument or document (including any enactment amended by Schedule 8) to

matrimonial home rights under, or within the meaning of, Part IV shall be construed as including, in relation to times, circumstances and purposes before the commencement of sections 30 to 32, a reference to rights of occupation under, or within the meaning of, the 1983 Act.

12 (1) Any reference (however expressed) in any enactment, instrument or document (whether passed or made before or after the passing of this Act) to registration under section 2(8) of the 1983 Act shall, in relation to any time after the commencement of sections 30 to 32, be construed as being or as the case requires including a reference to registration under section 31(10).

(2) Any reference (however expressed) in this Act or in any other enactment, instrument or document (including any enactment amended by Schedule 8) to registration under section 31(10) shall be construed as including a reference to—

(a) registration under section 2(7) of the Matrimonial Homes Act 1967 or section 2(8) of the 1983 Act, and
(b) registration by caution duly lodged under section 2(7) of the Matrimonial Homes Act 1967 before 14th February 1983 (the date of the commencement of section 4(2) of the Matrimonial Homes and Property Act 1981).

13 In sections 30 and 31 and Schedule 4—

(a) any reference to an order made under section 33 shall be construed as including a reference to an order made under section 1 of the 1983 Act, and
(b) any reference to an order made under section 33(5) shall be construed as including a reference to an order made under section 1 of the 1983 Act by virtue of section 2(4) of that Act.

14 Neither section 31(11) nor the repeal by the Matrimonial Homes and Property Act 1981 of the words 'or caution' in section 2(7) of the Matrimonial Homes Act 1967, affects any caution duly lodged as respects any estate or interest before 14th February 1983.

15 Nothing in this Schedule is to be taken to prejudice the operation of sections 16 and 17 of the Interpretation Act 1978 (which relate to the effect of repeals).

SCHEDULE 10

REPEALS

Chapter	Short title	Extent of repeal
1968 c. 63.	The Domestic and Appellate Proceedings (Restriction of Publicity) Act 1968.	Section 2(1)(b).
1973 c. 18.	The Matrimonial Causes Act 1973.	Sections 1 to 7. In section 8(1)(b), the words 'or before the decree nisi is made absolute'. Sections 9 and 10.

Chapter	Short title	Extent of repeal
		Sections 17 and 18. Section 20. Section 22. In section 24A(3), the words 'divorce or'. In section 25(2)(h), the words 'in the case of proceedings for divorce or nullity of marriage,'. In section 28(1), the words from 'in', in the first place where it occurs, to 'nullity of marriage' in the first place where those words occur. In section 29(2), the words from 'may begin' to 'but'. In section 30, the words 'divorce' and 'or judicial separation'. In section 31, in subsection (2)(a), the words 'order for maintenance pending suit and any'. In section 41, in subsection (1) the words 'divorce or' and 'or a decree of judicial separation' and in subsection (2) the words 'divorce or' and 'or that the decree of judicial separation is not to be granted.' Section 49. In section 52(2)(b), the words 'to orders for maintenance pending suit and', 'respectively' and 'section 22 and'. In Schedule 1, paragraph 8.
1973 c. 45.	The Domicile and Matrimonial Proceedings Act 1973.	In section 5, in subsection (1), the words 'subject to section 6(3) and (4) of this Act' and, in paragraph (a), 'divorce, judicial separation or' and subsection (2). Section 6(3) and (4). In Schedule 1, in paragraph 11, in sub-paragraph (2)(a), in sub-paragraph (2)(c), in the first place where they occur, and in sub-paragraph (3)(b) and (c), the words 'in connection with the stayed proceedings'.

Chapter	Short title	Extent of repeal
1976 c. 50.	The Domestic Violence and Matrimonial Proceedings Act 1976.	The whole Act.
1978 c. 22.	The Domestic Proceedings and Magistrates' Courts Act 1978.	In section 1, paragraphs (c) and (d) and the word 'or' preceding paragraph (c). In section 7(1), the words 'neither party having deserted the other'. Sections 16 to 18. Section 28(2). Section 63(3). In Schedule 2, paragraphs 38 and 53.
1980 c. 43.	The Magistrates' Courts Act 1980.	In Schedule 7, paragraph 159.
1981 c. 54.	The Supreme Court Act 1981.	In section 18(1)(d), the words 'divorce or'.
1982 c. 53.	The Administration of Justice Act 1982.	Section 16.
1983 c. 19.	The Matrimonial Homes Act 1983.	The whole Act.
1984 c. 42.	The Matrimonial and Family Proceedings Act 1984.	Section 1. In section 21(f) the words 'except subsection (2)(e) and subsection (4)'. In section 27, the definition of 'secured periodical payments order'. In Schedule 1, paragraph 10.
1985 c. 61.	The Administration of Justice Act 1985.	In section 34(2), paragraph (f) and the word 'and' immediately preceding it. In Schedule 2, in paragraph 37, paragraph (e) and the word 'and' immediately preceding it.
1985 c. 71.	The Housing (Consequential Provisions) Act 1985.	In Schedule 2, paragraph 56.
1986 c. 53.	The Building Societies Act 1986.	In Schedule 21, paragraph 9(f).
1986 c. 55.	The Family Law Act 1986.	In Schedule 1, paragraph 27.
1988 c. 34.	The Legal Aid Act 1988.	In section 16(9), the word 'and' at the end of paragraph (a).

Chapter	Short title	Extent of repeal
1988 c. 50.	The Housing Act 1988.	In Schedule 17, paragraphs 33 and 34.
1989 c. 41.	The Children Act 1989.	Section 8(4)(c) and (f). In Schedule 11, paragraph 6(b). In Schedule 13, paragraphs 33(1) and 65(1).
1990 c. 41.	The Courts and Legal Services Act 1990.	Section 58(10)(b) and (e). In Schedule 18, paragraph 21.
1995 c. 42.	The Private International Law (Miscellaneous Provisions) Act 1995.	In the Schedule, paragraph 3.

APPENDIX TWO

Matrimonial Causes Act 1973
(1973 c. 18)

NOTE: The text of the Act is set out as it would appear if all amendments made by the Family Law Act 1996 were in force. With this exception, only provisions in force on 1 September 1996 have been taken into account. Italics have been used to highlight text inserted or substituted by the new Act and dots have been used to denote sections or words which have been repealed.

ARRANGEMENT OF SECTIONS

PART I
DIVORCE, NULLITY AND OTHER MATRIMONIAL SUITS

PART II
FINANCIAL RELIEF FOR PARTIES TO MARRIAGE AND CHILDREN OF FAMILY

An Act to consolidate certain enactments relating to matrimonial proceedings, maintenance agreements, and declarations of legitimacy, validity of marriage and British nationality, with amendments to give effect to recommendations of the Law Commission.

[23 May 1973]

PART I
DIVORCE, NULLITY AND OTHER MATRIMONIAL SUITS
Divorce

1 Divorce on breakdown of marriage

[...]

2 Supplemental provisions as to facts raising presumption of breakdown

[...]

3 Bar on petitions for divorce within one year of marriage

[...]

4 Divorce not precluded by previous judicial separation

[...]

5 Refusal of decree in five year separation cases on grounds of grave hardship to respondent

[...]

6 Attempts at reconciliation of parties to marriage

[...]

7 Consideration by the court of certain agreements or arrangements

[...]

8 Intervention of Queen's Proctor

(1) In the case of *proceedings for a divorce order*—

   (a) the court may, if it thinks fit, direct all necessary papers in the matter to be sent to the Queen's Proctor, who shall under the directions of the Attorney-General instruct counsel to argue before the court any question in relation to the matter which the court considers it necessary or expedient to have fully argued;

   (b) any person may at any time during the progress of the proceedings [...] give information to the Queen's Proctor on any matter material to the due decision of the case, and the Queen's Proctor may thereupon take such steps as the Attorney-General considers necessary or expedient.

(2) Where the Queen's Proctor interviews or shows cause against *the making of a divorce order*, the court may make such order as may be just as to the payment by other parties to the proceedings of the costs incurred by him in so doing or as to the payment by him of any costs incurred by any of those parties by reason of his so doing.

(3) The Queen's Proctor shall be entitled to charge as part of the expenses of his office—

   (a) the costs of any proceedings under subsection (1)(a) above;

(b) where his reasonable costs of intervening or showing cause as mentioned in subsection (2) above are not fully satisfied by any order under that subsection, the amount of the difference;

(c) if the Treasury so directs, any costs which he pays to any parties under an order made under subsection (2).

9 Proceedings after decree nisi: general powers of court

[...]

10 Proceedings after decree nisi: special protection for respondent in separation cases

[...]

Nullity

11 Grounds on which a marriage is void

A marriage celebrated after 31st July 1971 shall be void on the following grounds only, that is to say—

(a) that it is not a valid marriage under the provisions of the Marriage Acts 1949 to 1986 (that is to say where—
  (i) the parties are within the prohibited degrees of relationship;
  (ii) either party is under the age of sixteen; or
  (iii) the parties have intermarried in disregard of certain requirements as to the formation of marriage);

(b) that at the time of the marriage either party was already lawfully married;

(c) that the parties are not respectively male and female;

(d) in the case of a polygamous marriage entered into outside England and Wales, that either party was at the time of the marriage domiciled in England and Wales.

For the purposes of paragraph (d) of this subsection a marriage is not polygamous if at its inception neither party has any spouse additional to the other.

12 Grounds on which a marriage is voidable

A marriage celebrated after 31st July 1971 shall be voidable on the following grounds only, that is to say—

(a) that the marriage has not been consummated owing to the incapacity of either party to consummate it;

(b) that the marriage has not been consummated owing to the wilful refusal of the respondent to consummate it;

(c) that either party to the marriage did not validly consent to it, whether in consequence of duress, mistake, unsoundness of mind or otherwise;

(d) that at the time of the marriage either party, though capable of giving a valid consent, was suffering (whether continuously or intermittently) from mental disorder within the meaning of the Mental Health Act 1983 of such a kind or to such an extent as to be unfitted for marriage;

(e) that at the time of the marriage the respondent was suffering from venereal disease in a communicable form;

(f) that at the time of the marriage the respondent was pregnant by some person other than the petitioner.

13 Bars to relief where marriage is voidable

(1) The court shall not, in proceedings instituted after 31st July 1971, grant a decree of nullity on the ground that a marriage is voidable if the respondent satisfies the court—

(a) that the petitioner, with knowledge that it was open to him to have the marriage avoided, so conducted himself in relation to the respondent as to lead the respondent reasonably to believe that he would not seek to do so; and

(b) that it would be unjust to the respondent to grant the decree.

(2) Without prejudice to subsection (1) above, the court shall not grant a decree of nullity by virtue of section 12 above on the grounds mentioned in paragraph (c), (d), (e) or (f) of that section unless—

(a) it is satisfied that proceedings were instituted within the period of three years from the date of the marriage, or

(b) leave for the institution of proceedings after the expiration of that period has been granted under subsection (4) below.

(3) Without prejudice to subsections (1) and (2) above, the court shall not grant a degree of nullity by virtue of section 12 above on the grounds mentioned in paragraph (e) or (f) of that section unless it is satisfied that the petitioner was at the time of the marriage ignorant of the facts alleged.

(4) In the case of proceedings for the grant of a decree of nullity by virtue of section 12 above on the grounds mentioned in paragraph (c), (d), (e) or (f) of that section, a judge of the court may, on an application made to him, grant leave for the institution of proceedings after the expiration of the period of three years from the date of the marriage if—

(a) he is satisfied that the petitioner has at some time during that period suffered from mental disorder within the meaning of the Mental Health Act 1983, and

(b) he considers that in all the circumstances of the case it would be just to grant leave for the institution of proceedings.

(5) An application for leave under subsection (4) above may be made after the expiration of the period of three years from the date of the marriage.

14 Marriages governed by foreign law or celebrated abroad under English law

(1) Where, apart from this Act, any matter affecting the validity of a marriage would fall to be determined (in accordance with the rules of private international law) by reference to the law of a country outside England and Wales, nothing in section 11, 12 or 13(1) above shall—

(a) preclude the determination of that matter as aforesaid; or

(b) require the application to the marriage of the grounds or bar there mentioned except so far as applicable in accordance with those rules.

(2) In the case of a marriage which purports to have been celebrated under the Foreign Marriage Acts 1892 to 1947 or has taken place outside England and Wales and purports to be a marriage under common law, section 11 above is without prejudice to

any ground on which the marriage may be void under those Acts or, as the case may be, by virtue of the rules governing the celebration of marriages outside England and Wales under common law.

15 Decrees of nullity to be decrees nisi

Every decree of nullity of marriage shall in the first instance be a decree nisi and shall not be made absolute before the end of six weeks from its grant unless—

(a)   the High Court by general order from time to time fixes a shorter period; or

(b)   in any particular case, the court in which the proceedings are for the time being pending from time to time by special order fixes a shorter period than the period otherwise applicable for the time being by virtue of this section.

15A Intervention of Queen's Proctor

(1) In the case of a petition for nullity of marriage—

(a)   the court may, if it thinks fit, direct all necessary papers in the matter to be sent to the Queen's Proctor, who shall under the directions of the Attorney-General instruct counsel to argue before the court any question in relation to the matter which the court considers it necessary or expedient to have fully argued;

(b)   any person may at any time during the progress of the proceedings or before the decree nisi is made absolute give information to the Queen's Proctor on any matter material to the due decision of the case, and the Queen's Proctor may thereupon take such steps as the Attorney-General considers necessary or expedient.

(2) If the Queen's Proctor intervenes or shows cause against a decree nisi in any proceedings for nullity of marriage, the court may make such order as may be just as to the payment by other parties to the proceedings of the costs incurred by him in so doing or as to the payment by him of any costs incurred by any of those parties by reason of him so doing.

(3) Subsection (3) of section 8 above applies in relation to this section as it applies in relation to that section.

15B Proceedings after decree nisi: general powers of the court

(1) Where a decree of nullity of marriage has been granted under this Act but not made absolute, then, without prejudice to section 15A above, any person (excluding a party to the proceedings other than the Queen's Proctor) may show cause why the decree should not be made absolute by reason of material facts not having been brought before the court; and in such a case the court may—

(a)   notwithstanding anything in section 15 above (but subject to section 41 below) make the decree absolute; or

(b)   rescind the decree; or

(c)   require further inquiry; or

(d)   otherwise deal with the case as it thinks fit.

(2) Where a decree of nullity of marriage has been granted under this Act and no application for it to be made absolute has been made by the party to whom it was granted, then, at any time after the expiration of three months from the earliest date on which that party could have made such an application, the party against whom it was granted may make an application to the court, and on that application the court may exercise any of the powers mentioned in paragraphs (a) to (d) of subsection (1) above.

16 Effect of decree of nullity in case of voidable marriage

A decree of nullity granted after 31st July 1971 in respect of a voidable marriage shall operate to annul the marriage only as respects any time after the decree has been made absolute, and the marriage shall, notwithstanding the decree, be treated as if it had existed up to that time.

Other matrimonial suits

17 Judicial separation

[. . .]

18 Effects of judicial separation

[. . .]

19 Presumption of death and dissolution of marriage

(1) Any married person who alleges that reasonable grounds exist for supposing that the other party to the marriage is dead may present a petition to the court to have it presumed that the other party is dead and to have the marriage dissolved, and the court may, if satisfied that such reasonable grounds exist, grant a degree of presumption of death and dissolution of the marriage.

(2) (*previously repealed*)

(3) In any proceedings under this section the fact that for a period of seven years or more the other party to the marriage has been continually absent from the petitioner and the petitioner has no reason to believe that the other party has been living within that time shall be evidence that the other party is dead until the contrary is proved.

(4) Sections *15, 15A and 15B* above shall apply to a petition and a decree under this section as they apply to a petition for *nullity of marriage* and a decree of *nullity of marriage* respectively.

(5) (*previously repealed*)

(6) It is hereby declared that neither collusion nor any other conduct on the part of the petitioner which has at any time been a bar to relief in matrimonial proceedings constitutes a bar to the grant of a decree under this section.

General

20 Relief for respondent in divorce proceedings

[. . .]

PART II
FINANCIAL RELIEF FOR PARTIES TO MARRIAGE AND CHILDREN OF FAMILY

21 Financial provision and property adjustment orders

(1) For the purposes of this Act, a financial provision order is—

    (a)   an order that a party must make in favour of another person such periodical payments, for such term, as may be specified (a 'periodical payments order');

(b)   *an order that a party must, to the satisfaction of the court, secure in favour of another person such periodical payments, for such term, as may be specified (a 'secured periodical payments order');*

(c)   *an order that a party must make a payment in favour of another person of such lump sum or sums as may be specified (an 'order for the payment of a lump sum').*

(2) For the purposes of this Act, a property adjustment order is—

(a)   *an order that a party must transfer such of his or her property as may be specified in favour of the other party or a child of the family;*

(b)   *an order that a settlement of such property of a party as may be specified must be made, to the satisfaction of the court, for the benefit of the other party and of the children of the family, or either or any of them;*

(c)   *an order varying, for the benefit of the parties and of the children of the family, or either or any of them, any marriage settlement;*

(d)   *an order extinguishing or reducing the interest of either of the parties under any marriage settlement.*

(3) Subject to section 40 below, where an order of the court under this Part of this Act requires a party to make or secure a payment in favour of another person or to transfer property in favour of any person, that payment must be made or secured or that property transferred—

(a)   *if that other person is the other party to the marriage, to that other party; and*

(b)   *if that other person is a child of the family, according to the terms of the order—*

    (i)   *to the child; or*

    (ii)   *to such other person as may be specified, for the benefit of that child.*

(4) References in this section to the property of a party are references to any property to which that party is entitled either in possession or in reversion.

(5) Any power of the court under this Part of this Act to make such an order as is mentioned in subsection (2)(b) to (d) above is exercisable even though there are no children of the family.

(6) In this section—

'marriage settlement' means an ante-nuptial or post-nuptial settlement made on the parties (including one made by will or codicil);
'party' means a party to a marriage; and
'specified' means specified in the order in question.

Ancillary relief in connection with divorce proceedings etc

22 Maintenance pending suit

[…]

22A Financial provision orders: divorce and separation

(1) On an application made under this section, the court may at the appropriate time make one or more financial provision orders in favour of—

(a)   *a party to the marriage to which the application relates; or*

(b)   *any of the children of the family.*

(2) The 'appropriate time' is any time—

- (a) after a statement of marital breakdown has been received by the court and before any application for a divorce order or for a separation order is made to the court by reference to that statement;
- (b) when an application for a divorce order or separation order has been made under section 3 of the 1996 Act and has not been withdrawn;
- (c) when an application for a divorce order has been made under section 4 of the 1996 Act and has not been withdrawn;
- (d) after a divorce order has been made;
- (e) when a separation order is in force.

(3) The court may make—

- (a) a combined order against the parties on one occasion,
- (b) separate orders on different occasions,
- (c) different orders in favour of different children,
- (d) different orders from time to time in favour of the same child,

but may not make, in favour of the same party, more than one periodical payments order, or more than one order for payment of a lump sum, in relation to any marital proceedings, whether in the course of the proceedings or by reference to a divorce order or separation order made in the proceedings.

(4) If it would not otherwise be in a position to make a financial provision order in favour of a party or child of the family, the court may make an interim periodical payments order, an interim order for the payment of a lump sum or a series of such orders, in favour of that party or child.

(5) Any order for the payment of a lump sum made under this section may—

- (a) provide for the payment of the lump sum by instalments of such amounts as may be specified in the order; and
- (b) require the payment of the instalments to be secured to the satisfaction of the court.

(6) Nothing in subsection (5) above affects—

- (a) the power of the court under this section to make an order for the payment of a lump sum; or
- (b) the provisions of this Part of this Act as to the beginning of the term specified in any periodical payments order or secured periodical payments order.

(7) Subsection (8) below applies where the court—

- (a) makes an order under this section ('the main order') for the payment of a lump sum; and
- (b) directs—
  - (i) that payment of that sum, or any part of it, is to be deferred; or
  - (ii) that that sum, or any part of it, is to be paid by instalments.

(8) In such a case, the court may, on or at any time after making the main order, make an order ('the order for interest') for the amount deferred, or the instalments, to carry interest (at such rate as may be specified in the order for interest)—

- (a) from such date, not earlier than the date of the main order, as may be so specified;
- (b) until the date when the payment is due.

(9) This section is to be read subject to any restrictions imposed by this Act and to section 19 of the 1996 Act.

22B Restrictions affecting section 22A

(1) No financial provision order, other than an interim order, may be made under section 22A above so as to take effect before the making of a divorce order or separation order in relation to the marriage, unless the court is satisfied—

    (a)   that the circumstances of the case are exceptional; and

    (b)   that it would be just and reasonable for the order to be so made.

(2) Except in the case of an interim periodical payments order, the court may not make a financial provision order under section 22A above at any time while the period for reflection and consideration is interrupted under section 7(8) of the 1996 Act.

(3) No financial provision order may be made under section 22A above by reference to the making of a statement of marital breakdown if, by virtue of section 5(3) or 7(9) of the 1996 Act (lapse of divorce or separation process), it has ceased to be possible—

    (a)   for an application to be made by reference to that statement; or

    (b)   for an order to be made on such an application.

(4) No financial provision order may be made under section 22A after a divorce order has been made, or while a separation order is in force, except—

    (a)   in response to an application made before the divorce order or separation order was made; or

    (b)   on a subsequent application made with the leave of the court.

(5) In this section, 'period for reflection and consideration' means the period fixed by section 7 of the 1996 Act.

23 Financial provision orders: nullity

(1) On or after granting a decree of nullity of marriage (whether before or after the decree is made absolute), the court may, on an application made under this section, make one or more financial provision orders in favour of—

    (a)   either party to the marriage; or

    (b)   any child of the family.

(2) Before granting a decree in any proceedings for nullity of marriage, the court may make against either or each of the parties to the marriage—

    (a)   an interim periodical payments order, an interim order for the payment of a lump sum, or a series of such orders, in favour of the other party;

    (b)   an interim periodical payments order, an interim order for the payment of a lump sum, a series of such orders or any one or more other financial provision orders in favour of each child of the family.

(3) Where any such proceedings are dismissed, the court may (either immediately or within a reasonable period after the dismissal) make any one or more financial provision orders in favour of each child of the family.

(4) An order under this section that a party to a marriage must pay a lump sum to the other party may be made for the purpose of enabling that other party to meet any liabilities or

expenses reasonably incurred by him or her in maintaining himself or herself or any child of the family before making an application for an order under this section in his or her favour.

(5) An order under this section for the payment of a lump sum to or for the benefit of a child of the family may be made for the purposes of enabling any liabilities or expenses reasonably incurred by or for the benefit of that child before the making of an application for an order under this section in his favour to be met.

(6) An order under this section for the payment of a lump sum may—

- (a)   *provide for the payment of that sum by instalments of such amount as may be specified in the order; and*
- (b)   *require the payment of the instalments to be secured to the satisfaction of the court.*

(7) Nothing in subsections (4) to (6) above affects—

- (a)   *the power under subsection (1) above to make an order for the payment of a lump sum; or*
- (b)   *the provision of this Act as to the beginning of the term specified in any periodical payments order or secured periodical payments order.*

(8) The powers of the court under this section to make one or more financial provision orders are exercisable against each party to the marriage by the making of—

- (a)   *a combined order on one occasion, or*
- (b)   *separate orders on different occasions,*

but the court may not make more than one periodical payments order, or more than one order for payment of a lump sum, in favour of the same party.

(9) The powers of the court under this section so far as they consist in power to make one or more orders in favour of the children of the family—

- (a)   *may be exercised differently in favour of different children; and*
- (b)   *except in the case of the power conferred by subsection (3) above, may be exercised from time to time in favour of the same child; and*
- (c)   *in the case of the power conferred by that subsection, if it is exercised by the making of a financial provision order of any kind in favour of a child, shall include power to make, from time to time, further financial provision orders of that or any other kind in favour of that child.*

(10) Where an order is made under subsection (1) above in favour of a party to the marriage on or after the granting of a decree of nullity of marriage, neither the order nor any settlement made in pursuance of the order takes effect unless the decree has been made absolute.

(11) Subsection (10) above does not affect the power to give a direction under section 30 below for the settlement of an instrument by conveying counsel.

(12) Where the court—

- (a)   *makes an order under this section ('the main order') for the payment of a lump sum; and*
- (b)   *directs—*
  - (i)   *that payment of that sum or any part of it is to be deferred; or*
  - (ii)   *that that sum or any part of it is to be paid by instalments,*

it may, on or at any time after making the main order, make an order ('the order for interest') for the amount deferred or the instalments to carry interest at such rate as may be specified by the order for interest from such date, not earlier than the date of the main order, as may be so specified, until the date when payment of it is due.

(13) This section is to be read subject to any restrictions imposed by this Act.

23A Property adjustment orders: divorce and separation

(1) On an application made under this section, the court may, at any time mentioned in section 22A(2) above, make one or more property adjustment orders.

(2) If the court makes, in favour of the same party to the marriage, more than one property adjustment order in relation to any marital proceedings, whether in the course of the proceedings or by reference to a divorce order or separation order made in the proceedings, each order must fall within a different paragraph of section 21(2) above.

(3) The court shall exercise its powers under this section, so far as is practicable, by making on one occasion all such provision as can be made by way of one or more property adjustment orders in relation to the marriage as it thinks fit.

(4) Subsection (3) above does not affect section 31 or 31A below.

(5) This section is to be read subject to any restrictions imposed by this Act and to section 19 of the 1996 Act.

23B Restrictions affecting section 23A

(1) No property adjustment order may be made under section 23A above so as to take effect before the making of a divorce order or separation order in relation to the marriage unless the court is satisfied—

   (a)   that the circumstances of the case are exceptional; and
   (b)   that it would be just and reasonable for the order to be so made.

(2) The court may not make a property adjustment order under section 23A above at any time while the period for reflection and consideration is interrupted under section 7(8) of the 1996 Act.

(3) No property adjustment order may be made under section 23A above by virtue of the making of a statement of marital breakdown if, by virtue of section 5(3) or 7(5) of the 1996 Act (lapse of divorce or separation process), it has ceased to be possible—

   (a)   for an application to be made by reference to that statement; or
   (b)   for an order to be made on such an application.

(4) No property adjustment order may be made under section 23A above after a divorce order has been made, or while a separation order is in force, except—

   (a)   in response to an application made before the divorce order or separation order was made; or
   (b)   on a subsequent application made with the leave of the court.

(5) In this section, 'period for reflection and consideration' means the period fixed by section 7 of the 1996 Act.

24 Property adjustment orders: nullity of marriage

(1) On or after granting a decree of nullity of marriage (whether before or after the decree is made absolute), the court may, on an application made under this section, make one or more property adjustment orders in relation to the marriage.

(2) The court shall exercise its powers under this section, so far as is practicable, by making on one occasion all such provision as can be made by way of one or more property adjustment orders in relation to the marriage as it thinks fit.

(3) Subsection (2) above does not affect section 31 or 31A below.

(4) Where a property adjustment order is made under this section on or after the granting of a decree of nullity of marriage, neither the order nor any settlement made in pursuance of the order is to take effect unless the decree has been made absolute.

(5) That does not affect the power to give a direction under section 30 below for the settlement of an instrument by conveyancing counsel.

(6) This section is to be read subject to any restrictions imposed by this Act.

24A Orders for sale of property

(1) Where the court makes under *any of sections 22A to 24 above a* secured periodical payments order, an order for the payment of a lump sum or a property adjustment order, then, on making that order or at any time thereafter, the court may make a further order for the sale of such property as may be specified in the order, being property in which or in the proceeds of sale of which either or both of the parties to the marriage has or have a beneficial interest, either in possession or reversion.

(2) Any order made under subsection (1) above may contain such consequential or supplementary provisions as the court thinks fit and without prejudice to the generality of the foregoing provision, may include—

(a) provision requiring the making of a payment out of the proceeds of sale of the property to which the order relates, and

(b) provision requiring any such property to be offered for sale to a person, or class of persons, specified in the order.

(3) Where an order is made under subsection (1) above on or after the grant of a decree of [...] nullity of marriage, the order shall not take effect unless the decree has been made absolute.

(4) Where an order is made under subsection (1) above, the court may direct that the order, or such provision thereof as the court may specify, shall not take effect until the occurrence of an event specified by the court or the expiration of a period so specified.

(5) Where an order under subsection (1) above contains a provision requiring the proceeds of sale of the property to which the order relates to be used to secure periodical payments to a party to the marriage, the order shall cease to have effect on the death or re-marriage of that person.

(6) Where a party to marriage has a beneficial interest in any property, or in the proceeds of sale thereof, and some other person who is not a party to the marriage also has a beneficial interest in that property or in the proceeds of sale thereof, then, before

deciding whether to make an order under this section in relation to that property, it shall be the duty of the court to give that other person an opportunity to make representations with respect to the order; and any representations made by that other person shall be included among the circumstances to which the court is required to have regard under section 25(1) below.

25 Matters to which court is to have regard in deciding how to exercise its powers under ss 23, 24 and 24A

(1) It shall be the duty of the court in deciding whether to exercise its powers under *any of sections 22A to 24A* above and, if so, in what manner, to have regard to all the circumstances of the case, first consideration being given to the welfare while a minor of any child of the family who has not attained the age of eighteen.

(2) As regards the exercise of the powers of the court under *section 22A or 23 above to make a financial provision order in favour of a party to a marriage or the exercise of its powers under section 23A*, 24 or 24A above in relation to a party to the marriage, the court shall in particular have regard to the following matters—

(a) the income, earning capacity, property and other financial resources which each of the parties to the marriage has or is likely to have in the foreseeable future, including in the case of earning capacity any increase in that capacity which it would in the opinion of the court be reasonable to expect a party to the marriage to take steps to acquire;

(b) the financial needs, obligations and responsibilities which each of the parties to the marriage has or is likely to have in the foreseeable future;

(c) the standard of living enjoyed by the family before the breakdown of the marriage;

(d) the age of each party to the marriage and the duration of the marriage;

(e) any physical or mental disability of either of the parties to the marriage;

(f) the contributions which each of the parties has made or is likely in the foreseeable future to make to the welfare of the family, including any contribution by looking after the home or caring for the family;

(g) the conduct of each of the parties, *whatever the nature of the conduct and whether it occurred during the marriage or after the separation of the parties or (as the case may be) dissolution or annulment of the marriage*, if that conduct is such that it would in the opinion of the court be inequitable to disregard it;

(h) […] the value to each of the parties to the marriage of any benefit […] which, by reason of the dissolution or annulment of the marriage, that party will lose the chance of acquiring.

(3) As regards the exercise of the powers of the court under *section 22A or 23 above to make a financial provision order in favour of a child of the family or the exercise of its powers under section 23A*, 24 or 24A above in relation to a child of the family, the court shall in particular have regard to the following matters—

(a) the financial needs of the child;

(b) the income, earning capacity (if any), property and other financial resources of the child;

(c) any physical or mental disability of the child;

(d) the manner in which he was being and in which the parties to the marriage expected him to be educated or trained;

(e)   the considerations mentioned in relation to the parties to the marriage in paragraphs (a), (b), (c) and (e) of subsection (2) above.

(4) As regards the exercise of the powers of the court under *any of sections 22A to 24A* above against a party to a marriage in favour of a child of the family who is not the child of that party, the court shall also have regard—

(a)   to whether that party assumed any responsibility for the child's maintenance, and, if so, to the extent to which, and the basis upon which, that party assumed such responsibility and to the length of time for which that party discharged such responsibility;

(b)   to whether in assuming and discharging such responsibility that party did so knowing that the child was not his or her own;

(c)   to the liability of any other person to maintain the child.

(5) In relation to any power of the court to make an interim periodical payments order or an interim order for the payment of a lump sum, the preceding provisions of this section, in imposing any obligation on the court with respect to the matters to which it is to have regard, shall not require the court to do anything which would cause such a delay as would, in the opinion of the court, be inappropriate having regard—

(a)   *to any immediate need for an interim order;*

(b)   *to the matters in relation to which it is practicable for the court to inquire before making an interim order; and*

(c)   *to the ability of the court to have regard to any matter and to make appropriate adjustments when subsequently making a financial provision order which is not interim.*

25A Exercise of court's powers in favour of party to marriage on decree of divorce or nullity of marriage

(1) *If the court decides to exercise any of its powers under any of sections 22A to 24A above in favour of a party to a marriage (other than its power to make an interim periodical payments order or an interim order for the payment of a lump sum)*, it shall be the duty of the court to consider whether it would be appropriate so to exercise those powers that the financial obligations of each party towards the other will be terminated as soon after the grant of a *divorce order or decree of nullity* as the court considers just and reasonable.

(2) Where the court decides in such a case to make a periodical payments or secured periodical payments order in favour of a party to the marriage, the court shall in particular consider whether it would be appropriate to require those payments to be made or secured only for such term as would in the opinion of the court be sufficient to enable the party in whose favour the order is made to adjust without undue hardship to the termination of his or her financial dependence on the other party.

(3) If the court—

(a)   *would have power under section 22A or 23 above to make a financial provision order in favour of a party to a marriage ('the first party'),but*

(b)   *considers that no continuing obligation should be imposed on the other party to the marriage ('the second party') to make or secure periodical payments in favour of the first party,*

it may direct that the first party may not at any time after the direction takes effect, apply to the court for the making against the second party of any periodical payments order or secured periodical payments order and, if the first party has already applied to the court for the making of such an order, it may dismiss the application.

(3A) If the court—

    (a) exercises, or has exercised, its power under section 22A at any time before making a divorce order, and

    (b) gives a direction under subsection (3) above in respect of a periodical payments order or a secured periodical payments order,

it shall provide for the direction not to take effect until a divorce order is made.

25B Pensions

(1) The matters to which the court is to have regard under section 25(2) above include—

    (a) in the case of paragraph (a), any benefits under a pension scheme which a party to the marriage has or is likely to have, and

    (b) in the case of paragraph (h), any benefits under a pension scheme which, by reason of the dissolution or annulment of the mariage, a party to the marriage will lose the chance of acquiring,

and, accordingly, in relation to benefits under a pension scheme, section 25(2)(a) above shall have effect as if 'in the foreseeable future' were omitted.

(2) In any proceedings for a financial provision order under *section 22A or 23* above in a case where a party to the marriage has, or is likely to have, any benefit under a pension scheme, the court shall, in addition to considering any other matter which it is required to consider apart from this subsection, consider—

    (a) whether, having regard to any matter to which it is required to have regard in the proceedings by virtue of subsection (1) above, such an order (whether deferred or not) should be made, and

    (b) where the court determines to make such an order, how the terms of the order should be affected, having regard to any such matter.

    (c) in particular, where the court determines to make such an order, whether the order should provide for the accrued rights of the party with pension rights ('the pension rights') to be divided between that party and the other party in such a way as to reduce the pension rights to the party with those rights and to create pension rights for the other party.

(3) The following provisions apply where, having regard to any benefits under a pension scheme, the court determines to make an order under *section 22A or 23* above.

(4) To the extent to which the order is made having regard to any benefits under a pension scheme, the order may require the trustees or managers of the pension scheme in question, if at any time any payment in respect of any benefits under the scheme becomes due to the party with pension rights, to make a payment for the benefit of the other party.

(5) The amount of any payment which, by virtue of subsection (4) above, the trustees or managers are required to make under the order at any time shall not exceed the amount of the payment which is due at that time to the party with pension rights.

(6) Any such payment by the trustees or managers—

(a)   shall discharge so much of the trustees' or managers' liability to the party with pension rights as corresponds to the amount of the payment, and

(b)   shall be treated for all purposes as a payment made by the party with pension rights in or towards the discharge of his liability under the order.

(7) Where the party with pension rights may require any benefits which he has or is likely to have under the scheme to be commuted, the order may require him to commute the whole or part of those benefits; and this section applies to the payment of any amount commuted in pursuance of the order as it applies to other payments in respect of benefits under the scheme.

(8) If a pensions adjustment order under subsection (2)(c) above is made, the pension rights shall be reduced and pension rights of the other party shall be created in the prescribed manner with benefits payable on prescribed conditions, except that the court shall not have the power—

(a)   *to require the trustees or managers of the scheme to provide benefits under their own scheme if they are able and willing to create the rights for the other party by making a transfer payment to another scheme and the trustees and managers of that other scheme are able and willing to accept such a payment and to create those rights; or*

(b)   *to require the trustees or managers of the scheme to make a transfer to another scheme—*

   (i)   *if the scheme is an unfunded scheme (unless the trustees or managers are able and willing to make such a transfer payment); or*

   (ii)   *in prescribed circumstances.*

(9) No pensions adjustment order may be made under subsection (2)(c) above—

(a)   *if the scheme is a scheme of a prescribed type, or*

(b)   *in prescribed circumstances, or*

(c)   *insofar as it would affect benefits of a prescribed type.*

25C Pensions: lump sums

(1) The power of the court under *section 22A or 23* above to order a party to a marriage to pay a lump sum to the other party includes, where the benefits which the party with pension rights has or is likely to have under a pension scheme include any lump sum payable in respect of his death, power to make any of the following provision by the order.

(2) The court may—

(a)   if the trustees or managers of the pension scheme in question have power to determine the person to whom the sum, or any part of it, is to be paid, require them to pay the whole or part of that sum, when it becomes due, to the other party,

(b)   if the party with pension rights has power to nominate the person to whom the sum, or any part of it, is to be paid, require the party with pension rights to nominate the other party in respect of the whole or part of that sum,

(c)   in any other case, require the trustees or managers of the pension scheme in question to pay the whole or part of that sum, when it becomes due, for the benefit of the other party instead of to the person to whom, apart from the order, it would be paid.

(3) Any payment by the trustees or managers under an order made under *section 22A or 23* above by virtue of this section shall discharge so much of the trustees, or managers, liability in respect of the party with pension rights as corresponds to the amount of the payment.

25D Pensions: supplementary

(1) Where—

(a)   an order made under *section 22A or 23* above by virtue of section 25B or 25C above imposes any requirement on the trustees or managers of a pension scheme ('the first scheme') and the party with pension rights acquires transfer credits under another pension scheme ('the new scheme') which are derived (directly or indirectly) from a transfer from the first scheme of all his accrued rights under that scheme (including transfer credits allowed by that scheme), and

(b)   the trustees or managers of the new scheme have been given notice in accordance with regulations,

the order shall have effect as if it has been made instead in respect of the trustees or managers of the new scheme; and in this subsection 'transfer credits' has the same meaning as in the Pension Schemes Act 1993.

(2) Regulations may—

(a)   in relation to any provision of sections 25B or 25C above which authorises the court making an order under *section 22A or 23* above to require the trustees or managers of a pension scheme to make a payment for the benefit of the other party, make provision as to the person to whom, and the terms on which, the payment is to be made *or prescribe the rights of the other party under the pension scheme,*

(aa) *make such consequential modifications of any enactment or subordinate legislation as appear to the Lord Chancellor necessary or expedient to give effect to the provisions of section 25B; and an order under this paragraph may make provision applying generally in relation to enactments and subordinate legislation of a description specified in the order,*

(b)   require notices to be given in respect of changes of circumstances relevant to such orders which include provision made by virtue of section 25B and 25C above,

(c)   make provision for the trustees or managers of any pension scheme to provide, for the purposes of orders under *section 22A or 23* above, information as to the value of any benefits under the scheme,

(d)   make provision for the recovery of the administrative expenses of—

(i)   complying with such orders, so far as they include provision made by virtue of sections 25B or 25C above, and

(ii)   providing such information,

from the party with pension rights or the other party,

(e)   make provision for the value of any benefits under a pension scheme to be calculated and verified, for the purposes of orders under *section 22A or 23* above, in a prescribed manner, and regulations made by virtue of paragraph (e) above may provide for that value to be calculated and verified in accordance with guidance which is prepared and from time to time revised by a prescribed person and approved by the Secretary of State.

(3) In this section and sections 25B and 25C above—

 (a) references to a pension scheme include—
  (i) a retirement annuity contract, or
  (ii) an annuity, or insurance policy, purchased or transferred for the purpose of giving effect to rights under a pension scheme,
 (b) in relation to such a contract or annuity, references to the trustees or managers shall be read as references to the provider of the annuity,
 (c) in relation to such a policy, references to the trustees or managers shall be read as references to the insurer,

and in section 25B(1) and (2) above, references to benefits under a pension scheme include any benefits by way of pension, whether under a pension scheme or not.

(4) In this section and sections 25B and 25C above—

'the party with pension rights' means the party to the marriage who has or is likely to have benefits under a pension scheme and 'the other party' means the other party to the marriage.

'funded scheme' means a scheme under which the benefits are provided for by setting aside resources related to the value of the members' rights as they accrue (and 'unfunded scheme' shall be construed accordingly);

'pension scheme' means an occupational pension scheme or a personal pension scheme (applying the definitions in section 1 of the Pension Schemes Act 1993,. but as if the reference to employed earners in the definition of 'personal pension scheme' were to any earners),

'prescribed' means prescribed by regulations, and

'regulations' means regulations made by the Lord Chancellor;

'subordinate legislation' has the same meaning as in the Interpretation Act 1978;

and the power to make regulations under this section shall be exercisable by statutory instrument, which shall be subject to annulment in pursuance of a resolution of either House of Parliament.

(4A) Other expressions used in section 25B above shall be construed in accordance with section 124 (interpretation of Part I) of the Pensions Act 1995.

26 Commencement of proceedings for ancillary relief etc

(1) *If a petition for nullity of marriage has been presented, then, subject to subsection (2) below, proceedings* for a financial provision order under section 23 above, or for a property adjustment order may be begun, subject to and in accordance with rules of court, at anytime after the presentation of the petition.

(2) Rules of court may provide, in such cases as may be prescribed by the rules—

 (a) that applications for any such relief as is mentioned in subsection (1) above shall be made in the petition or answer; and

(b) that applications for any such relief which are not so made, or are not made until after the expiration of such period following the presentation of the petition or filing of the answer as may be so prescribed, shall be made only with the leave of the court.

Financial provision in case of neglect to maintain

27 Financial provision orders, etc, in case of neglect by party to marriage to maintain other party or child of the family

(1) Either party to a marriage may apply to the court for an order under this section on the ground that the other party to the marriage (in this section referred to as the respondent)—

(a) has failed to provide reasonable maintenance for the applicant, or

(b) has failed to provide, or to make a proper contribution towards, reasonable maintenance for any child of the family.

(2) The court shall not entertain an application under this section unless—

(a) the applicant or the respondent is domiciled in England and Wales on the date of the application; or

(b) the applicant has been habitually resident there throughout the period of one year ending with that date; or

(c) the respondent is resident there on that date.

(3) Where an application under this section is made on the ground mentioned in subsection (1)(a) above, then, in deciding—

(a) whether the respondent has failed to provide reasonable maintenance for the applicant, and

(b) what order, if any, to make under this section in favour of the applicant,

the court shall have regard to all the circumstances of the case including the matters mentioned in section 25(2) above, and where an application is also made under this section in respect of a child of the family who has not attained the age of eighteen, first consideration shall be given to the welfare of the child while a minor.

(3A) Where an application under this section is made on the ground mentioned in subsection (1)(b) above then, in deciding—

(a) whether the respondent has failed to provide, or to make a proper contribution towards, reasonable maintenance for the child of the family to whom the application relates, and

(b) what order, if any, to make under this section in favour of the child,

the court shall have regard to all the circumstances of the case including the matters mentioned in section 25(3)(a) to (e) above, and where the child of the family to whom the application relates is not the child of the respondent, including also the matters mentioned in section 25(4) above.

(3B) In relation to an application under this section on the ground mentioned in subsection (1)(a) above, section 25(2)(c) above shall have effect as if for the reference therein to the breakdown of the marriage there were substituted a reference to the failure to provide reasonable maintenance for the applicant, and in relation to an application under this section on the ground mentioned in subsection (1)(b) above, section 25(2)(c) above (as it applies by virtue of section 25(3)(e) above) shall have effect as if for the reference therein to the breakdown of the marriage there were substituted a reference to the failure to provide, or to make a proper contribution towards, reasonable maintenance for the child of the family to whom the application relates.

(5) Where on an application under this section it appears to the court that the applicant or any child of the family to whom the application relates is in immediate need of financial assistance, but it is not yet possible to determine what order, if any, should be made on the application, the court may make an interim order for maintenance, that is to say, an order requiring the respondent—

(a)   *to make to the applicant until the determination of the application such periodical payments as the court thinks reasonable, or*

(b)   *to pay to the applicant such sum or sums as the court thinks reasonable.*

(6) Subject to the restrictions imposed by the following provisions of this Act, if on an application under this section the applicant satisfies the court of any ground mentioned in subsection (1) above, the court may make one or more financial provision orders against the respondent in favour of the applicant or a child of the family.

(6A) An application for the variation under section 31 of this Act of a periodical payments order or secured periodical payments order made under this section in favour of a child may, if the child has attained the age of sixteen, be made by the child himself.

(6B) Where a periodical payments order made in favour of a child under this section ceases to have effect on the date on which the child attains the age of sixteen or at any time after that date but before or on the date on which he attains the age of eighteen, then, if at any time before he attains the age of twenty-one an application is made by the child for an order under this subsection, the court shall have power by order to revive the first-mentioned order from such date as the court may specify, not being earlier than the date of the making of the application, and to exercise its powers under section 13 of this Act in relation to any order so revived.

(7) Without prejudice to the generality of subsection *(6)* above, an order under this section for the payment of a lump sum—

(a)   may be made for the purpose of enabling any liabilities or expenses reasonably incurred in maintaining the applicant or any child of the family to whom the application relates before the making of the application to be met;

(b)   may provide for the payment of that sum by instalments of such amount as may be specified in the order and may require the payment of the instalments to be secured to the satisfaction of the court.

(8) (*previously repealed*)

Additional provisions with respect to financial provision and property adjustment orders

28 Duration of continuing financial provision orders in favour of party to marriage, and effect of remarriage

(1) Subject [. . .] to the provisions of sections 25A(2) above and 31(7) below, the term to be specified in a periodical payments or secured periodical payments order in favour

of a party to a marriage shall be such term as the court thinks fit, except that the term shall not begin before or extend beyond the following limits, that is to say—

(a) *a term specified in the order which is to begin before the making of the order shall begin no earlier—*

    (i) *where the order is made by virtue of section 22A(2)(a) or (b) above, unless sub-paragraph (ii) below applies, than the beginning of the day on which the statement of marital breakdown in question was received by the court;*

    (ii) *where the order is made by virtue of section 22A(2)(b) above and the application for the divorce order was made following cancellation of an order preventing divorce under section 10 of the 1996 Act, than the date of the making of that application;*

    (iii) *where the order is made by virtue of section 22A(2)(c) above, than the date of the making of the application for the divorce order; or*

    (iv) *in any other case, than the date of the making of the application on which the order is made;*

(b) *a term specified in a periodical payments order or secured periodical payments order shall be so defined as not to extend beyond—*

    (i) *in the case of a periodical payments order, the death of the party by whom the payments are to be made; or*

    (ii) *in either case, the death of the party in whose favour the order was made or the remarriage of that party following the making of a divorce order or decree of nullity.*

(1A) *At any time when—*

(a) *the court exercises, or has exercised, its power under section 22A or 23 above to make a financial provision order in favour of a party to a marriage,*

(b) *but for having exercised that power, the court would have power under one of those sections to make such an order, and*

(c) *an application for a divorce order or a petition for a decree of nullity of marriage is outstanding or has been granted in relation to the marriage,*

the court may direct that that party shall not be entitled to apply under section 31 below for the extension of the term specified in the order.

(1B) *If the court—*

(a) *exercises, or has exercised, its power under section 22A at any time before making a divorce order, and*

(b) *gives a direction under subsection (1A) above in respect of a periodical payments order or a secured periodical payments order,*

it shall provide for the direction not to take effect until a divorce order is made.

(2) Where a periodical payments or secured periodical payments order in favour of a party to a marriage is made otherwise than *at such a time as is mentioned in subsection (1A)(c) above*, and the marriage in question is subsequently dissolved or annulled but the order continues in force, the order shall, notwithstanding anything in it, cease to have effect on the remarriage of that party, except in relation to any arrears due under it on the date of the remarriage.

(3) If after the grant of *an order or decree* dissolving or annulling a marriage either party to that marriage remarries whether at any time before or after the commencement of

this Act, that party shall not be entitled to apply, by reference to grant of *that order or decree*, for a financial provision order in his or her favour, or for a property adjustment order, against the other party to that marriage.

29 Duration of continuing financial provision orders in favour of children, and age limit on making certain orders in their favour

(1) Subject to subsection (3) below, no financial provision order and no order for a transfer of property *such as is mentioned in section 21(2)(a)* above shall be made in favour of a child who has attained the age of eighteen.

(1A) The term specified in a periodical payments order or secured periodical payments order made in favour of a child shall be such term as the court thinks fit.

(1B) If that term is to begin before the making of the order, it may do so no earlier than—

   (a)   *in the case of an order made by virtue of section 22A(2)(a) or (b) above, except where paragraph (b) below applies, the beginning of the day on which the statement of marital breakdown in question was received by the court;*

   (b)   *in the case of an order made by virtue of section 22A(2)(b) above where the application for the divorce order was made following cancellation of an order preventing divorce under section 10 of the 1996 Act, the date of the making of that application;*

   (c)   *in the case of an order made by virtue of section 22A(2)(c) above, the date of the making of the application for the divorce order; or*

   (d)   *in any other case, the date of the making of the application on which the order is made.*

(2) The term to be specified in a periodical payments or secured periodical payments order in favour of a child [. . .]—

   (a)   shall not in the first instance extend beyond the date of the birthday of the child next following his attaining the upper limit of the compulsory school age (that is to say, the age that is for the time being that limit by virtue of section 35 of the Education Act 1944 together with any Order in Council made under that section) unless the court considers that in the circumstances of the case the welfare of the child requires that it should extend to a later date; and

   (b)   shall not in any event, subject to subsection (3) below, extend beyond the date of the child's eighteenth birthday.

(3) Subsection (1) above, and paragraph (b) of subsection (2), shall not apply in the case of a child, if it appears to the court that—

   (a)   the child is, or will be, or if an order were made without complying with either or both of those provisions would be, receiving instruction at an educational establishment or undergoing training for a trade, profession or vocation, whether or not he is also, or will also be, in gainful employment; or

   (b)   there are special circumstances which justify the making of an order without complying with either or both of those provisions.

(4) Any periodical payments order in favour of a child shall, notwithstanding anything in the order, cease to have effect on the death of the person liable to make payments under the order, except in relation to any arrears due under the order on the date of the death.

(5) Where—

(a) a maintenance assessment ('the current assessment') is in force with respect to a child; and

(b) an application is made under Part II of this Act for a periodical payments or secured periodical payments order in favour of that child—

(i) in accordance with section 8 of the Child Support Act 1991, and

(ii) before the end of the period of 6 months beginning with the making of the current assessment

the term to be specified in any such order made on that application may be expressed to begin on, or at any time after, the earliest permitted date.

(6) For the purposes of subsection (5) above, 'the earliest permitted date' is whichever is the later of—

(a) the date 6 months before the application is made; or

(b) the date on which the current assessment took effect or, where successive maintenance assessments have been continuously in force with respect to a child, on which the first of those assessments took effect.

(7) Where—

(a) a maintenance assessment ceases to have effect or is cancelled by or under any provision of the Child Support Act 1991; and

(b) an application is made, before the end of the period of 6 months beginning with the relevant date, for a periodical payments or secured periodical payments order in favour of a child with respect to whom that maintenance assessment was in force immediately before it ceased to have effect or was cancelled.

the term to be specified in any such order made on that application may begin with the date on which that maintenance assessment ceased to have effect or, as the case may be, the date with effect from which it was cancelled, or any later date.

(8) In subsection (7)(b) above—

(a) where the maintenance assessment ceased to have effect, the relevant date is the date on which it so ceased; and

(b) where the maintenance assessment was cancelled, the relevant date is the later of—

(i) the date on which the person who cancelled it did so, and

(ii) the date from which the cancellation first had effect.

30 Direction for settlement of instrument for securing payments or effecting property adjustment

Where the court decides to make a financial provision order requiring any payments to be secured or a property adjustment order—

(a) it may direct that the matter be referred to one of the conveyancing counsel of the court for him to settle a proper instrument to be executed by all necessary parties; and

(b) where the order is to be made in proceedings for [. . .] nullity of marriage [. . .] it may, if it thinks fit, defer the grant of the decree in question until the instrument has been duly executed.

Variation, discharge and enforcement of certain orders, etc.

31 Variation, discharge, etc., of certain orders for financial relief

(1) Where the court has made an order to which this section applies, then, subject to the provisions of this section and of section 28(1A) above, the court shall have power to vary or discharge the order or to suspend any provision thereof temporarily and to revive the operation of any provision so suspended.

(2) This section applies to the following orders *under this Part of this Act*, that is to say—

- (a)   any [...] interim order for maintenance;
- (b)   any periodical payments order;
- (c)   any secured periodical payments order;
- (d)   *an order for the payment of a lump sum in a case in which the payment is to be made by instalments;*
- (dd) any deferred order made by virtue of section *21(1)(c)* (lump sums) which includes provision made by virtue of—
  - (i)   section 25B(4), or
  - (ii)   section 25C,

  (provision in respect of pension rights);
- (de) *any other order for the payment of a lump sum, if it is made at a time when no divorce order has been made, and no separation order is in force, in relation to the marriage;*
- (e)   *any order under section 23A of a kind referred to in section 21(2)(b), (c) or (d) which is made on or after the making of a separation order;*
- (ea) *any order under section 23A which is made at a time when no divorce order has been made, and no separation order is in force, in relation to the marriage;*
- (f)   any order made under section 24A(1) above for the sale of property.

(2A) Where the court has made an order referred to in subsection (2)(a), (b) or (c) above, then, subject to the provisions of this section, the court shall have power to remit the payment of any arrears due under the order or of any part thereof.

(2B) Where the court has made an order referred to in subsection (2)(dd)(ii) above, this section shall cease to apply to the order on the death of either of the parties to the marriage.

(3) The powers exercisable by the court under this section in relation to an order shall be exercisable also in relation to any instrument executed in pursuance of the order.

(4) The court shall not exercise the powers conferred by this section in relation to an order *referred to in subsection (2)(e)* above except on an application made in proceedings *on an application for a divorce order in relation to the marriage.*

(4A) In relation to an order which falls within subsection (2)(de) or (ea) above ('the subsection (2) order')—

- (a)   *the powers conferred by this section may be exercised—*
  - (i)   *only on an application made before the subsection (2) order has or, but for paragraph (b) below, would have taken effect; and*
  - (ii)   *only if, at the time when the application is made, no divorce order has been made in relation to the marriage and no separation order has been so made since the subsection (2) order was made; and*

(b)   *an application made in accordance with paragraph (a) above prevents the subsection (2) order from taking effect before the application has been dealt with.*

(4B) No variation—

(a)   *of a financial provision order made under section 22A above, other than an interim order, or*

(b)   *of a property adjustment order made under section 23A above,*

shall be made so as to take effect before the making of a divorce order or separation order in relation to the marriage, unless the court is satisfied that the circumstances of the case are exceptional, and that it would be just and reasonable for the variation to be so made.

(5) *Subject to subsections (7A) to (7F) below and without prejudice to any power exercisable by virtue of subsection (2)(d), (dd) or (e) above or otherwise than by virtue of this section,* no property adjustment order shall be made on an application for the variation of a periodical payments or secured periodical payments order made (whether in favour of a party to a marriage or in favour of a child of the family) under *section 22A or 23* above, and no order for the payment of a lump sum shall be made on an application for the variation of a periodical payments or secured periodical payments order in favour of a party to a marriage (whether made under *section 22A or 23* or under section 27 above).

(6) Where the person liable to make payments under a secured periodical payments order has died, an application under this section relating to that order (and to any order made under section 24A(1) above which requires the proceeds of sale of property to be used for securing those payments) may be made by the person entitled to payments under the periodical payments order or by the personal representatives of the deceased person, but no such application shall, except with the permission of the court, be made after the end of the period of six months from the date on which representation in regard to the estate of that person is first taken out.

(7) In exercising the powers conferred by this section the court shall have regard to all the circumstances of the case, first consideration being given to the welfare while a minor of any child of the family who has not attained the age of eighteen, and the circumstances of the case shall include any change in any of the matters to which the court was required to have regard when making the order to which the application relates, and—

(a)   in the case of a periodical payments or secured periodical payments order made *in favour of a party to a marriage, the court shall, if the marriage has been dissolved or annulled, consider* whether in all the circumstances and after having regard to any such change it would be appropriate to vary the order so that payments under the order are required to be made or secured only for such further period as will in the opinion of the court be sufficient (*in the light of any proposed exercise by the court, where the marriage has been dissolved, of its powers under subsection (7B) below*) to enable the party in whose favour the order was made to adjust without undue hardship to the termination of those payments;

(b)   in a case where the party against whom the order was made has died, the circumstances of the case shall also include the changed circumstances resulting from his or her death.

(7A) Subsection (7B) below applies where, after the dissolution of a marriage, the court—

(a)   *discharges a periodical payments order or secured periodical payments order made in favour of a party to the marriage, or*

(b)   *varies such an order so that payments under the order are required to be made or secured only for such further period as is determined by the court.*

(7B) The court has power, in addition to any power it has apart from this subsection, to make supplemental provision consisting of any of—

(a)   *an order for the payment of a lump sum in favour of a party to the marriage;*

(b)   *one or more property adjustment orders in favour of a party to the marriage;*

(c)   *a direction that the party in whose favour the original order discharged or varied was made is not entitled to make any further application for—*

 (i)   *a periodical payments or secured periodical payments order, or*

 (ii)   *an extension of the period to which the original order is limited by any variation made by the court.*

(7C) An order for the payment of a lump sum made under subsection (7B) above may—

(a)   *provide for the payment of that sum by instalments of such amount as may be specified in the order; and*

(b)   *require the payment of the instalments to be secured to the satisfaction of the court.*

(7D) Subsections (7) and (8) of section 22A above apply where the court makes an order for the payment of a lump sum under subsection (7B) above as they apply where it makes such an order under section 22A above.

(7E) If under subsection (7B) above the court makes more than one property adjustment order in favour of the same party to the marriage, each of those orders must fall within a different paragraph of section 21(2) above.

(7F) Sections 24A and 30 above apply where the court makes a property adjustment order under subsection (7B) above as they apply where it makes such an order under section 23A above.

(8) The personal representatives of a deceased person against whom a secured periodical payments order was made shall not be liable for having distributed any part of the estate of the deceased after the expiration of the period of six months referred to in subsection (6) above on the ground that they ought to have taken into account the possibility that the court might permit an application under this section to be made after that period by the person entitled to payments under the order; but this subsection shall not prejudice any power to recover any part of the estate so distributed arising by virtue of the making of an order in pursuance of this section.

(9) In considering for the purposes of subsection (6) above the question when representation was first taken out, a grant limited to settled land or to trust property shall be left out of account and a grant limited to real estate or to personal estate shall be left out of account unless a grant limited to the remainder of the estate has previously been made or is made at the same time.

(10) Where the court, in exercise of its powers under this section, decides to vary or discharge a periodical payments or secured periodical payments order, then, subject to section 28(1) and (2) above, the court shall have power to direct that the variation or discharge shall not take effect until the expiration of such period as may be specified in the order.

(11) Where—

(a) a periodical payments or secured periodical payments order in favour of more than one child ('the order') is in force;

(b) the order requires payments specified in it to be made to or for the benefit of more than one child without apportioning those payments between them;

(c) a maintenance assessment ('the assessment') is made with respect to one or more, but not all, of the children with respect to whom those payments are to be made; and

(d) an application is made, before the end of the period of 6 months beginning with the date on which the assessment was made, for the variation or discharge of the order, the court may, in exercise of its powers under this section to vary or discharge the order, direct that the variation or discharge shall take effect from the date on which the assessment took effect or any later date.

(12) Where—

(a) an order ('the child order') of a kind prescribed for the purposes of section 10(1) of the Child Support Act 1991 is affected by a maintenance assessment;

(b) on the date on which the child order became so affected there was in force a periodical payments or secured periodical payments order ('the spousal order') in favour of a party to a marriage having the care of the child in whose favour the child order was made; and

(c) an application is made, before the end of the period of 6 months beginning with the date on which the maintenance assessment was made, for the spousal order to be varied or discharged,

the court may, in exercise of its powers under this section to vary or discharge the spousal order, direct that the variation or discharge shall take effect from the date on which the child order became so affected or any later date.

(13) For the purposes of subsection (12) above, an order is affected if it ceases to have effect or is modified by or under section 10 of the Child Support Act 1991.

(14) Subsections (11) and (12) above are without prejudice to any other power of the court to direct that the variation of discharge of an order under this section shall take effect from a date earlier than that on which the order for variation or discharge was made.

31A Variation etc. following reconciliations

(1) Where, at a time before the making of a divorce order—

(a) *an order ('a paragraph (a) order') for the payment of a lump sum has been made under section 22A above in favour of a party,*

(b) *such an order has been made in favour of a child of the family but the payment has not yet been made, or*

(c) *a property adjustment order ('a paragraph (c) order') has been made under section 23A above,*

the court may, on an application made jointly by the parties to the marriage, vary or discharge the order.

(2) Where the court varies or discharges a paragraph (a) order, it may order the repayment of an amount equal to the whole or any part of the lump sum.

(3) Where the court varies or discharges a paragraph (c) order, it may (if the order has taken effect)—

    (a)   order any person to whom property was transferred in pursuance of the paragraph (c) order to transfer—

        (i)   the whole or any part of that property, or

        (ii)   the whole or any part of any property appearing to the court to represent that property,

    in favour of a party to the marriage or a child of the family; or

    (b)   vary any settlement to which the order relates in favour of any person or extinguish or reduce any person's interest under that settlement.

(4) Where the court acts under subsection (3) it may make such supplemental provision (including a further property adjustment order or an order for the payment of a lump sum) as it thinks appropriate in consequence of any transfer, variation, extinguishment or reduction to be made under paragraph (a) or (b) of that subsection.

(5) Sections 24A and 30 above apply for the purposes of this section as they apply where the court makes a property adjustment order under section 23A or 24 above.

(6) The court shall not make an order under subsection (2), (3) or (4) above unless it appears to it that there has been a reconciliation between the parties to the marriage.

(7) The court shall also not make an order under subsection (3) or (4) above unless it appears to it that the order will not prejudice the interests of—

    (a)   any child of the family; or

    (b)   any person who has acquired any right or interest in consequence of the paragraph (c) order and is not a party to the marriage or a child of the family.

32 Payment of certain arrears unenforceable without the leave of the court

(1) A person shall not be entitled to enforce through the High Court or any county court the payment of any arrears due under *any financial provision order under this Part of this Act or any interim order for maintenance* without the leave of that court if those arrears became due more than twelve months before proceedings to enforce the payment of them are begun.

(2) The court hearing an application for the grant of leave under this section may refuse leave, or may grant leave subject to such restrictions and conditions (including conditions as to the allowing of time for payment or the making of payment by instalments) as that court thinks proper, or may remit the payment of the arrears or of any part thereof.

(3) An application for the grant of leave under this section shall be made in such manner as may be prescribed by rules of court.

33 Orders for repayment in certain cases of sums paid under certain orders

(1) Where on an application made under this section in relation to an order to which this section applies it appears to the court that by reason of—

    (a)   a change in the circumstances of the person entitled to, or liable to make, payments under the order since the order was made, or (b)　the changed circumstances resulting from the death of the person so liable,

the amount received by the person entitled to payments under the order in respect of a period after those circumstances changed or after the death of the person liable to make payments under the order, as the case may be, exceeds the amount which the person so liable or his or her personal representatives should have been required to pay, the court may order the respondent to the application to pay to the applicant such sum, not exceeding the amount of the excess, as the court thinks just.

(2) This section applies to the following orders under this Part of this Act—

(a)　*any periodical payments order;*

(b)　*any secured periodical payments order; and*

(c)　*any interim order for maintenance, so far as it requires the making of periodical payments.*

(3) An application under this section may be made by the person liable to make payments under an order to which this section applies or his or her personal representatives and may be made against the person entitled to payments under the order or her or his personal representatives.

(4) An application under this section may be made in proceedings in the High Court or a county court for—

(a)　the variation or discharge of the order to which this section applies, or

(b)　leave to enforce, or the enforcement of, the payment of arrears under that order;

but when not made in such proceedings shall be made to a county court, and accordingly references in this section to the court are references to the High Court or a county court, as the circumstances require.

(5) The jurisdiction conferred on a county court by this section shall be exercisable notwithstanding that by reason of the amount claimed in the application the jurisdiction would not but for this subsection be exercisable by a county court.

(6) An order under this section for the payment of any sum may provide for the payment of that sum by instalments of such amount as may be specified in the order.

Consent orders

33A　Consent orders for financial provision or property adjustment

(1) Notwithstanding anything in the preceding provisions of this Part of this Act, on an application for a consent order for financial relief the court may, unless it has reason to think that there are other circumstances into which it ought to inquire, make an order in the terms agreed on the basis only of the prescribed information furnished with the application.

(2) Subsection (1) above applies (*subject, in the case of the powers of the court under section 31A above, to subsections (6) and (7) of that section*) to an application for a consent order varying or discharging an order for financial relief as it applies to an application for an order for financial relief.

(3) In this section—

'consent order', in relation to an application for an order, means an order in the terms applied for to which the respondent agrees;

'order for financial relief' means *any of the following orders under this Part of this Act, that is to say, any financial provision order, any property adjustment order, any order for the sale of property or any interim order for maintenance*; and

'prescribed' means prescribed by rules of court.

Maintenance agreements

34 Validity of maintenance agreements

(1) If a maintenance agreement includes a provision purporting to restrict any right to apply to a court for an order containing financial arrangements, then—

  (a)   that provision shall be void; but
  (b)   any other financial arrangements contained in the agreement shall not thereby be rendered void or unenforceable and shall, unless they are void or unenforceable for any other reason (and subject to sections 35 and 36 below), be binding on the parties to the agreement.

(2) In this section and in section 35 below—

  'maintenance agreement' means any agreement in writing made, whether before or after the commencement of this Act, between the parties to a marriage, being—
  (a)   an agreement containing financial arrangements, whether made during the continuance or after the dissolution or annulment of the marriage; or
  (b)   a separation agreement which contains no financial arrangements in a case where no other agreement in writing between the same parties contains such arrangements;

  'financial arrangements' means provisions governing the rights and liabilities towards one another when living separately of the parties to a marriage (including a marriage which has been dissolved or annulled) in respect of the making or securing of payments or the disposition or use of any property, including such rights and liabilities with respect to the maintenance or education of any child, whether or not a child of the family.

35 Alteration of agreements by court during lives of parties

(1) Where a maintenance agreement is for the time being subsisting and each of the parties to the agreement is for the time being either domiciled or resident in England and Wales, then, subject to subsection (3) below, either party may apply to the court or to a magistrates' court for an order under this section.

(2) If the court to which the application is made is satisfied either—

  (a)   that by reason of a change in the circumstances in the light of which any financial arrangements contained in the agreement were made or, as the case may be, financial arrangements were omitted from it (including a change foreseen by the parties when making the agreement), the agreement should be altered so as to make different, or, as the case may be, so as to contain, financial arrangements, or
  (b)   that the agreement does not contain proper financial arrangements with respect to any child of the family,

then subject to subsections (3), (4) and (5) below, that court may by order make such alterations in the agreement—

    (i)   by varying or revoking any financial arrangements contained in it, or

    (ii)   by inserting in it financial arrangements for the benefit of one of the parties to the agreement or of a child of the family,

as may appear to that court to be just having regard to all the circumstances, including, if relevant, the matters mentioned in section 25(4) above; and the agreement shall have effect thereafter as if any alteration made by the order has been made by agreement between the parties and for valuable consideration.

(3) A magistrates' court shall not entertain an application under subsection (1) above unless both the parties to the agreement are resident in England and Wales and at least one of the parties is resident within the commission area (within the meaning of the Justices of the Peace Act 1979) for which the court is appointed; and shall not have power to make any order on such an application except—

    (a)   in a case where the agreement includes no provision for periodical payments by either of the parties, an order inserting provision for the making by one of the parties of periodical payments for the maintenance of the other party or for the maintenance of any child of the family;

    (b)   in a case where the agreement includes provision for the making by one of the parties of periodical payments, an order increasing or reducing the rate of, or terminating, any of those payments.

(4) Where a court decides to alter, by order under this section, an agreement by inserting provision for the making or securing by one of the parties to the agreement of periodical payments for the maintenance of the other party or by increasing the rate of the periodical payments which the agreement provides shall be made by one of the parties for the maintenance of the other, the term for which the payments or, as the case may be, the additional payments attributable to the increase are to be made under the agreement as altered by the order shall be such term as the court may specify, subject to the following limits, that is to say—

    (a)   where the payments will not be secured, the term shall be so defined as not to extend beyond the death of either of the parties to the agreement or the remarriage of the party to whom the payment are to be made;

    (b)   where the payments will be secured, the term shall be so defined as not to extend beyond the death or remarriage of that party.

(5) Where a court decides to alter, by order under this section, an agreement by inserting provision for the making or securing by one of the parties to the agreement of periodical payments for the maintenance of a child of the family or by increasing the rate of the periodical payments which the agreement provides shall be made or secured by one of the parties for the maintenance of such a child, then, in deciding the term for which under the agreement as altered by the order the payments, or as the case may be, the additional payments attributable to the increase are to be made or secured for the benefit of the child, the court shall apply the provisions of section 29(2) and (3) above as to age limits as if the order in question were a periodical payments or secured periodical payments order in favour of the child.

(6) For the avoidance of doubt it is hereby declared that nothing in this section or in section 34 above affects any power of a court before which any proceedings between

the parties to a maintenance agreement are brought under any other enactment (including a provision of this Act) to make an order containing financial arrangements or any right of either party to apply for such an order in such proceedings.

(7) Subject to subsection (5) above, references in this Act to any such order as is mentioned in section 21 above shall not include references to any order under this section.

36 Alteration of agreements by court after death of one party

(1) Where a maintenance agreement within the meaning of section 34 above provides for the continuation of payments under the agreement after the death of one of the parties and that party dies domiciled in England and Wales, the surviving party or the personal representatives of the deceased party may, subject to subsections (2) and (3) below, apply to the High Court or a county court for an order under section 35 above.

(2) An application under this section shall not, except with the permission of the High Court or a county court, be made after the end of the period of six months from the date on which representation in regard to the estate of the deceased is first taken out.

(3) A county court shall not entertain an application under this section, or an application for permission to make an application under this section, unless it would have jurisdiction by virtue of section 22 of the Inheritance (Provision for Family and Dependants) Act 1975 (which confers jurisdiction on county courts in proceedings under that Act if the value of the property mentioned in that section does not exceed £5,000 or such larger sum as may be fixed by order of the Lord Chancellor) to hear and determine proceedings for an order under section 2 of that Act in relation to the deceased's estate.

(4) If a maintenance agreement is altered by a court on an application made in pursuance of subsection (1) above, the like consequences shall ensue as if the alteration had been made immediately before the death by agreement between the parties and for valuable consideration.

(5) The provisions of this section shall not render the personal representatives of the deceased liable for having distributed any part of the estate of the deceased after the expiration of the period of six months referred to in subsection (2) above on the ground that they ought to have taken into account the possibility that a court might permit an application by virtue of this section to be made by the surviving party after that period; but this subsection shall not prejudice any power to recover any part of the estate so distributed arising by virtue of the making of an order in pursuance of this section.

(6) Section 31(9) above shall apply for the purposes of subsection (2) above as it applies for the purposes of subsection (6) of section 31.

(7) Subsection (3) of section 22 of the Inheritance (Provision for Family and Dependants) Act 1975 (which enables rules of court to provide for the transfer from a county court to the High Court or from the High Court to a county court of proceedings for an order under section 2 of that Act) and paragraphs (a) and (b) of subsection (4) of that section (provisions relating to proceedings commenced in county court before coming into force of order of the Lord Chancellor under that section) shall apply in relation to proceedings consisting of any such application as is referred to in subsection (3) above as they apply in relation to proceedings for an order under section 2 of that Act.

Miscellaneous and supplemental

37 Avoidance of transactions intended to prevent or reduce financial relief

(1) For the purposes of this section 'financial relief' means relief under any of the provisions of sections *22A to 24, 27, 31 (except subsection (6)), 31A* and 35 above, and any reference in this section to defeating a person's claim for financial relief is a reference to preventing financial relief from being granted to that person, or to that person for the benefit of a child of the family, or reducing the amount of any financial relief which might be so granted, or frustrating or impeding the enforcement of any order which might be or has been made at his instance under any of those provisions.

(2) Where proceedings for financial relief are brought by one person against another, the court may, on the application of the first-mentioned person—

(a)　if it is satisfied that the other party to the proceedings is, with the intention of defeating the claim for financial relief, about to make any disposition or to transfer out of the jurisdiction or otherwise deal with any property, make such order as it thinks fit for restraining the other party from so doing or otherwise from protecting the claim;

(b)　if it is satisfied that the other party has, with that intention, made a reviewable disposition and that if the disposition were set aside financial relief or different financial relief would be granted to the applicant, make an order setting aside the disposition;

(c)　if it is satisfied, in a case where an order has been obtained under any of the provisions mentioned in subsection (1) above by the applicant against the other party, that the other party has, with that intention, made a reviewable disposition, make an order setting aside the disposition;

and an application for the purposes of paragraph (b) above shall be made in the proceedings for the financial relief in question.

(3) Where the court makes an order under subsection (2)(b) or (c) above setting aside a disposition it shall give such consequential directions as it thinks fit for giving effect to the order (including requiring the making of any payments or the disposal of any property).

(4) Any disposition made by the other party to the proceedings for financial relief in question (whether before or after the commencement of those proceedings) is a reviewable disposition for the purposes of subsection (2)(b) and (c) above unless it was made for valuable consideration (other than marriage) to a person who, at the time of the disposition, acted in relation to it in good faith and without notice of any intention on the part of the other party to defeat the applicant's claim for financial relief.

(5) Where an application is made under this section with respect to a disposition which took place less than three years before the date of the application or with respect to a disposition or other dealing with property which is about to take place and the court is satisfied—

(a)　in a case falling within subsection (2)(a) or (b) above, that the disposition or other dealing would (apart from this section) have the consequence, or

(b)　in a case falling within subsection (2)(c) above, that the disposition has had the consequence, of defeating the applicant's claim for financial relief, it shall be presumed, unless the contrary is shown, that the person who disposed of or is about to dispose of or deal with the property did so or, as the case may be, is about to do so, with the intention of defeating the applicant's claim for financial relief.

(6) In this section 'disposition' does not include any provision contained in a will or codicil but, with that exception, includes any conveyance, assurance or gift of property of any description, whether made by an instrument or otherwise.

(7) This section does not apply to a disposition made before 1st January 1968.

38 Orders for repayment in certain cases of sums paid after cessation of order by reason of remarriage

(1) Where—

(a) a periodical payments or secured periodical payments order in favour of a party to a marriage (hereafter in this section referred to as 'a payments order') has ceased to have effect by reason of the remarriage of that party, and

(b) the person liable to make payments under the order or his or her personal representatives made payments in accordance with it in respect of a period after the date of the remarriage in the mistaken belief that the order was still subsisting,

the person so liable or his or her personal representatives should not be entitled to bring proceedings in respect of a cause of action arising out of the circumstances mentioned in paragraphs (a) and (b) above against the person entitled to payments under the order or her or his personal representatives, but may instead make an application against that person or her or his personal representatives under this section.

(2) On an application under this section the court may order the respondent to pay to the applicant a sum equal to the amount of the payments made in respect of the period mentioned in subsection (1)(b) above or, if it appears to the court that it would be unjust to make that order, it may either order the respondent to pay to the applicant such lesser sum as it thinks fit or dismiss the application.

(3) An application under this section may be made in proceedings in the High Court or a county court for leave to enforce, or the enforcement of, payment of arrears under the order in question, but when not made in such proceedings shall be made to a county court; and accordingly references in this section to the court are references to the High Court or a county court, as the circumstances require.

(4) The jurisdiction conferred on a county court by this section shall be exercisable notwithstanding that by reason of the amount claimed in the application the jurisdiction would not but for this subsection be exercisable by a county court.

(5) An order under this section for the payment of any sum may provide for the payment of that sum by instalments of such amount as may be specified in the order.

(6) The clerk of a magistrates' court to whom any payments under a payments order are required to be made, and the collecting officer under an attachment of earnings order made to secure payments under a payments order, shall not be liable—

(a) in the case of the clerk, for any act done by him in pursuance of the payments order after the date on which that order ceased to have effect by reason of the remarriage of the person entitled to payments under it, and

(b) in the case of the collecting officer, for any act done by him after that date in accordance with any enactment or rule of court specifying how payments made to him in compliance with the attachment of earnings order are to be dealt with,

if, but only if, the act was one which he would have been under a duty to do had the payments order not so ceased to have effect and the act was done before notice in writing of the fact that the person so entitled had remarried was given to him by or on behalf of that person, the person liable to make payments under the payments order or the personal representatives of either of those persons.

(7) In this section 'collecting officer', in relation to an attachment of earnings order, means the officer of the High Court, the registrar of a county court or the clerk of a magistrates' court to whom a person makes payments in compliance with the order.

39 Settlement, etc, made in compliance with a property adjustment order may be avoided on bankruptcy of settlor

The fact that a settlement or transfer of property had to be made in order to comply with a property adjustment order shall not prevent that settlement or transfer from being a transaction in respect of which an order may be made under section 339 or 340 of the Insolvency Act 1986 (transactions at an undervalue and preferences).

40 Payments, etc, under order made in favour of person suffering from mental disorder

Where the court makes an order under this Part of this Act requiring payments (including a lump sum payment) to be made, or property to be transferred, to a party to a marriage and the court is satisfied that the person in whose favour the order is made is incapable, by reason of mental disorder within the meaning of the Mental Health Act 1959, of managing and administering his or her property and affairs then, subject to any order, direction or authority made or given in relation to that person under Part VIII of that Act, the court may order the payments to be made, or as the case may be, the property to be transferred, to such persons having charge of that person as the court may direct.

PART III
PROTECTION, CUSTODY, ETC, OF CHILDREN

41 Restrictions on decrees of annulment affecting children

(1) In any proceedings for a decree of [...] nullity of marriage, [...] the court shall consider—

(a) whether there are any children of the family to whom this section applies; and
(b) where there are any such children, whether (in the light of the arrangements which have been, or are proposed to be, made for their upbringing and welfare) it should exercise any of its powers under the Children Act 1989 with respect to any of them.

(2) Where, in any case to which this section applies, it appears to the court that—

(a) the circumstances of the case require it, or are likely to require it, to exercise any of its powers under the Act of 1989 with respect to any such child;

(b)   it is not in a position to exercise the power or (as the case may be) those powers without giving further consideration to the case; and

(c)   there are exceptional circumstances which make it desirable in the interests of the child that the court should give a direction under this section,

it may direct that the decree of [. . .] nullity is not to be made absolute [. . .] until the court orders otherwise.

(3) This section applies to—

(a)   any child of the family who has not reached the age of sixteen at the date when the court considers the case in accordance with the requirements of this section; and

(b)   any child of the family who has reached that age at the date and in relation to whom the court directs that this section shall apply.

PART IV
MISCELLANEOUS AND SUPPLEMENTAL

47 Matrimonial relief and declarations of validity in respect of polygamous marriages

(1) A court in England and Wales shall not be precluded from granting matrimonial relief or making a declaration concerning the validity of a marriage by reason only that either party to the marriage is, or has during the subsistence of the marriage been, married to more than one person.

(2) In this section 'matrimonial relief' means—

(a)   any *divorce order, any separation order under the 1996 Act or any* decree under Part I of this Act;

(b)   a financial provision order under section 27 above;

(c)   an order under section 35 above altering a maintenance agreement;

(d)   an order under any provision of this Act *or the 1996 Act* which confers a power exercisable in connection with, or in connection with proceedings for, *a statement of marital breakdown or any such order or decree* as is mentioned in paragraphs (a) to (c) above;

(dd) an order under Part III of the Matrimonial and Family Proceedings Act 1984;

(e)   an order under Part I of the Domestic Proceedings and Magistrates' Courts Act 1978.

(3) In this section 'a declaration concerning the validity of a marriage' means any declaration under Part III of the Family Law Act 1986 involving a determination as to the validity of a marriage.

(4) Provision may be made by rules of court—

(a)   for requiring notice of proceedings brought by virtue of this section to be served on any additional spouse of a party to the marriage in question; and

(b)   for conferring on any such additional spouse the right to be heard in the proceedings,

in such cases as may be specified in the rules.

48 Evidence

(1) The evidence of a husband or wife shall be admissible in any proceedings to prove that marital intercourse did or did not take place between them during any period.

(2) In any proceedings for nullity of marriage, evidence on the question of sexual capacity shall be heard in camera unless in any case the judge is satisfied that in the interests of justice any such evidence ought to be heard in open court.

49 Parties to proceedings under this Act

[. . .]

52 Interpretation

(1) In this Act—

'*the 1996 Act*' *means the Family Law Act 1996*;
'child', in relation to one or both of the parties to a marriage, includes an illegitimate child of that party, or as the case may be, of both parties;
'child of the family', in relation to the parties to a marriage, means—
   (a)   a child of both of those parties; and
   (b)   any other child, not being a child who is placed with those parties as foster parents by a local authority or voluntary organisation, who has been treated by both of those parties as a child of their family;
      'the court' (except where the context otherwise requires) means the High Court or, where a county court has jurisdiction by virtue of Part V of the Matrimonial and Family Proceedings Act 1984, a county court;
'education' includes training.
'maintenance assessment' has the same meaning as it has in the Child Support Act 1991 by virtue of section 54 of that Act as read with any regulations in force under that section.
'*statement of marital breakdown*' *has the same meaning as in the Family Law Act 1996*.

(2) In this Act—

   (a)   references to financial provision orders, periodical payments and secured periodical payments orders and orders for the payment of a lump sum, and references to property adjustment orders, shall be construed in accordance *(subject to section 35(7) above) with section 21 above and*—
      (i)   *in the case of a financial provision order or periodical payments order, as including (except where the context otherwise requires) references to an interim periodical payments order under section 22A or 23 above; and*
      (ii)   *in the case of a financial provision order or order for the payment of a lump sum, as including (except where the context otherwise requires) references to an interim order for the payment of a lump sum under section 22A or 23 above;* and
   (b)   references [. . .] and to interim orders for maintenance shall be construed [. . .] in accordance with [. . .] section 27(5) above.

(3) For the avoidance of doubt it is hereby declared that references in this Act to remarriage include references to a marriage which is by law void or voidable.

(4) Except where the contrary intention is indicated, references in this Act to any enactment include references to that enactment as amended, extended or applied by or under any subsequent enactment, including this Act.

53 Transitional provisions and savings

Schedule 1 to this Act shall have effect for the purpose of—

(a) the transition to the provisions of this Act from the law in force before the commencement of this Act;

(b) the preservation for limited purposes of certain provisions superseded by provisions of this Act or by enactments repealed and replaced by this Act; and

(c) the assimilation in certain respects to orders under this Act of orders made, or deemed to have been made, under the Matrimonial Causes Act 1965.

54 Consequential amendments and repeals

(1) Subject to the provisions of Schedule 1 to this Act—

(a) the enactments specified in Schedule 2 to this Act shall have effect subject to the amendments specified in that Schedule, being amendments consequential on the provisions of this Act or on enactments repealed by this Act; and

(b) (*previously repealed*)

(2) The amendment of any enactment by Schedule 2 to this Act shall not be taken as prejudicing the operation of section 38 of the Interpretation Act 1889 (which relates to the effect of repeals).

55 Citation, commencement and extent

(1) This Act may be cited as the Matrimonial Causes Act 1973.

(2) This Act shall come into force on such day as the Lord Chancellor may appoint by order made by statutory instrument.

(3) Subject to the provisions of paragraphs 3(2) of Schedule 2 below, this Act does not extend to Scotland or Northern Ireland.

NOTE
Sch 1 (Transitional Provisions and Savings) and Sch 2 (Consequential Amendments) are not set out. Sch 3 has been previously repealed.

INDEX

References are to paragraph numbers.